THIRTY-TWO
#32
Eagle Rock Branch Library
5027 Caspar Avenue
Los Angeles, CA 90041

D0086233

State Trooper Exam

JUN 0 1 2007

State
Trooper
Exam

351.3STA
S7975-2
2007

LEARNING EXPRESS®

NEW YORK

176617927

Copyright © 2007 LearningExpress, LLC.

All rights reserved under International and Pan-American Copyright Conventions.
Published in the United States by LearningExpress, LLC, New York.

Library of Congress Cataloging-in-Publication Data:
State trooper exam.
     p. cm.
  ISBN: 978-1-57685-583-6
  1. Police, State—United States—Examinations, questions, etc. 2. Police—United
States—Examinations, questions, etc.
  I. LearningExpress (Organization)
  HV8143.S73 2007
  363.2076—dc22

               2006036561

Printed in the United States of America

9 8 7 6 5 4 3 2 1

ISBN: 978-1-57685-583-6

For information on LearningExpress, other LearningExpress products,
or bulk sales, please write to us at:
  LearningExpress
  55 Broadway
  8th Floor
  New York, NY 10006

Or visit us at:
  www.learnatest.com

List of Contributors ▶

The following people contributed to the content of this book.

Dorothy Moses Schulz, PhD, is a professor at John Jay College of Criminal Justice (CUNY). She is a retired captain with the Metro-North Commuter Railroad Police Department and its predecessor railroad, Conrail. She was the first woman to hold a management rank in both departments. Dr. Schulz is a life member of the International Association of Chiefs of Police (IACP) and other police and history associations; speaks frequently at police and academic gatherings; and has published on a variety of historical and current police topics, particularly in areas concerning transit and railroad police and women in policing.

Walter Signorelli was a member of the New York City Police Department for 31 years. He retired with the rank of inspector after serving in the Patrol Bureau, the Narcotics Division, the Detective Division, the Organized Crime Control Bureau, and the Personnel Bureau. He is a graduate of the St. John's University School of Law and is admitted to practice law in New York State. He is an assistant professor of law and police science at John Jay College of Criminal Justice.

Contents

Introduction

State Trooper Exam is more than just a guide to taking and passing the state trooper exam. It is also more than merely a collection of practice tests. This book provides you with an overview of who state police officers are, what they do, the steps in the hiring process, academy training, and conditions of employment. It also explains how you should design your approach to taking the exam so that you have the best possible chance of passing it.

When you take the practice tests, do not just answer the questions and hope for the best—if you do that on the exam, you are not likely to do your best. If you use this book, though, as a guide to understanding *how* the exam is structured and *what* you are being asked to do, your chances of passing will increase considerably. No book can promise you a higher score, but a book can offer you tips and hints to better understand how to study for an exam and how to analyze the patterns of the skills that are being tested. To help you understand each of those skills, there are sections devoted to different types of questions you might see on the written state trooper exam.

Most state police departments begin the formal hiring process with a written exam. In virtually all states, it will be the first step you take after applying for the job and after your application is checked to assure you have the minimum requirements for entry into the department you are testing for.

Because the written test is only the first step you must take to become a state trooper, there are also chapters on how to prepare the oral appraisal, the physical and medical exams, and the psychological exam. Not all agencies make use of an oral appraisal; some consider it too costly or time-consuming to have applicants from all over the state—or even all over the nation—come to a test site to be interviewed by a panel of policing experts. Even if the agency you are applying for does not require an oral exam, the chapter on oral appraisal exams can help you prepare for any type of interview that may occur in the hiring process.

Physical, medical, and psychological exams are common steps in the applicant process for almost all police positions. The exams may not be exactly the same and they may not take place in the same order in every agency, but eventually, if you are successful in passing the written exam, you will be called to appear for one or all of these tests. Of the three, the physical exam is the easiest to prepare for. Not only can you work to get yourself into excellent physical condition, but many state police agencies now provide information on their websites about what you will be asked to do when you report for the physical exam. Statistics show that this is the most difficult portion of the exam for female applicants, but "difficult" does not mean "impossible." In addition to publicizing the physical test requirements, a number of agencies also provide training plans to prepare an applicant for what will be expected. Some schedule pre-physical meetings or even training sessions to help applicants prepare for this rigorous step in the hiring process.

With a volunteer military having replaced the draft and computer skills having replaced outdoor sports for many people, all applicants can benefit from learning what they will be asked to do at the physical exam and starting a training program at least six months before they hope to be tested. Remember that even if you never get to take the physical, the healthy habits you have learned will stay with you and benefit you throughout your lifetime. A sound mind and a sound body will better prepare you for any law enforcement career.

It is more difficult to prepare for the medical and psychological exams, although the training program you develop to pass the physical may help you to pass the medical if you have no serious ailments. The medical may also include a drug test. This is one area where different agencies set different standards as to past drug use, but no agency will hire an applicant who tests positive for drugs at the medical exam. Check your desired employer's minimum qualifications for past drug experimentation so you are neither disappointed nor embarrassed when you appear for testing.

The psychological exam is the hardest to study or practice for. Although policies differ among agencies, you will most likely be asked to complete a number of paper-and-pencil tests that have been determined successful at assessing the traits considered most important for a successful police career. Generally, these traits include self-confidence (but not arrogance), honesty, integrity, compatibility (ability to work with a team), diplomacy, independence, dependability, and decisiveness. To you, some of these may actually appear contradictory, but the series of tests you will take have been shown to analyze whether you have these traits in the proper combination. The best way to prepare for this test is to be relaxed, minimize stress in your life before appearing for the test, and answer honestly. Do not try to fool the test; you may be asked a different version of the same question more than once, and if you answer dishonestly, it is very likely that the results will show this.

▶ How to Use This Book

Now that you have a good idea of what the book contains, you should consider how you will use it to your best advantage. The first thing to remember is that, just as in the test you will be taking, there are no shortcuts. Do not practice only the tests; practice the *skills* you will need for the test. Do this by carefully reading the material in each chapter and by thinking about how that topic will help you become a state police officer. Even if you have done well in high school or college, you need to remember that careful reading is not the same as just reading the words. Reading this book carefully is an important way to practice for the test. If you do not read the test questions carefully, you will probably answer them incorrectly.

Throughout the United States, educators have been worrying about the drop in SAT scores within the last decade. Maybe you were faced with concern over the SAT when you were in high school and thinking about attending college. Because many state police agencies now require some college or even a four-year degree from their applicants, it is likely that you have already faced timed aptitude tests that can play a large role in your future. One of the findings of those studying the drop in SAT scores was that students took too many shortcuts in studying. For instance, they studied vocabulary lists rather than more complex reading material. This did not help the students, because reading is more than just a list of words; it also means understanding the words in context so that you understand a situation.

Thus, reading this book carefully will help you in a number of ways. Just by reading each section carefully, you will enhance your comprehension skills; these skills are exactly what will be tested in the reading portions of the entry exam.

Many states include math on their entry exams. You might wonder why. While the average trooper may not need advanced calculus to get through the day, basic math is required when estimating speed or distance, when totaling the value of found or stolen property, and even for calculating such simple things as mileage or expenses. Your math skills will be tested in conjunction with your reading skills; rather than just being asked to add up a list of numbers or determine a percentage of items lost or found, you might be asked to read a passage on a situation and then asked to do some arithmetical calculations. If you haven't read the situation properly, there is a good chance you will not calculate properly, either.

None of this information is meant to intimidate you, only to impress on you the importance of studying for the written exam, and to help you understand how *State Trooper Exam* can give you an extra boost of knowledge and confidence that may translate into the difference between passing and failing.

1 ▶ What State Troopers Do

CHAPTER SUMMARY

State police and highway patrols provide many services, although the roles of officers in highway patrol departments may be somewhat more limited than those in full-service state police departments.

State police have concurrent (or shared) jurisdiction or responsibility with local police departments. Forty-nine of the 50 states in the United States have some form of state police agency; Hawaii is the only state without such an agency. In about half the states, state troopers, whether in full-service agencies or in highway patrols, have primary responsibility for enforcing traffic laws on interstate highways, turnpikes, and other major roadways.

In some states, state police are responsible for criminal investigation and are frequently called upon by small local police departments and some small sheriffs' offices to provide leadership and expertise in many complex criminal investigations. Full-service state police agencies are sometimes referred to as operating in the centralized model of state law enforcement because all the state's policing functions are combined in one large department.

These full-service departments also provide crime lab services for local police and sheriffs. This might include ballistic and drug testing, DNA analysis, and analysis of evidence in major crimes. These departments may also maintain the state records on criminal history of offenders, including sex offender records, and may operate a state computer network that is similar to the one maintained at the federal level by the Federal Bureau of Investigation (FBI). About two-thirds of state police agencies operate recruit training academies; some of these permit officers from local departments to attend. Many state police departments also take leadership roles in supervisory, management, and specialized training for local police officers, particularly those in small rural police departments.

Some state police even fulfill the role of local police in small towns and unincorporated areas of a state. This may be because there is no local police department or because the local department is too small to provide coverage 24 hours a day, seven days a week. In these cases, troopers may be assigned full-time to provide all general police services to a town or area, in effect becoming the town's police force. In some states, such as New Jersey, towns may pay the state police to act as their police force; this is often termed *contract policing*, and obligates the state police to provide whatever services are outlined in the contract just as a private security firm might do for a client.

Some states limit the roles of the state police because they also have formed bureaus of investigation to undertake criminal and civil investigations on a statewide basis. This is often referred to as a decentralized model of state law enforcement because there is a distinction between highway traffic enforcement and other state-level law enforcement functions. In these states, agencies, often with names like *bureau of investigation*, are state versions of the FBI; agents are sworn police officers but rarely, if ever, work in uniform or are involved in non-investigatory police activities.

The decentralized model is more often found in southern and midwestern states, although some western states also follow this type of organization. Generally, the state police agencies that operate in a decentralized model can be recognized by the word *highway* or *patrol* in their name. Examples are the Ohio State Highway Patrol, the North Carolina Highway Patrol, and the Wyoming Highway Patrol. Many of the decentralized agencies have fewer officers than the full-service state police agencies, in part because their responsibilities are more limited, but also because they are often found in states with smaller populations and

lower population density. This means that highway patrol officers must often patrol long stretches of roadway alone, with their backup many miles away.

Interestingly, both the largest and the smallest state patrol agencies are decentralized. The largest is also the best known—the California Highway Patrol (CHP). Despite its fame through a television show and its almost 7,000 sworn officers, the CHP shares law enforcement duties with the California Division of Law Enforcement, the state's investigative agency. And as an indication that labels do not always tell the entire story, in 2001 and 2002, CHP was honored with the Herman Goldstein Award by the Police Executive Research Forum (PERF) for its efforts in problem-oriented policing, a philosophy more commonly associated with municipal policing than with highway patrol. In contrast with the size of CHP, the North Dakota Highway Patrol is the smallest decentralized agency, with approximately 150 officers patrolling throughout the entire state.

What does all this mean to you—the applicant? It means that there are many career paths to follow. Although virtually all state police agencies assign new officers to uniformed patrol in marked vehicles on roadways, there are many career options to which a trooper may aspire.

The New Jersey State Police (NJSP), for instance, lists more than 120 units in which its officers might work. Although the choices do not run from A to Z, they do run from A to V. Troopers may work in Alcoholic Beverage Control enforcement, or as armorers (those who test, maintain, and repair firearms), or in the aviation unit, or in the victims services unit. The range between these duties is vast; some assignments are action-oriented and require working mostly nights with teams of other officers, while other assignments may appeal to those who require a more normal workweek to care for children or other dependents. To say there is something for everyone is not an exaggeration, although, of course, no one is guaranteed the assignment of his or her choice. The NJSP's range of duties is particularly wide, but is not that different from other full-service state agencies. In the New York State Police (NYSP), for instance, officers might work in crime analysis, forensics, drug enforcement, the warrant squad, SCUBA, or marine unit. The Illinois State Police (ISP), which began as a highway patrol in 1919 but grew into a full-service agency, maintains the state's criminal statistics and criminal history records, registers firearms owners, and has gained an enviable reputation for its various labs and its electronic data processing and computer center.

With this wide range of assignments open to you, it is important not to forget that the most basic responsibilities of any state trooper are to protect life and property and to promote highway safety. You may respond to all types of crime calls, including burglaries, assaults, robberies, and homicides, and also to such service calls as finding lost or missing children or adults, evacuating those in danger due to natural disasters or vehicle accidents, or assisting fire or medical personnel in handling other health or safety emergencies.

These basic requirements mean that all troopers must know how to operate a motor vehicle; must be prepared to work all hours of the day and night, including weekends; must be prepared to carry a firearm and use it if the situation warrants deadly physical force; patrol wide areas, generally in one-officer patrol cars; interact with people of all races and from all social classes; investigate crimes; take notes based on a series of events or interviews; make arrests; conduct searches; testify in court or before a grand jury; and fulfill a number of roles that may develop on short notice and that require exercising tact and good judgment.

▶ Contemporary Concerns Lead to New Roles

In addition to these varied tasks that state police have performed for decades, the twenty-first century has brought new responsibilities. Since September 11, 2001, state police have become involved in antiterrorism and homeland security activities. Most Americans know that after the 9/11 attacks, the federal government passed the Homeland Security Act of 2002, forming the Department of Homeland Security (DHS). This new cabinet-level department has brought together about 170,000 employees working for 22 agencies that protect Americans overseas and domestically, and maintain safe transportation, cargo, and borders. Less well known are the state-level activities to increase homeland security, many of which were assigned to state police departments, resulting in career paths that had not previously existed. State police officers are now involved in investigating suspected terrorists or terrorist-inspired crimes.

Although foreign terrorists have received considerable press and law enforcement attention, there are numerous domestic terrorist groups operating around the nation. Additionally, whether the terrorists themselves are foreign or domestic, acts of terrorism are essentially local issues that must be addressed primarily by local police acting in conjunction with state and federal agencies. State police departments participate in multiagency joint terrorism task forces and serve as the lead agency for many new statewide intelligence-gathering networks. In rural areas, antiterrorism resources are usually staffed by state police officers, who also frequently provide training for local police.

State homeland security directors, whether working out of the offices of their respective governors or other arrangements, frequently rely on the state police for expertise and personnel to undertake specialist assignments. The NYSP worked closely with U.S. Customs and Border Patrol officers who were assigned to checkpoints along the Canadian border, a task that the NYSP was not assigned prior to the September 11 attacks. Additional emerging areas of specialization are enforcement of regulations to control or safeguard the handling and shipping of hazardous materials; conducting threat analyses to prevent terrorist acts such as bombings; and assistance in such newly emerging specialties as risk analysis and threat and vulnerability recognition and resolution. State police are also working to prevent terrorist acts involving weapons of mass destruction, including chemical, biological, and radiological weapons.

Just as computers have become a way of life in many parts of the country and a lifeline for teens and businesspeople, they have also fostered new types of crimes that are often beyond the capability of local police to investigate but are not broad enough to involve federal law enforcement agencies. Many state police agencies have assumed investigative and enforcement responsibilities for computer-generated crimes, particularly those involving financial fraud, identity theft, or dissemination of prohibited material. Although computer crime is vast, like many more traditional modes of criminal behavior, it can be divided into categories. Cyber-criminals who strike businesses are often insiders (current or former employees); hackers are outsiders who want to hurt a company or institution or, sometimes, just prove they are able to break into an institution's computer network; virus writers may be motivated by financial gain or, again, just want to impress those in the know with their ability to curtail or even stop computer traffic; and criminal groups mostly use computers to engage in some form of theft or fraud.

Another large category of computer criminals are sex offenders, who use the Internet to prey on young victims. State police have been involved in so-called "stings," posing as underage boys and girls online and then arranging to meet those who seek sexual contact with minors. Pornographers, too, have been able to use the Internet to circulate pictures and movies of children engaged in sexual behavior. The resources to investigate these types of complex crimes are often beyond the capabilities of most small police departments, and to fill the void, in many states, state police investigators have gained expertise in these areas and are working with federal agents, and with banks and financial institutions, to prosecute cyber-criminals.

► The History of State Policing

The history of state police agencies in the United States is not as long as the histories of municipal or federal policing, but it is far more varied and colorful than you might expect. Many applicants who take the exams for state police departments are surprised to learn that the job is far more than patrolling state highways and rural byways. This surprise often comes because books on policing have portrayed the creation of state police merely as attempts to provide highway enforcement at a time when cars were becoming commonplace throughout the country. The development of state police agencies is one of the most neglected areas of police history.

The roots of state policing can be traced to experiments that began when, upon gaining independence from Mexico in 1835, Texas formed the Texas Rangers. Since Texas was a republic at the time, rather than a state, the Rangers did not officially become a state police force until 1845, when Texas became a state. Similar mounted forces were formed in 1901 and 1905 by the territories of Arizona and New Mexico, respectively. Although today these forces are considered the pioneers in state policing, since most of their tasks involved patrolling the border with Mexico, they were actually more like today's federal Border Patrol than like the state police departments that followed in their footsteps.

The earliest state police department that would be familiar to today's applicants was formed in Connecticut in 1903, followed by the Pennsylvania State Constabulary (now the Pennsylvania State Police) in 1905. Eventually, all 50 states except Hawaii formed some type of state police agency—either a full-service department, such as those in New York, Connecticut, New Jersey, Pennsylvania, and Illinois, or an agency primarily assigned to highway patrol, such as the California Highway Patrol, the Ohio State Highway Patrol, and the South Carolina Highway Patrol.

The Pennsylvania State Constabulary in some ways set the tone for all state police agencies. Although it has changed over the years, the Pennsylvania force was highly centralized and as much like a militia as a police force. Its organization, and the fact that officers played a large role in controlling strikes, led to its unpopularity with both business leaders and laborers. Setting the tone for many later controversies involving police, business leaders felt the constabulary was unreliable as a strike-breaking force and laborers believed they were the victims of unnecessary police violence, going so far as to compare them to Cossacks.

Although the Pennsylvania State Police (PSP) has changed considerably over the years, state police agencies to this day are more formal in their manner and more military in training and attitude than most municipal police departments. They also tend to demand a higher level of physical agility during training and throughout a trooper's career.

The creation of the state police in New York was also controversial; again, the issues revolved around business versus labor and urban versus rural interests. Many of those who favored the state police tried to convince those in rural portions of the country that they were being overrun by crime, in part due to the new availability of vehicles. This perception, and the fact that many state police agencies were not formed until the 1920s and 1930s, is part of the reason the development of state policing is generally viewed as primarily a response to the newfound mobility of criminals. Other departments that formed before the 1920s, and prior to the advent of the automobile as a major issue in crime control, include Michigan in 1917 and West Virginia in 1919.

Despite a number of critics who argued that small, rural police and sheriffs' departments were unable to meet the crime-fighting needs of rural America, many residents of these areas, including New York state, were concerned that supporting state police forces would result in higher taxes and that the forces could become agents of repression, particularly in labor disputes. Organized labor was also against state police, but in New York, a coalition of upstate and suburban legislators overcame the opposition by including the bill a prohibition against using the state police within city limits to suppress riots and disorders, unless directed to do so by the governor or unless requested by the mayor of the city and approved by the governor. With this limitation, the authorization passed both houses of the New York State Legislature and the bill was signed into law by Governor Charles S. Whitman.

Setting the early military style of the department, Governor Whitman named his friend Dr. George Fletch Chandler, a surgeon who had served in the U.S. Army's 10th Infantry, as the first commander. The first recruits trained at a National Guard camp and appeared in public for the first time in September 1917, when 232 troopers were assigned to the New York State Fairgrounds near Syracuse. Troopers were appointed for two years subject to the approval of the superintendent. It was a misdemeanor to quit without consent until 1938, the year appointments became permanent. Although early NYSP troopers were required to know how to ride horseback, and many did so in the course of their duties, by 1918 the force had added Model T Fords and motorcycles, especially for what were termed *hurried calls*.

Troopers in many states lived in barracks, worked long hours, and needed permission to marry. In 1958 troopers in New York State saw their average workday change to an eight-hour, five day a week schedule from the previous 12-hour schedule. Although no troopers are still required to live in barracks, state police agencies are generally more military in their training styles and have a much smaller percentage of women in their ranks than municipal police departments and most federal law enforcement agencies.

CHAPTER

2

Becoming a State Trooper

CHAPTER SUMMARY

Not only is state policing newer than municipal and federal policing, it also has the fewest agencies and employs the fewest number of officers of the three branches (federal, state, local) of policing. In the year 2000, the 49 state police agencies employed about 56,000 full-time, sworn officers. Reflecting that patrol is the major component of the job, more than 65% of the officers spent their workday on patrol. This small number of positions compared to municipal policing, which in 2000 employed more than 440,000 sworn officers, means that each applicant for a state police position will face intense competition for the few positions that become available.

▶ Eligibility/Basic Qualifications

It is very important for anyone who aspires to a position as a state police officer to review the eligibility requirements carefully. Although it might seem surprising, considering the similarity in the organization and roles of many state police departments, the basic requirements may differ substantially from agency to agency. The differences may have little to do with job responsibilities or with geography. As an example, the NYSP requires an applicant to be 20 years old on application date and 21 at the time of appointment, and no older than 30 without a military-service exemption, but the NJSP requires that applicants be at least 21 on the date of the written exam but may attend and graduate from the academy up to age 35. The ISP demands that an applicant be at least 21 (although there is an option that permits 20-year-olds to apply) but does not list a maximum age on its website. The PSP accepts applicants who are least 20 when they complete the application, but new troopers must be at least 21 and under 40 at the time of appointment.

Educational requirements are also different. The NYSP requires a high school diploma or equivalent at the time of application and completion of 60 college credits by the time of appointment, although there are at least two categories of exemptions to the educational requirements. The NJSP requires a four-year bachelor's degree or 60 college credits plus at least two years of satisfactory employment or military experience. The ISP has a number of educational options, all of which require an applicant to have an average of C or better, and to have some combination of education and work experience, with military duty often substituting for the years of work. The PSP requires an associate's degree or 60 college credits at the time of application (different from the time of appointment), but will accept some waivers if the candidate has military training or has two years of full-time police experience, including having been certified by the state's Municipal Police Officers' Education and Training Commission (MPOETC). The departments also differ as to how military training counts in place of other education or work experience, and whether and how veterans' preference points are added to an applicant's test score.

Just as with other types of police employment, candidates must be U.S. citizens by the time of appointment but need not always have attained citizenship at the time of application. Virtually all state police agencies require an applicant to have a valid driver's license, sometimes from the state of appointment, sometimes from any state. Similarly, some require that you be a resident of the state at the time of appointment, others at the time you begin or graduate from the police academy.

Other areas that may differ are past drug use, past conviction records (although no agency will employ someone who has a felony on his or her record), and past driving or credit records. Having been less than honorably discharged from any branch of the military will usually disqualify an applicant, as will having been fired from a government job, espe-

cially if that job is with another law enforcement agency. Testing positive for current drug use will also disqualify a candidate.

Few agencies have specific height and weight standards any longer, instead requiring that candidates pass the physical ability test. The vision requirements, once universally set at 20/20 uncorrected, are now more flexible. Color blindness remains an automatic disqualification for virtually all police jobs. A new standard in many police departments concerns tattoos. The NYSP, for instance, according to its website, requires all officers to "present a neat and professional appearance at all times" and specifies that this means that tattoos, brands, body piercings, and other body art may not be visible while an officer is in uniform or dressed in other business attire. The NJSP does not mention this issue at all. The PSP website also mentions tattoos, stating that non-facial tattoos are permissible as long as they are neither objectionable nor demeaning to the department's image. The department retains the right to make that determination and requires that those that do not conform be altered or removed.

Regulations on other matters are equally specific for many of the agencies. Applicants should become familiar with the requirements of the agency or agencies they plan to apply to. Because the regulations may be similar in some cases or substantially different in others, understanding the specific requirements of the agency is vital to your job search.

▶ Career Information Resources

For those who want to apply to only one state police agency or to multiple agencies that do not require residency, the best place to begin a search for information is on the Internet. All state police agencies, like many municipal and virtually all federal agencies, have web pages, and they are full of useful information. Use any search engine to find the website of your agency of choice. Once you've gotten to the pages you are seeking, bookmark them so you can go back anytime you want to check something or to see if the requirements or other information provided have changed. Because the headquarters of state police agencies are often located in rural parts of their states, it may be hardest for those living in big cities to learn about their state police agencies firsthand. It is for these applicants that the websites will be exceptionally useful. Many of the websites are interactive and provide you with the opportunity to ask questions and receive personalized answers from a member of the force.

If you are in college, attend your school's career fairs or visit with a career counselor. Many state police agencies, even those that do not require a college education, are eager to recruit college students into their ranks. Particularly if you are attending a college with a criminal justice or a police studies program, there is a strong possibility that your own state's police agency will be at the career fair; often, neighboring states will also attend to increase interest in their agencies. Some job fairs are strictly informational, offering material for further study. Others will provide you with an opportunity to talk to officers from the department who are assigned to the recruitment office. Come prepared with resumes, since some departments will take your information and place you on a list to receive the latest test applications and schedules as they are developed. If you attend a college that does not have a criminal justice program, contact a local college that does and see if you might be permitted access to its fair. Be forewarned; a number of colleges are instituting dress codes to attend job fairs.

Many state police agencies exhibit at state and county fairs. While their primary purpose at these events may be to promote highway safety or various community-based programs, general career information will probably be available. Because these exhibits are usually staffed by troopers, they present excellent opportunities to speak with someone on the job who can give you a good idea of what the work is like and

can help you decide if the position fits your interests and aspirations.

State police agencies tend to have smaller percentages of women and racial and ethnic minorities than large municipal police departments. To help them find candidates who often do not look for them, agencies have expanded their recruitment to some less traditional venues. Some agencies have begun recruiting at gyms and sporting events; others have set up career events with scouting groups and with groups that have large minority or female memberships. If you belong to any such groups and are interested in a career in state policing, have your group leader contact the state police recruitment unit, which may be happy to send information or even a recruiter to talk personally with potential applicants.

▶ The Job Search

Similar to learning basic eligibility standards and information about your agency of choice, the best way to learn about vacancies, exam periods, steps in the application process, and whatever else you need to know leading up to the actual written test is from the agency's website. If you have met with a recruitment officer or contacted the agency via mail or phone, you may already have received an applicant package. If not, requirements, samples, and actual applications may be available on the agency's website. Even if the application itself is not there, you can often fill out a form to request this material.

Generally, the first step in the selection process will be completing the application. Read carefully what you are being asked and make sure you answer everything correctly. The application may ask you to list every place you have lived for the past seven or ten years. "Every" means just that; do not decide that somewhere you lived for only four or five months doesn't count. If you lived in a college dorm but it wasn't your legal address for voting, reread the form to see what is being asked of you. If you can't determine, consider e-mailing or calling to be sure. A form that is incorrectly filled out may disqualify you if the reader finds lies or inconsistencies. This is not a good time to guess. Make a copy of the application so you can make edits and corrections should the need arise. Once you have thoroughly reviewed your draft, neatly complete the final application and submit it to the agency.

What you write on the application will form the basis of your initial screening and your more detailed background investigation. The initial check is to assure you meet the minimum entry requirements. Are you the correct age to be eligible to sit for the written exam? If there is a residency requirement, have you fulfilled it? Do you have a valid driver's license, or is it only necessary for you to have this at the time of actual appointment? If it is determined that you have intentionally made a false statement, you will be disqualified before you even get to the written exam.

Some applicants are disqualified not because they lied—but simply because they did not follow instructions. Did you complete the application? Did you sign and date the application?

Most state police agencies have specific filing periods for upcoming exams. Only a few agencies have rolling applications, which means you may apply at any time and your application will be held until the next test date. If you are filing for a specific exam, the easiest way to be disqualified is by not mailing the application in enough time for it to be postmarked before the application deadline. Parents and teachers may have given you second chances; it is unlikely the state police will. The first step in the early elimination of applicants is the application process. Just as the written exam is meant to test your reading and comprehension skills, so is the application. Read carefully and follow the instructions.

If you have read carefully and followed the instructions and you meet all the minimum eligibility requirements, you will be advised, usually by mail, of

the next steps in the applicant process. Some agencies may ask you for a resume, but many will not. This is where the hiring process differs from many civilian positions. You may be asked to submit documents to support your claim of minimum eligibility, such as a birth certificate, a high school diploma, a college transcript, or military discharge papers, but even these may not be asked of you until after you have passed the written exam. The reason for this is that the written exam eliminates many applicants, and many agencies do not want to invest the time and costs related to checking documentation of applicants who may not pass the written exam. You probably know this already, which may be the reason you have invested in this study guide to help you get over the first hurdle.

▶ Steps in the Hiring Process

Although different agencies may arrange the steps in the hiring process slightly differently, virtually all will include the following steps:

1. Completing the written application (possibly online)
2. Successfully passing the written exam
3. Passing the physical fitness (or ability) tests
4. Passing the background investigation
5. Passing the medical and psychological examinations

Depending on the agency to which you have applied, other steps might include an oral appraisal exam and a polygraph exam. A drug-screening exam (generally a urinalysis) will also be administered, either at the physical fitness test or during the medical exam. Generally, you must pass each step in the process to be permitted to move on to the next phase of the application process.

Some agencies may ask for letters of recommendation; others, such as the PSP, specifically advise candidates that no recommendations will be accepted and that, in fact, they will be discarded if received. Some agencies may ask for a traditional resume, while others will expect you to provide all required information on the application form itself. Agencies that accept military service in lieu of educational requirements or that offer veterans' preference points will ask you to provide a non-returnable copy of the Certificate of Release or Discharge from Active Duty (Form DD-214, Member 4 copy). If you are applying while still an active duty member of the military, there are other requirements you must fulfill, which are generally available on the agency's website or obtainable by a telephone call or e-mail to the recruitment section.

▶ Hiring Trends

It is difficult to discuss hiring trends in state policing because the sizes of the agencies vary so greatly. Remember that the smallest state police agency has only about 150 employees, while the largest has over 7,000. In addition, state policing is not a career that someone enters casually. Most of those who become state troopers have sought the position for many years. The voluntary turnover rates are low; most of those who pass all the steps in the hiring process and who successfully complete the academy remain for their entire work lives, usually retiring after 20 or 25 years of service. It can be estimated that even the larger agencies hire no more than 100 or 200 troopers each year. Because there are mandatory retirement ages for troopers in many states (usually 55 or 60), the number of vacancies may depend on whether the agency increased in size at particular times in its history. If there was a large increase in staff at particular periods, this may mean that there will be a disproportionately large number of retirements in a particular year. Current applicants are at somewhat of an advantage because new roles for state police agencies in combat-ing terrorism and computer-related crimes have resulted in some increases in staff complements.

Regardless of these small increases, the position is selective. The NYSP is an excellent example. In 2006, the agency reported on its website that for its most recent exam, more than 19,500 applicants took the exam and slightly over 17,000 passed. The NYSP usually conducts two academy classes each year. Although class size may vary from about 100 to 250 recruit officers per class, what generally does not vary is the statistic that it takes about ten candidates to fill one vacancy. What this means is that for every ten people who pass the written exam, nine do not pass the later portions of the applicant process. This means that about 1,000 people who passed the written exam are contacted for processing to fill 100 positions. Other states do not differ substantially.

Some agencies may have even higher rates of applicants who pass the written exam but do not reach the point of entering an academy. Rather than making the written exam less important, this fact highlights the importance of doing well. Most agencies contact applicants in the order they ranked on the written exam. Thus, the higher your score, the earlier you will have the opportunity to enter into the rest of the hiring process—and the sooner you may be called to attend an academy class.

▶ Training

What can you expect when you attend an academy class? The first thing to know is that state police training is not like a vacation at camp. Depending on the state in which you are hired, you can expect to attend the academy for between five and eight months. Generally, you will be expected to live on the academy grounds at least from Sunday evening to Friday night. Some academies do not permit recruit officers to go home at all until they are partway through the training period. This means that if you have dependent children or other relatives, you will have to make provisions for their care in your absence. The same is true if you have pets.

Academy training is a full-time responsibility; the PSP considers the normal training day to begin at 5:30 A.M. and end at 10:45 P.M. While you may not be busy for all these hours, you should expect some nighttime training and other activities that may be scheduled for after the dinner period. You will not be permitted to hold any type of job or attend any other schools while in the academy. You can expect to be up early in the morning, generally starting the day with an inspection of your living space and your uniform, participating in some physical activity, and then attending a full day of classroom activities. You will be advised on what you are expected to bring with you on the first day of training; the PSP's website lists 20 items of training uniforms and materials you are to have on the first day of the academy. The list ranges from uniforms to gym clothing, civilian attire, toiletry and bath items, and 30 hangers of the same color. In that respect, it might seem like summer camp or a college dorm, but the discipline will be far stricter than at either of those places. Candidates with a military background will have a more realistic idea of what to expect. Other agencies may be somewhat less specific, but the expectations are similar.

Much has been written about the rigors of the physical training at most state police academies. Of course, you will have gotten yourself into excellent physical shape to pass the preemployment physical, but the regimen may still be taxing. Remember that by the time you get to most academies, you will already have passed a strenuous physical ability test, but you will be expected to stay in top shape and can expect to be tested frequently on your flexibility, strength, and cardiovascular health. Using the PSP, one of the most rigorous academies, as an example, upon arrival at the academy, cadets are expected to pass the same physical fitness test they took for entry, and to participate in a program that includes calisthenics, weight training, fighting techniques, boxing, and defensive tactics.

Depending on the policies of your department, you may be taught to drive a variety of vehicles in addition to a passenger vehicle. In every state, you will receive firearms training, at least in your sidearm and a shotgun, and, in some states, in a wider variety of weapons. Expect to run daily in the morning, the evening, or both. You can also expect swimming and water rescue and emergency medical training, although only a few states expect you to go beyond Red Cross basic first-aid training. Those who are or want to become certified emergency medical technicians or even paramedics may be provided with the opportunity to take this training or refresh their certifications.

Although physical training is a vital part of the state police academy training, mental activity is also emphasized. You will also have a full range of classroom activities, including pencil-and-paper exams, oral presentations, and projects that you will have to work on individually or as part of a group. Virtually all academies expect you to maintain an academic average of at least 70% to successfully complete the classroom portion of the training. Recruits at the NJSP Academy are issued laptop computers that are used throughout the training.

Classroom instruction will range from the history of policing and the history of your agency to modern theories of community policing and crime prevention. You will study all aspects of law, including criminal law, motor vehicle law, drug law, and various aspects of civil law. You will also learn about crimes against children and how to interview juveniles and adults, including elderly persons who may need special attention. There are explanations of what constitutes domestic violence and how best to respond to these types of complaints. Additional training topics include decision making, responding to critical incidents, accident investigation and reconstruction, and other investigatory techniques. Practical police training will include how and when to make an arrest, how and when to search someone or something (particularly a motor vehicle), and general patrol techniques. There is also ethical training, dealing with moral dilemmas and how to deal with the authority and power that comes with being a police officer. This is all in addition to your other practical training on firearms, first aid, water safety, and, possibly, fire rescue and extracting injured persons from motor vehicles.

Most of your courses will be taught by senior members of the department, but outside experts, including attorneys, medical personnel, and community leaders, may be brought in for certain subjects. Many academies encourage student officers to form study groups in the evening and many candidates also spend evening hours in the gym to help them meet the rigorous physical requirements.

The last set of academy requirements will involve personal grooming and maintaining your living quarters. Again, different from high school or college but similar to the military, state police recruits are expected to maintain military-style personal grooming standards, as well as keeping their dorm rooms and bunks clean. The length of hair and the permissibility of sideburns will be specified. Men can expect that beards and/or mustaches will be prohibited. Women may be expected to cut their hair so that it does not extend beyond the bottom of the uniform collar, or they may be permitted to keep their hair longer as long as it can be pinned up under all agency hats, helmets, or other headgear. Jewelry is generally not permitted, and cologne or makeup may also be prohibited.

▶ Conditions of Employment

What will the job be like after all this and how much can you expect to earn? Once again, the second part of the question especially will depend on the agency. Salaries can normally be found on the agency's website. Full-service agencies may pay slightly higher than some highway patrol agencies, but because salaries come from government sources and because many agencies are unionized, the salary will be based in part on what

a state can pay and what the officers' union representatives are able to obtain at the collective bargaining table. Some examples based on 2005 and 2006 salaries may not be representative of all agencies, but can give you some idea of annual wage levels.

The NYSP starting salary as of April 1, 2006 was over $50,000 during academy training, rising to more than $61,500 upon graduation. After annual raises, based on the current contract, troopers with five years' experience earned more than $77,000. There are also location expenses for certain urban counties and New York City. NJSP salaries are comparable; in 2006, troopers earned a starting salary of more than $53,500 (which included a uniform allowance), and almost $60,000 in their second year of service. Salaries are lower in Illinois; new officers in 2006 could expect to earn about $37,000 while in the academy (including overtime) and almost $45,000 in base salary their first year out of the academy. There is also often overtime pay or compensatory time off and, in some cases, additional pay or time off for working holidays or nights or weekends. Obviously, if you take and pass a promotion exam, your salary will be considerably higher in each of the agencies.

Each of the departments offers full medical benefits, including dental and life insurance for yourself and for your dependents, although you may have to contribute to dependents' coverage. All departments offer vacation benefits, generally starting at a minimum of two weeks and increasing with longevity. Such benefits are usually accrued monthly (often, one sick day for each month worked), and most agencies have policies that give you time off for work-related injuries and do not require you to use your own time. Candidates who are active in sports, where they may become injured, or candidates who are thinking of becoming parents at some point in their careers should investigate policies pertaining to use of time off for non-work-related events that may limit the ability to work full duty.

One reason that vacancies do not occur frequently in state police agencies is that retirement policies are usually more generous than in private industry. Once again, different agencies may differ, but generally, troopers are able to retire at half-pay or higher with some combination of age and years of service. A common combination is age 50 with 25 years of service or age 55 with 20 years of service. In many agencies, if you stay beyond the minimum age and years of service formula, you add considerably to your retirement package. Although many agencies have eliminated mandatory retirement regulations, some require you to retire at age 55, 60, or 63.

In return for this generous benefit package, you will be asked to give up some other benefits that you might have in your present employment. As explained earlier, virtually all agencies will expect you to live at the training facility while you are in the academy and to give up personal freedom as to going out, grooming, and other decisions you may now take for granted. Virtually all agencies assign new troopers to road patrol, and you will generally have no say in what part of the state you are assigned to and the hours and days you will work, although generally you will not be expected to work more than 40 hours a week without overtime pay.

You will be expected to work armed and in uniform in all types of weather and to handle all types of police calls to which you are dispatched. Most often, you will work in a marked patrol car alone and will be expected to handle your calls independently until another officer is available to respond. This is a major difference between state policing and policing in a large metropolitan police department. In a large department, you may work with a partner, or other officers may be only minutes away; in state policing, the closest member of your own department may be hours away, and even officers from smaller neighboring departments may be 30 minutes or more away. This is why physical training, judgment, and handling yourself in emergencies are such an important part of academy training.

CHAPTER

3 ▶ About the State Trooper Written Exam

CHAPTER SUMMARY
To select the best candidates to become state police officers, state governments employ a series of screening devices, including medical and physical examinations, character and background investigations, psychological assessments, and written tests. The written test is competitive.

▶ How the Exam Is Scored

Those who score the highest marks have the greatest chance of being selected, but others who pass the exam also can be selected. Merely passing the exam is not to be disparaged. These exams are challenging, and the passing mark is set at a point deemed effective for selecting qualified candidates.

When the cutoff mark is set, one point on the grading scale becomes the difference between passing and failing. It may seem arbitrary that, for example, a candidate who scores 80% passes the exam, while a candidate who scores 79% fails, but a line must be drawn somewhere; otherwise, the administration of a written examination would be meaningless.

For candidates, the lesson to be drawn from this is that every point counts, and because the exams are competitive, every point counts whether the exam is difficult or relatively easy. Most of the exams are organized and graded like exams you have taken throughout your educational career, and are also similar to many of the exams given in the military to test candidates for entry and for specific specializations. These are traditional paper-and-pencil tests that for ease of scoring will usually be based on a total of 100 points. This may mean either 100 or 200 questions; most often, your score will be expressed as a percentage.

Your goal must be to score a higher mark than most of the other candidates. If the candidate is exceptionally brilliant, perhaps he or she need not worry about the competition; but for most candidates taking the exam, their preparation, practice, and perseverance—rather than sheer brilliance—is what separates the winners from the losers.

► Establish a Study Game Plan

Establishing a study schedule is essential. These schedules are like game plans, and just like a football or basketball coach's game plan, they must be carried out successfully on the field or on the court. Going through the motions will not result in a win; full commitment to the game plan is required.

A candidate cannot succeed by going through the motions of reading the material and logging in the hours on the schedule. You must thoroughly study and master the material. This includes concentrating, making notes, restudying questions that you answered incorrectly, and working until you get 100% of the practice questions right. This is hard work, and requires motivation. Therefore, the first step is to find the motivation.

The desire to succeed on any test provides a basic level of motivation for most people, especially when passing the test opens an opportunity for employment. However, the best motivation for a candidate is to decide that becoming a state police officer is his or her number one career choice. That is the kind of commitment and motivation that a candidate needs to compete successfully, because the majority of the other candidates are just as committed to becoming state troopers.

A career as a state trooper is not an ordinary job. It is not merely a civil service position; it is an extraordinary position. It is a career that gives the officer a special status in society. It is a career that engenders respect and admiration for those who carry out their responsibilities honorably, courageously, fairly, and intelligently. A state trooper is endowed with substantial authority and responsibility to protect life and property, to preserve the peace, to protect the rights of citizens, to prevent crime, and to apprehend criminals. When necessary, a state trooper has the authority to use physical force and even deadly physical force.

We entrust the trooper with this authority, and we expect him or her to perform these duties in an exemplary manner. The functions that state troopers perform cover a wide spectrum of activities, including, but not limited to, investigating reported crimes, arresting lawbreakers, counseling youths, disarming dangerous criminals, enforcing traffic laws, investigating organized crime and terrorist networks, rendering aid and assistance to accident victims, reconstructing accident scenes, handling demonstrations and disorders, and testifying at hearings and trials.

Each state trooper may be called upon to perform any of these functions, and all need to possess the skills that will enable them to do so. With training, they learn to perform these functions efficiently and effectively. However, before candidates are hired and before they are trained, they must demonstrate that they have the capability to perform these functions properly. They must demonstrate that they have the ability to assess situations and to make the proper judgments as to what action, if any, to employ.

The written test is the primary means of ascertaining whether a candidate possesses the necessary capabilities. Written tests are not the perfect means of assessing candidates, but they have proven to be the most practical and effective. The written exam is, in many ways, the most important step in the hiring process, because it serves an important gate-keeping function. The candidate who does not pass the written exam may be in excellent physical condition or may have other qualifications, but it will make no difference if he or she is unable to pass the written exam.

▶ The Three Ps

Some states, in addition to the written test, employ oral question and answer tests to select candidates, but you must pass the written test before moving on to the oral test. Whether the process includes only a written test or requires both oral and written tests, the three Ps—preparation, practice, and perseverance—are the keys to success.

Preparation

Preparation includes not only the time spent studying the relevant material and guides, but also a full-time commitment to obtaining the knowledge and abilities that will make you a successful candidate and an excellent state police officer. You should study previous tests that were given for the position. Every day, you should devote a substantial amount of time to reading about law-enforcement topics. You should have a comprehensive, up-to-date police administration textbook as a reference. You should also read newspaper articles pertaining to police work, and focus on current police-related issues and controversies that are raised in the print or broadcast media.

As part of your preparation, you should endeavor to improve your vocabulary. In the course of your studies and when taking practice tests, you must look up every word about which you are unsure. In law enforcement, as in any specialized profession, there are words, terms, and jargon (specialized expressions used primarily in certain professions but not in others) that are repeatedly used. Candidates should be familiar with them and should understand how they are used in the context of law-enforcement terminology. Unfamiliarity with or an erroneous understanding of a word during the written exam can cause substantial difficulty, especially in a reading comprehension question. Because many exam questions are structured in a series format, an erroneous interpretation of one word can cause a series of errors.

Practice

Practice tests are invaluable tools for candidates to improve their test-taking skills. The best way to take practice tests is to replicate as closely as possible the actual test conditions. Uninterrupted privacy is a must, and the tests should be completed in one sitting. Training for written exams is similar to training for physical contests. Endurance is essential. The exams can be viewed as mental marathons. An exam of several hours tests a person's mental and emotional endurance. Those who have not trained will tire and, as a result, will make mistakes. Those who have trained will be better suited to remain focused and clearheaded to the end of the exam.

With rare exceptions, your written exam will be similar to the exams given in past years. Familiarity with previous exams is invaluable. Being familiar with the structures of individual questions and of questions in a series will allow you to quickly note the question format and proceed to the content of the questions. This will save time and considerable mental energy.

The types of questions are each described in later chapters of this book. The most common types of questions are reading-based (comprehension); writing and information ordering; mathematics; spatial and directional orientation (generally map reading); memory and observation; and problem solving, which includes reasoning, judgment, and sensitivity. Generally, there will be anywhere between five and 15 questions in each category, although some categories may be stressed more strongly than others. The most common response pattern will be multiple choice (select from **a** through **d**), although true/false or short response questions may also be included.

Sometimes, the examiners will employ a new format for the entire exam or for a section of the exam. In the event that the exam uses a new format, candidates who are thoroughly familiar with past exams will recognize that a new format is being employed. With this knowledge, you can avoid panic, because you will know that all the other candidates taking the exam will be as unfamiliar with the new format as you are.

Perseverance

Perseverance is the product of motivation and commitment. Studying past exam questions repeatedly until you get them all right, constantly working to improve your vocabulary, working out math problems, and sticking to good and consistent study habits all are hard work. If you have a year to prepare, it is a long haul. If you have only a few short months, the concentrated effort to prepare can be arduous. To overcome any discouragement that may arise, to overcome any tendency to put off work that needs to be done today, you must periodically revisit and, if necessary, revise your motivations and commitments. You should have in mind a set of articulated goals, and remember the benefits of becoming a state police officer—the pride, the respect, the accomplishment. State police officers have the opportunity to help others, to make a difference in society, and to preserve and improve the community. Success in these things brings success in life.

By any measure, the yearly salary is not exorbitant, but over the course of a career, the security of the steady salary, pay raises, health benefits, pension benefits, and the opportunity for promotions provide substantial value that many higher paying jobs do not offer.

Moreover, becoming a state police officer may be only the first step on the ladder to higher ranks, further career advancement, higher salaries, and greater opportunities. To become a sergeant, a lieutenant, a captain, a colonel, or a chief, you must first pass the initial written exam for entry into the agency. To move up the ranks, you must do your best at the very beginning of your career, because the higher the mark you score, the sooner you will be hired, and the sooner you will have the opportunity to take the exam for promotion to sergeant. The written promotion exam will follow the same format as the entry exam, so the good study habits you developed at the beginning of your career will help you excel again. Then, of course, the sooner you become a sergeant, the sooner you can move up further in the ranks.

With these opportunities for advancement, you should realize that the written exam to become a state police officer is much more than a single test. It is only the first step on the ladder. In a cost/benefit analysis, you should not calculate the time and effort you expend preparing and practicing versus the benefit of becoming an officer, but rather the expenditure versus the opportunity of achieving higher rank and the opportunities that will follow.

Just as you did for initial information about job qualifications and other portions of the hiring process, visit the website of the agency of your choice to learn more about the written exam. Some agencies post sample questions and study hints similar to those in this book. Equally important is the information on test dates and application deadlines. Most agencies test no more than twice a year, some less frequently than that. There are also cut-off dates by which your application must have been received for you to be permitted entry into a test site. If this information is not available on the website, contact the agency by e-mail or telephone or reach out to your recruiter for relevant details.

CHAPTER

4 ▶ The LearningExpress Test Preparation System

CHAPTER SUMMARY

Taking a state trooper exam can be tough, and your career in law enforcement depends on your passing the exam. The LearningExpress Test Preparation System, developed exclusively for LearningExpress by leading test experts, gives you the discipline and attitude you need to succeed.

Taking the state trooper written exam is no picnic, and neither is getting ready for it. Your future career depends on passing the test, but there are all sorts of pitfalls that can keep you from doing your best on this all-important exam. Here are some of the obstacles that can stand in the way of your success:

- Being unfamiliar with the format of the exam
- Being paralyzed by test anxiety
- Leaving your preparation to the last minute
- Not preparing at all
- Not knowing vital test-taking skills: how to pace yourself through the exam, how to use the process of elimination, and when to guess
- Not being in tip-top mental and physical shape
- Arriving late at the test site, having to work on an empty stomach, or shivering through the exam because the room is cold

What's the common denominator in all these test-taking pitfalls? One word: control. Who's in control, you or the exam?

Now the good news: The LearningExpress Test Preparation System puts you in control. In just nine easy-to-follow steps, you will learn everything you need to know to make sure that you are in charge of your preparation and your performance on the exam. Other test takers may let the test get the better of them; other test takers may be unprepared or out of shape—but not you. You will have taken all the steps you need to take to get a high score on the state trooper written exam.

Here's how the LearningExpress Test Preparation System works: Nine easy steps lead you through everything you need to know and do to get ready to master your exam. Each of the steps listed below includes both reading about the step and one or more activities. It is important that you do the activities along with the reading, or you won't be getting the full benefit of the system.

Step 1: Get Information
Step 2: Conquer Test Anxiety
Step 3: Make a Plan
Step 4: Learn to Manage Your Time
Step 5: Learn to Use the Process of Elimination
Step 6: Know When to Guess
Step 7: Reach Your Peak Performance Zone
Step 8: Get Your Act Together
Step 9: Do It!

If you have several hours, you can work through the whole LearningExpress Test Preparation System in one sitting. Otherwise, you can break it up and do just one or two steps a day for the next several days. It is up to you—remember, you are in control.

▶ Step 1: Get Information

Activities: Read Chapter 3, "About the State Trooper Written Exam," and use the suggestions there to find out about your requirements.
Knowledge is power. Therefore, first, you have to find out everything you can about the state trooper exam. Once you have your information, the next steps will show you what to do about it.

Part A: Straight Talk about the State Trooper Written Exam

Why do you have to take this exam, anyway? State policing is an attractive career option to many people, and the number of candidates often exceeds the number of job openings. To ensure that they hire the most qualified candidates, your state or the agency you want to work for will require you to take a written exam.

It is important for you to remember that your score on the written exam does not determine how smart you are or even whether you will make a good state trooper. There are all kinds of things a written exam like this can't test: whether you are likely to show up late or call in sick a lot, whether you can follow orders, or whether you can become part of a unit that works together to accomplish a task. Those kinds of things are hard to evaluate on a written exam. Meanwhile, it is easy to evaluate whether you can correctly answer questions about your job duties.

This is not to say that correctly answering the questions on the written exam is not important! The knowledge tested on the exam is knowledge you will need to do your job, and your ability to enter the profession depends on your passing this exam. And that's why you are here—to achieve control over the exam.

Part B: What's on the Test

If you haven't already done so, stop here and read Chapter 3 of this book, which gives you an overview of the written exam. Later, you will have the opportunity to take the sample practice exams in Chapters 5, 12, 13, 14, 15, and 16.

▶ Step 2: Conquer Test Anxiety

Activity: Take the Test Anxiety Quiz on page 22.
Having complete information about the exam is the first step in getting control of the exam. Next, you have to overcome one of the biggest obstacles to test success: test anxiety. Test anxiety can not only impair your performance on the exam itself; it can even keep you from preparing! In this step, you will learn stress management techniques that will help you succeed on your exam. Learn these strategies now, and practice them as you complete the exams in this book so that they will be second nature to you by exam day.

Combating Test Anxiety

The first thing you need to know is that a little test anxiety is a good thing. Everyone gets nervous before a big exam—and if that nervousness motivates you to prepare thoroughly, so much the better. Many well-known people throughout history have experienced anxiety or nervousness—from performers such as actor Sir Laurence Olivier and singer Aretha Franklin to writers such as Charlotte Brontë and Alfred, Lord Tennyson. In fact, anxiety probably gave them a little extra edge—just the kind of edge you need to do well, whether on a stage or in an examination room.

Stop here and complete the Test Anxiety Quiz on the next page to find out whether your level of test anxiety is something you should worry about.

Stress Management before the Test

If you feel your level of anxiety getting the best of you in the weeks before the test, here is what you need to do to bring the level down again:

- **Get prepared**. There's nothing like knowing what to expect and being prepared for it to put you in control of test anxiety. That's why you are reading this book. Use it faithfully, and remind yourself that you are better prepared than most of the people taking the test.
- **Practice self-confidence**. A positive attitude is a great way to combat test anxiety. This is no time to be humble or shy. Stand in front of the mirror and say to your reflection, "I'm prepared. I'm full of self-confidence. I'm going to ace this test. I know I can do it." If you hear it often enough, you will come to believe it.
- **Fight negative messages**. Every time someone starts telling you how hard the exam is or how it is almost impossible to get a high score, start telling them your self-confidence messages above. If the someone with the negative messages is you, telling yourself *you don't do well on exams* or *you just can't do this*, don't listen.
- **Visualize**. Imagine yourself reporting for duty on your first day as a state trooper. Visualizing success can help make it happen—and it reminds you of why you are working so hard to pass the exam.
- **Exercise**. Physical activity helps calm down your body and focus your mind. Besides, being in good physical shape can actually help you do well on the exam. Go for a run, lift weights, go swimming—and do it regularly.

Test Anxiety Quiz

You need to worry about test anxiety only if it is extreme enough to impair your performance. The following questionnaire will provide a diagnosis of your level of test anxiety. In the blank before each statement, write the number that most accurately describes your experience.

0 = Never
1 = Once or twice
2 = Sometimes
3 = Often

___I have gotten so nervous before an exam that I simply put down the books and didn't study for it.
___I have experienced disabling physical symptoms such as vomiting and severe headaches because I was nervous about an exam.
___I have simply not showed up for an exam because I was scared to take it.
___I have experienced dizziness and disorientation while taking an exam.
___I have had trouble filling in the little circles because my hands were shaking too hard.
___I have failed an exam because I was too nervous to complete it.
___**Total:** Add up the numbers in the blanks above.

Your Test Anxiety Score
Here are the steps you should take, depending on your score. If you scored:

- **Below 3**, your level of test anxiety is nothing to worry about; it is probably just enough to give you that little extra edge.
- **Between 3 and 6**, your test anxiety may be enough to impair your performance, and you should practice the stress management techniques listed in this section to try to bring your test anxiety down to manageable levels.
- **Above 6**, your level of test anxiety is a serious concern. In addition to practicing the stress management techniques listed in this section, you may want to seek additional, personal help. Call your local high school or community college and ask for the academic counselor. Tell the counselor that you have a level of test anxiety that sometimes keeps you from being able to take an exam. The counselor may be willing to help you or may suggest someone else you should talk to.

Stress Management on Test Day

There are several ways you can bring down your level of test anxiety on test day. They will work best if you practice them in the weeks before the test, so you know which ones work best for you.

- **Deep breathing**. Take a deep breath while you count to five. Hold it for a count of one, then let it out for a count of five. Repeat several times.
- **Move your body**. Try rolling your head in a circle. Rotate your shoulders. Shake your hands from the wrist. Many people find these movements very relaxing.
- **Visualize again**. Think of the place where you are most relaxed: lying on the beach in the sun, walking through the park, or whatever makes you feel good. Now close your eyes and imagine you are actually there. If you practice in advance, you will find that you need only a few seconds of this exercise to experience a significant increase in your sense of well-being.

When anxiety threatens to overwhelm you right there during the exam, there are still things you can do to manage the stress level.

- **Repeat your self-confidence messages**. You should have them memorized by now. Say them quietly to yourself, and believe them!
- **Visualize one more time**. This time, visualize yourself moving smoothly and quickly through the test, answering every question correctly, and finishing just before time is up. Like most visualization techniques, this one works best if you have practiced it ahead of time.
- **Find an easy question**. Skim over the test until you find an easy question, and answer it. Getting even one circle filled in gets you into the test-taking groove.
- **Take a mental break**. Everyone loses concentration once in a while during a long test. It is normal, so you shouldn't worry about it. Instead, accept what has happened. Say to yourself, "Hey, I lost it there for a minute. My brain is taking a break." Put down your pencil, close your eyes, and do some deep breathing for a few seconds. Then you will be ready to go back to work.

Try these techniques ahead of time, and see which ones work best for you.

▶ Step 3: Make a Plan

Activity: Construct a study plan.

Maybe the most important thing you can do to get control of yourself and your exam is to make a study plan. Too many people fail to prepare simply because they fail to plan. Spending hours poring over sample test questions the day before the exam not only raises your level of test anxiety, but also will not replace careful preparation and practice over time.

Don't fall into the cram trap. Take control of your preparation time by mapping out a study schedule.

Even more important than making a plan is making a commitment. You can't review everything that might be on the test in one night. You need to set aside some time every day for study and practice. Try for at least 20 minutes a day. Twenty minutes daily will do you much more good than two hours on Saturday—divide your test preparation into smaller pieces of the larger work. In addition, making study notes, creating visual aids, and memorizing can be quite useful as you prepare. Each time you begin to study, quickly review your last lesson. This routine will help you retain all you have learned and help you assess whether you are studying effectively. You may realize you are not remembering some of the material you studied earlier. Approximately one week before your exam, try to determine the areas that are still most difficult for you.

Don't put off your study until the day before the exam. Start now. A few minutes a day, with half an hour or more on weekends, can make a big difference in your score.

Learning Styles

Each of us absorbs information differently. Whichever way works best for you is called your dominant learning method. If someone asks you for help constructing a new bookcase, which may be in many pieces, how do you begin? Do you need to read the directions and see the diagram? Would you rather hear someone read the directions to you—telling you which part connects to another? Or do you draw your own diagram?

The three main learning methods are visual, auditory, and kinesthetic. Determining which type of learner you are will help you create tools for studying.

1. **Visual learners** need to see the information in the form of maps, pictures, text, words, or math examples. Outlining notes and important points in colorful highlighters and taking note of diagrams and pictures may be key in helping you study.
2. **Auditory learners** retain information when they can hear directions, the spelling of a word, a math theorem, or poem. Repeating information aloud or listening to your notes on a tape recorder may help. Many auditory learners also find working in study groups or having someone quiz them is beneficial.
3. **Kinesthetic learners** must *do*! They need to draw diagrams, or write directions. Rewriting notes on index cards or making margin notes in your textbooks also helps kinesthetic learners to retain information.

Mnemonics

Mnemonics are memory tricks that help you remember what you need to know. The three basic principles in the use of mnemonics are imagination, association, and location. Acronyms (words created from the first letters in a series of words) are common mnemonics. One acronym you may already know is **HOMES**, for the names of the Great Lakes (**H**uron, **O**ntario, **M**ichigan, **E**rie, and **S**uperior). **ROY G. BIV** reminds people of the colors in the spectrum (**R**ed, **O**range, **Y**ellow,

Green, Blue, Indigo, and Violet). Depending on the type of learner you are, mnemonics can also be colorful or vivid images, stories, word associations, or catchy rhymes such as "Thirty days hath September . . ." created in your mind. Any type of learner, whether visual, auditory, or kinesthetic, can use mnemonics to help the brain store and interpret information.

▶ Step 4: Learn to Manage Your Time

Activities: Practice these strategies as you take the sample tests in this book.

Steps 4, 5, and 6 of the LearningExpress Test Preparation System put you in charge of your exam by showing you test-taking strategies that work. Practice these strategies as you take the sample tests in this book, and then you will be ready to use them on test day.

First, you will take control of your time on the exam. Most state trooper exams have a time limit, which may give you more than enough time to complete all the questions—or may not. It is a terrible feeling to hear the examiner say, "Five minutes left," when you are only three-quarters of the way through the test. Here are some tips to keep that from happening to you.

- **Follow directions**. If the directions are given orally, listen to them. If they are written on the exam booklet, read them carefully. Ask questions before the exam begins if there's anything you don't understand. If you are allowed to write in your exam booklet, write down the beginning time and the ending time of the exam.
- **Pace yourself**. Glance at your watch every few minutes, and compare the time to how far you have gotten in the test. When one-quarter of the time has elapsed, you should be a quarter of the way through the test, and so on. If you are falling behind, pick up the pace a bit.

- **Keep moving**. Don't spend too much time on one question. If you don't know the answer, skip the question and move on. Circle the number of the question in your test booklet in case you have time to come back to it later.
- **Keep track of your place on the answer sheet**. If you skip a question, make sure that you also skip the question on the answer sheet. Check yourself every 5–10 questions to make sure that the number of the question still corresponds with the number on the answer sheet.
- **Don't rush**. Though you should keep moving, rushing won't help. Try to keep calm and work methodically and quickly.

▶ Step 5: Learn to Use the Process of Elimination

Activity: Complete worksheet on Using the Process of Elimination (see page 27).

After time management, your next most important tool for taking control of your exam is using the process of elimination wisely. It is standard test-taking wisdom that you should always read all the answer choices before choosing your answer. This helps you find the right answer by eliminating wrong answer choices. And, sure enough, that standard wisdom applies to your state trooper exam, too.

Let's say you are facing a vocabulary question that goes like this:

"Biology uses a binomial system of classification." In this sentence, the word *binomial* most nearly means
a. understanding the law.
b. having two names.
c. scientifically sound.
d. having a double meaning.

If you happen to know what *binomial* means, of course, you don't need to use the process of elimination, but let's assume you don't. So, you look at the answer choices. "Understanding the law" sure doesn't sound very likely for something having to do with biology. So you eliminate choice **a**—and now you have only three answer choices to deal with. Mark an X next to choice **a**, so you never have to read it again.

Now, move on to the other answer choices. If you know that the prefix *bi-* means *two*, as in *bicycle*, you will flag choice **b** as a possible answer. Mark a check mark beside it, meaning "good answer, I might use this one."

Choice **c**, "scientifically sound," is a possibility. At least it's about science, not law. It could work here, though, when you think about it, having a "scientifically sound" classification system in a scientific field is kind of redundant. You remember the *bi-* in *binomial*, and probably continue to like answer **b** better. But you're not sure, so you put a question mark next to **c**, meaning "well, maybe."

Now, choice **d**, "having a double meaning." You're still keeping in mind that *bi-* means *two*, so this one looks possible at first. But then you look again at the sentence the word belongs in, and you think, "Why would biology want a system of classification that has two meanings? That wouldn't work very well!" If you're really taken with the idea that *bi-* means *two*, you might put a question mark here. But if you're feeling a little more confident, you'll put an X. You have already got a better answer picked out.

Now your question looks like this:

"Biology uses a binomial system of classification." In this sentence, the word *binomial* most nearly means
X **a.** understanding the law.
✓ **b.** having two names.
? **c.** scientifically sound.
? **d.** having a double meaning.

You've got just one check mark for a good answer. If you're pressed for time, you should simply mark choice **b** on your answer sheet. If you have the time to be extra careful, you could compare your check-mark answer to your question-mark answers to make sure that it's better. (It is: The *binomial* system in biology is the one that gives a two-part genus and species name like *Homo sapiens*.)

It is good to have a system for marking good, bad, and maybe answers. We recommend this one:

X = bad
✓ = good
? = maybe

If you don't like these marks, devise your own system. Just make sure you do it long before test day—while you are working through the practice exams in this book—so you won't have to worry about it during the test.

Even when you think you are absolutely clueless about a question, you can often use the process of elimination to get rid of at least one answer choice. If so, you are better prepared to make an educated guess, as you will see in Step 6. More often, you can eliminate answers until you have only two possible answers. Then you are in a strong position to guess.

Try using your powers of elimination on the questions in the worksheet on page 27, Using the Process of Elimination. The questions are not about law enforcement; they are just designed to show you how the process of elimination works. The answer explanations for this worksheet show one possible way you might use the process to arrive at the right answer.

▶ Step 6: Know When to Guess

Activity: Complete worksheet on Your Guessing Ability (see page 28).

Armed with the process of elimination, you are ready to take control of one of the big questions in test taking: Should I guess? The answer is *Yes*. Some exams have what's called a "guessing penalty," in which a fraction of your wrong answers is subtracted from your right answers—but state trooper exams don't tend to work like that. The number of questions you answer correctly yields your raw score. So you have nothing to lose and everything to gain by guessing.

The more complicated answer to the question "Should I guess?" depends on you—your personality and your guessing intuition. There are two things you need to know about yourself before you go into the exam:

1. Are you a risk-taker?
2. Are you a good guesser?

You will have to decide about your risk-taking quotient on your own. To find out if you are a good guesser, complete the Your Guessing Ability worksheet, on page 28.

▶ Step 7: Reach Your Peak Performance Zone

Activity: Complete the Physical Preparation Checklist.
To get ready for a challenge like a big exam, you have to take control of your physical, as well as your mental, state. Exercise, proper diet, and rest in the weeks prior to the test will ensure that your body works with, rather than against, your mind on test day, as well as during your preparation.

Use the process of elimination to answer the following questions.

1. Ilsa is as old as Meghan will be in five years. The difference between Ed's age and Meghan's age is twice the difference between Ilsa's age and Meghan's age. Ed is 29. How old is Ilsa?
   a. 4
   b. 10
   c. 19
   d. 24

2. "All drivers of commercial vehicles must carry a valid commercial driver's license whenever operating a commercial vehicle."

   According to this sentence, which of the following people need NOT carry a commercial driver's license?
   a. a truck driver idling his engine while waiting to be directed to a loading dock
   b. a bus operator backing her bus out of the way of another bus in the bus lot
   c. a taxi driver driving his personal car to the grocery store
   d. a limousine driver taking the limousine to her home after dropping off her last passenger of the evening

3. Smoking tobacco has been linked to
   a. increased risk of stroke and heart attack.
   b. all forms of respiratory disease.
   c. increasing mortality rates over the past ten years.
   d. juvenile delinquency.

4. Which of the following words is spelled correctly?
   a. incorrigible
   b. outragous
   c. domestickated
   d. understandible

Answers

Here are the answers, as well as some suggestions as to how you might have used the process of elimination to find them.

1. d. You should have eliminated choice a off the bat. Ilsa can't be four years old if Meghan is going to be Ilsa's age in five years. The best way to eliminate other answer choices is to try plugging them in to the information given in the problem. For instance, for choice b, if Ilsa is 10, then Meghan must be 5. The difference in their ages is 5. The difference between Ed's age, 29, and Meghan's age, 5, is 24. Is 24 two times 5? No. Then choice b is wrong. You could eliminate choice c in the same way and be left with choice d.

2. c. Note the word *not* in the question, and go through the answers one by one. Is the truck driver in choice a "operating a commercial vehicle"? Yes, idling counts as "operating," so he needs to have a commercial driver's license. Likewise, the bus operator in choice b is operating a commercial vehicle; the question doesn't say the operator has to be on the street. The limo driver in choice d is operating a commercial vehicle, even if it doesn't have a passenger in it. However, the cabbie in choice c is not operating a commercial vehicle, but his own private car.

Using the Process of Elimination (continued)

3. a. You could eliminate choice **b** simply because of the presence of the word *all*. Such absolutes hardly ever appear in correct answer choices. Choice **c** looks attractive until you think a little about what you know—aren't fewer people smoking these days, rather than more? So how could smoking be responsible for a higher mortality rate? (If you didn't know that *mortality rate* means the rate at which people die, you might keep this choice as a possibility, but you would still be able to eliminate two answers and have only two to choose from.) And choice **d** is unlikely, so you could eliminate that one, too. You are left with the correct choice, **a**.

4. a. How you used the process of elimination here depends on which words you recognized as being spelled incorrectly. If you knew that the correct spellings were outrageous, domesticated, and understandable, then you were home free.

Your Guessing Ability

The following are ten really hard questions. You are not supposed to know the answers. Rather, this is an assessment of your ability to guess when you don't have a clue. Read each question carefully, just as if you did expect to answer it. If you have any knowledge of the subject, use that knowledge to help you eliminate wrong answer choices.

1. September 7 is Independence Day in
   a. India.
   b. Costa Rica.
   c. Brazil.
   d. Australia.

2. Which of the following is the formula for determining the momentum of an object?
   a. $p = MV$
   b. $F = ma$
   c. $P = IV$
   d. $E = mc^2$

3. Because of the expansion of the universe, the stars and other celestial bodies are all moving away from each other. This phenomenon is known as
   a. Newton's first law.
   b. the big bang.
   c. gravitational collapse.
   d. Hubble flow.

4. American author Gertrude Stein was born in
   a. 1713.
   b. 1830.
   c. 1874.
   d. 1901.

5. Which of the following is NOT one of the Five Classics attributed to Confucius?
   a. *I Ching*
   b. *Book of Holiness*
   c. *Spring and Autumn Annals*
   d. *Book of History*

6. The religious and philosophical doctrine that holds that the universe is constantly in a struggle between good and evil is known as
   a. Pelagianism.
   b. Manichaeanism.
   c. neo-Hegelianism.
   d. Epicureanism.

7. The third chief justice of the U.S. Supreme
Court was
   a. John Blair.
   b. William Cushing.
   c. James Wilson.
   d. John Jay.

8. Which of the following is the poisonous portion
of a daffodil?
   a. the bulb
   b. the leaves
   c. the stem
   d. the flowers

9. The winner of the Masters golf tournament in
1953 was
   a. Sam Snead.
   b. Cary Middlecoff.
   c. Arnold Palmer.
   d. Ben Hogan.

10. The state with the highest per capita personal
income in 1980 was
   a. Alaska.
   b. Connecticut.
   c. New York.
   d. Texas.

Answers

Check your answers against the correct answers
below.
   1. c.
   2. a.
   3. d.
   4. c.
   5. b.
   6. b.
   7. b.
   8. a.
   9. d.
   10. a.

How Did You Do?

You may have simply gotten lucky and actually known the answers to one or two questions. In addition, your guessing was probably more successful if you were able to use the process of elimination on any of the questions. Maybe you didn't know who the third chief justice was (question 7), but you knew that John Jay was the first. In that case, you would have eliminated choice **d** and therefore improved your odds of guessing right from one in four to one in three.

According to probability, you should get two and a half answers correct, so getting either two or three right would be average. If you got four or more right, you may be a really terrific guesser. If you got one or none right, you may be a really bad guesser.

Keep in mind, though, that this is only a small sample. You should continue to keep track of your guessing ability as you work through the sample questions in this book. Circle the numbers of questions you guess on as you make your guess; or, if you don't have time while you take the practice tests, go back afterward and try to remember which questions you guessed at. Remember, on a test with four answer choices, your chance of guessing correctly is one in four. So keep a separate "guessing" score for each exam. How many questions did you guess on? How many did you get right? If the number you got right is at least one-fourth of the number of questions you guessed on, you are at least an average guesser—maybe better—and you should always go ahead and guess on the real exam. If the number you got right is significantly lower than one-fourth of the number you guessed on, you would be safe in guessing anyway, but maybe you would feel more comfortable if you guessed only selectively, when you can eliminate a wrong answer or at least have a good feeling about one of the answer choices.

Because the state trooper exam has no guessing penalty, even if you are a play-it-safe person with lousy intuition, you are still safe guessing every time.

Exercise

If you don't already have a regular exercise program going, the time during which you are preparing for an exam is actually an excellent time to start one. And if you are already keeping fit—or trying to get that way—don't let the pressure of preparing for an exam fool you into quitting now. Exercise helps reduce stress by pumping feel-good hormones called *endorphins* into your system. It also increases the oxygen supply throughout your body, including in your brain, so you will be at peak performance on test day.

A half hour of vigorous activity—enough to raise a sweat—every day should be your aim. If you are really pressed for time, every other day is OK. Choose an activity you like and get out there and do it. Jogging with a friend always makes the time go faster, or take a portable radio or CD player.

But don't overdo it. You don't want to exhaust yourself. Moderation is the key.

Diet

First of all, cut out the junk. Go easy on caffeine and nicotine, and eliminate alcohol from your system at least two weeks before the exam. What your body needs for peak performance is simply a balanced diet. Eat plenty of fruits and vegetables, along with protein and carbohydrates. Foods that are high in lecithin (an amino acid), such as fish and beans, are especially good "brain foods."

The night before the exam, you might carbo-load the way athletes do before a contest. Eat a big plate of spaghetti, rice and beans, or whatever your favorite carbohydrate is.

Rest

You probably know how much sleep you need every night to be at your best, even if you don't always get it. Make sure you do get that much sleep, though, for at least a week before the exam. Moderation is important here, too. Extra sleep will just make you groggy.

If you are not a morning person and your exam will be given in the morning, you should reset your internal clock so that your body doesn't think you are taking an exam at 3 A.M. You have to start this process well before the exam. The way it works is to get up half an hour earlier each morning, and then go to bed half an hour earlier that night. Don't try it the other way around; you will just toss and turn if you go to bed early without having gotten up early. The next morning, get up another half an hour earlier, and so on. How long you will have to do this depends on how late you are used to getting up.

▶ Step 8: Get Your Act Together

Activity: Complete the Final Preparations worksheet. You are in control of your mind and body; you are in charge of test anxiety, your preparation, and your test-taking strategies. Now it is time to take charge of external factors, like the testing site and the materials you need to take the exam.

Find out Where the Test Is and Make a Trial Run

The testing agency or your recruiter will notify you when and where your exam is being held. Do you know how to get to the testing site? Do you know how long it will take to get there? If not, make a trial run, preferably on the same day of the week at the same time of day. Make note, on the worksheet Final Preparations on page 31, of the amount of time it will take you to get to the exam site. Plan on arriving at least 10–15 minutes early so you can get the lay of the land, use the bathroom, and calm down. Then figure out how early you will have to get up that morning, and make sure you get up that early every day for a week before the exam.

Physical Preparation Checklist

For the week before the test, write down what physical exercise you engaged in and for how long and what you ate for each meal. Remember, you're trying for at least half an hour of exercise every other day (preferably every day) and a balanced diet that's light on junk food.

Exam minus 7 days

Exercise: _____ for _____ minutes

Breakfast: _____

Lunch: _____

Dinner: _____

Snacks: _____

Exam minus 6 days

Exercise: _____ for _____ minutes

Breakfast: _____

Lunch: _____

Dinner: _____

Snacks: _____

Exam minus 5 days

Exercise: _____ for _____ minutes

Breakfast: _____

Lunch: _____

Dinner: _____

Snacks: _____

Exam minus 4 days

Exercise: _____ for _____ minutes

Breakfast: _____

Lunch: _____

Dinner: _____

Snacks: _____

Exam minus 3 days

Exercise: _____ for _____ minutes

Breakfast: _____

Lunch: _____

Dinner: _____

Snacks: _____

Exam minus 2 days

Exercise: _____ for _____ minutes

Breakfast: _____

Lunch: _____

Dinner: _____

Snacks: _____

Exam minus 1 day

Exercise: _____ for _____ minutes

Breakfast: _____

Lunch: _____

Dinner: _____

Snacks: _____

Gather Your Materials

The night before the exam, lay out the clothes you will wear and the materials you have to bring with you to the exam. Plan on dressing in layers; you won't have any control over the temperature of the examination room. Have a sweater or jacket you can take off if it is warm. Use the checklist on the Final Preparations worksheet on the following page to help you pull together what you will need.

Don't Skip Breakfast

Even if you don't usually eat breakfast, do so on exam morning. A cup of coffee doesn't count. Don't eat doughnuts or other sweet foods, either. A sugar high will leave you with a sugar low in the middle of the exam. A mix of protein and carbohydrates is best: Cereal with milk, or eggs with toast, will do your body a world of good.

▶ Step 9: Do It!

Activity: Ace the state trooper exam!

Fast forward to exam day. You are ready. You made a study plan and followed through. You practiced your test-taking strategies while working through this book. You are in control of your physical, mental, and emotional states. You know when and where to show up and what to bring with you. In other words, you are better prepared than most of the other people taking the state trooper exam with you.

Just one more thing: When you are done with the exam, you deserve a reward. Plan a celebration. Call up your friends and plan a party, or have a nice dinner for two—whatever your heart desires. Give yourself something to look forward to.

And then do it. Go into the exam, full of confidence, armed with test-taking strategies you have practiced until they are second nature. You are in control of yourself, your environment, and your performance on the exam. You are ready to succeed. So do it. Go in there and ace the exam. And look forward to your future career as a state trooper!

Final Preparations

Getting to the Exam Site

Location of exam site: _____

Date: _____

Departure time: _____

Do I know how to get to the exam site?   Yes ____   No ____   (If no, make a trial run.)

Time it will take to get to exam site: _____

Things to Lay out the Night Before

Clothes I will wear   ____

Sweater/jacket   ____

Watch   ____

Photo ID   ____

Four #2 pencils   ____

Other Things to Bring/Remember

_____   _____

_____   _____

_____   _____

5 ▶ State Trooper Practice Test 1

CHAPTER SUMMARY

This is the first practice test in the book based on the most commonly tested areas on the state trooper exam. By taking Practice Test 1 before you begin studying for the state trooper exam, you will get an idea of how much you already know and how much you need to learn.

The skills tested on the exam that follows are the ones that have been tested in the past on state trooper exams that focus on job-related skills. The exam you take may look somewhat different from this exam, but you'll find that this exam provides vital practice in the skills you need to pass a state trooper exam. The practice test consists of 100 multiple-choice questions in the following areas: reading comprehension, writing and information ordering, mathematics, spatial and directional orientation, memory and observation, and problem solving. You should give yourself two hours to take this practice test. The time limit of the actual state trooper exam can vary from region to region.

State Trooper Practice Test 1

1.	(a) (b) (c) (d)	36.	(a) (b) (c) (d)	71.	(a) (b) (c) (d)
2.	(a) (b) (c) (d)	37.	(a) (b) (c) (d)	72.	(a) (b) (c) (d)
3.	(a) (b) (c) (d)	38.	(a) (b) (c) (d)	73.	(a) (b) (c) (d)
4.	(a) (b) (c) (d)	39.	(a) (b) (c) (d)	74.	(a) (b) (c) (d)
5.	(a) (b) (c) (d)	40.	(a) (b) (c) (d)	75.	(a) (b) (c) (d)
6.	(a) (b) (c) (d)	41.	(a) (b) (c) (d)	76.	(a) (b) (c) (d)
7.	(a) (b) (c) (d)	42.	(a) (b) (c) (d)	77.	(a) (b) (c) (d)
8.	(a) (b) (c) (d)	43.	(a) (b) (c) (d)	78.	(a) (b) (c) (d)
9.	(a) (b) (c) (d)	44.	(a) (b) (c) (d)	79.	(a) (b) (c) (d)
10.	(a) (b) (c) (d)	45.	(a) (b) (c) (d)	80.	(a) (b) (c) (d)
11.	(a) (b) (c) (d)	46.	(a) (b) (c) (d)	81.	(a) (b) (c) (d)
12.	(a) (b) (c) (d)	47.	(a) (b) (c) (d)	82.	(a) (b) (c) (d)
13.	(a) (b) (c) (d)	48.	(a) (b) (c) (d)	83.	(a) (b) (c) (d)
14.	(a) (b) (c) (d)	49.	(a) (b) (c) (d)	84.	(a) (b) (c) (d)
15.	(a) (b) (c) (d)	50.	(a) (b) (c) (d)	85.	(a) (b) (c) (d)
16.	(a) (b) (c) (d)	51.	(a) (b) (c) (d)	86.	(a) (b) (c) (d)
17.	(a) (b) (c) (d)	52.	(a) (b) (c) (d)	87.	(a) (b) (c) (d)
18.	(a) (b) (c) (d)	53.	(a) (b) (c) (d)	88.	(a) (b) (c) (d)
19.	(a) (b) (c) (d)	54.	(a) (b) (c) (d)	89.	(a) (b) (c) (d)
20.	(a) (b) (c) (d)	55.	(a) (b) (c) (d)	90.	(a) (b) (c) (d)
21.	(a) (b) (c) (d)	56.	(a) (b) (c) (d)	91.	(a) (b) (c) (d)
22.	(a) (b) (c) (d)	57.	(a) (b) (c) (d)	92.	(a) (b) (c) (d)
23.	(a) (b) (c) (d)	58.	(a) (b) (c) (d)	93.	(a) (b) (c) (d)
24.	(a) (b) (c) (d)	59.	(a) (b) (c) (d)	94.	(a) (b) (c) (d)
25.	(a) (b) (c) (d)	60.	(a) (b) (c) (d)	95.	(a) (b) (c) (d)
26.	(a) (b) (c) (d)	61.	(a) (b) (c) (d)	96.	(a) (b) (c) (d)
27.	(a) (b) (c) (d)	62.	(a) (b) (c) (d)	97.	(a) (b) (c) (d)
28.	(a) (b) (c) (d)	63.	(a) (b) (c) (d)	98.	(a) (b) (c) (d)
29.	(a) (b) (c) (d)	64.	(a) (b) (c) (d)	99.	(a) (b) (c) (d)
30.	(a) (b) (c) (d)	65.	(a) (b) (c) (d)	100.	(a) (b) (c) (d)
31.	(a) (b) (c) (d)	66.	(a) (b) (c) (d)		
32.	(a) (b) (c) (d)	67.	(a) (b) (c) (d)		
33.	(a) (b) (c) (d)	68.	(a) (b) (c) (d)		
34.	(a) (b) (c) (d)	69.	(a) (b) (c) (d)		
35.	(a) (b) (c) (d)	70.	(a) (b) (c) (d)		

▶ State Trooper Practice Test 1

Directions: Read the following passage, then answer questions 1 through 4.

Hearsay evidence, which is the secondhand reporting of a statement, is allowed in court only when the truth of the statement is irrelevant. Hearsay that depends on the statement's truthfulness is inadmissible because the witness does not appear in court and swear an oath to tell the truth; his or her demeanor when making the statement is not visible to the jury; the accuracy of the statement cannot be tested under cross-examination; or to introduce it would be to deprive the accused of the constitutional right to confront the accuser. Hearsay is admissible, however, when the truth of the statement is unimportant. If, for example, a defendant claims to have been unconscious at a certain time, and a witness claims that the defendant actually spoke to her at that time, this evidence would be admissible because the truth of what the defendant actually said is irrelevant.

1. The main purpose of the passage is to
   a. explain why hearsay evidence abridges the rights of the accused.
   b. question the truth of hearsay evidence.
   c. argue that rules about the admissibility of hearsay evidence should be changed.
   d. specify which use of hearsay evidence is inadmissible and why.

2. Which of the following is not a reason given in the passage for the inadmissibility of hearsay evidence?
   a. Rumors are not necessarily credible.
   b. The person making the original statement was not under oath.
   c. The jury should be able to watch the gestures and facial expressions of the person making the statement.
   d. The person making the statement cannot be cross-examined.

3. How does the passage explain the proper use of hearsay evidence?
   a. by listing a set of criteria
   b. by providing a hypothetical example
   c. by referring to the Constitution
   d. by citing case law

4. The passage suggests that the criterion used for deciding that most hearsay evidence is inadmissible is most likely
   a. the unreliability of most hearsay witnesses.
   b. the importance of physical evidence to corroborate witness testimony.
   c. concern for discerning the truth in a fair manner.
   d. doubt about the relevance of hearsay testimony.

Directions: Read the following passage, then answer questions 5 through 8.

Police officers must read suspects their Miranda rights upon taking them into custody. When a suspect who is merely being questioned incriminates himself or herself, he or she might later claim to have been in custody, and seek to have the case dismissed on the grounds of not having been apprised of his or her Miranda rights. In such cases, a judge must make a determination as to whether or not a reasonable person would have believed himself or herself to have been in custody, based on certain criteria. The judge must determine whether the suspect was questioned in a threatening manner (for example, if the suspect was seated while both officers remained standing) and whether the suspect was aware that he or she was free to leave at any time. Officers must be aware of these criteria and take care not to give suspects grounds for later claiming themselves to have been in custody.

5. What is the main idea of the passage?
  a. Officers must remember to read suspects their Miranda rights.
  b. Judges, not police officers, make the final determination as to whether or not a suspect was in custody.
  c. Officers who are merely questioning a suspect must not give the suspect the impression that he or she is in custody.
  d. Miranda rights needn't be read to all suspects before questioning.

6. According to the passage, a suspect is not in custody when he or she is
  a. free to refuse to answer questions.
  b. free to leave the police station.
  c. apprised of his or her Miranda rights.
  d. not apprised of his or her Miranda rights.

7. When must police officers read Miranda rights to a suspect?
  a. while questioning the suspect
  b. before taking the suspect to the police station
  c. while placing the suspect under arrest
  d. before releasing the suspect

8. A police officer questioning a suspect who is not under arrest must
  a. read the suspect his or her Miranda rights.
  b. allow the suspect a phone call.
  c. advise the suspect of his or her right to a lawyer.
  d. inform the suspect that he or she is free to leave.

Directions: Read the following passage, then answer questions 9 through 14.

Stalking is defined as the "willful, malicious, and repeated following and harassing of another person." The act of stalking can probably be traced back to the earliest episodes of human history, but in the United States, no substantive law existed to protect the victims of stalkers until 1990. Prior to this, the most that police officials could do was arrest the stalker for a minor offense or suggest the victim obtain a restraining order, a civil remedy often ignored by the offender. Frightened victims had their worst fears confirmed: They would have to be harmed—or killed—before anything could be done.

Stalking was brought into the public eye in 1989 by the stalker-murder of television star Rebecca Schaeffer and then by the 1990 stalker-murders of four women in Orange County, California, in a single six-week period. When it was discovered that one of the Orange County victims had a restraining order in her purse when her stalker murdered her, California reacted by drafting the first anti-stalking law. Now most states have similar laws.

The solution is not perfect: Some stalkers are too mentally deranged or obsessed to fear a prison term, and on the flip side, there is the danger, however small, of abuse of the law, particularly in marital disputes. Most importantly, law enforcement officials and general society need to be better educated about stalking, especially about its gender-related issues. (The majority of stalking victims are women terrorized by former husbands or boyfriends.)

But the laws are a vast improvement, and they carry the threat of felony penalties of up to ten years in prison for those who would attempt to control or possess others through intimidation and terror.

9. Based on the passage, which of the following is likely the most common question asked of police by stalking victims prior to 1990?
- **a.** How can I get a restraining order?
- **b.** Does he have to hurt me before you'll arrest him?
- **c.** Why is this person stalking me?
- **d.** Is it legal for me to carry a weapon to protect myself?

10. Which of the following best expresses the main idea of the passage?
- **a.** More education is needed about sexism, because sexism is the most important element in the crime of stalking.
- **b.** Stalking is thought of as a new kind of crime, but has probably existed throughout human history.
- **c.** The new anti-stalking legislation is an important weapon against the crime of stalking, though it is not a complete answer.
- **d.** Today, almost every state in the United States has a very effective, if not perfect, anti-stalking law.

11. Which of the following is NOT mentioned in the passage as a weakness in the new anti-stalking legislation?
- **a.** The laws alone might not deter some stalkers.
- **b.** A person might be wrongly accused of being a stalker.
- **c.** The police and public do not completely understand the crime.
- **d.** Victims do not yet have adequate knowledge about anti-stalking laws.

12. Based on the passage, why are restraining orders ineffective in preventing stalking?
- **a.** Only civil charges can be leveled against the violator.
- **b.** Prior to 1990, restraining orders could not be issued against stalkers.
- **c.** Law enforcement officials do not take such orders seriously.
- **d.** Restraining orders apply only to married couples.

13. Which of the following is NOT a stated or implied motive for stalking?
- **a.** to own the victim
- **b.** to terrify the victim
- **c.** to rob the victim
- **d.** to badger the victim

14. Based on the information in the passage, which of the following did the murders of Rebecca Schaeffer and the Orange County women mentioned in the second paragraph have in common?
- **a.** The murders provided impetus for anti-stalking laws.
- **b.** The victims sought, but could not obtain, legal protection.
- **c.** The victims were stalked and killed by a husband or lover.
- **d.** The murders were the result of sexism.

Directions: Read the following passage, then answer questions 15 through 17.

Law enforcement officers often do not like taking time from their regular duties to testify in court, but testimony is an important part of an officer's job. To be good witnesses, officers should keep complete notes detailing any potentially criminal or actionable incidents. When on the witness stand, officers may refer to those notes to refresh their memory about particular events. It is also very important for officers to listen carefully to the questions asked by the lawyers and to provide only the information requested. Officers should never volunteer opinions or any extra information that is beyond the scope of a question.

15. According to the passage, an officer who is testifying in court
  a. will be questioned by the judge.
  b. may refer to his or her notes while on the witness stand.
  c. must do so without pay.
  d. appreciates taking a break from routine assignments.

16. This passage is probably taken from a(n)
  a. memo entitled "Proper Arrest Procedure."
  b. newspaper article about crime prevention.
  c. recruitment pamphlet for law enforcement officers.
  d. officers' training manual.

17. According to the passage, testifying in court is
  a. an important part of a law enforcement officer's job.
  b. difficult, because lawyers try to trick witnesses.
  c. less stressful for law enforcement officers than for other witnesses.
  d. a waste of time, because judges usually let criminals off.

Directions: Read the following passage, then answer questions 18 through 20.

Most criminals do not suffer from antisocial personality disorder; however, nearly all persons with this disorder have been in trouble with the law. Sometimes labeled *sociopaths*, they are a grim problem for society. Their crimes range from con games to murder, and they are set apart by what appears to be a complete lack of conscience. Often attractive and charming, and always inordinately self-confident, they nevertheless demonstrate a disturbing emotional shallowness, as if they had been born without a faculty as vital as sight or hearing. These individuals are not legally insane, nor do they suffer from the distortions of thought associated with mental illness; however, some experts believe they are mentally ill. If so, it is an illness that is exceptionally resistant to treatment, particularly since these individuals have a marked inability to learn from the past. It is this latter trait that makes them a special problem for law enforcement officials. Their ability to mimic true emotion enables them to convince prison officials, judges, and psychiatrists that they feel remorse. When released from incarceration, however, they go back to their old tricks, to their con games, their impulsive destructiveness, and their sometimes lethal deceptions.

18. Based on the preceding passage, which of the following is NOT likely a characteristic of the person with antisocial personality disorder?
  a. delusions of persecution
  b. feelings of superiority
  c. inability to suffer deeply
  d. inability to feel joy

19. Which of the following careers would probably best suit the person with an antisocial personality?
  a. soldier with ambition to make officer
  b. warden of a large penitentiary
  c. loan officer in a bank
  d. salesperson dealing in nonexistent real estate

20. Based on the passage, which of the following words best sums up the inner emotional life of the person with an antisocial personality?
   a. angry
   b. empty
   c. anxious
   d. repressed

Directions: For questions 21 through 24, choose the answer choice that best rephrases the underlined portion of the given sentence.

21. <u>This was the fifth of five speeches the mayor gave during this the month of May.</u>
   a. This was the fifth of the five speeches the mayor gave during this the month of May.
   b. Of the five speeches the mayor gave during May, this was the fifth one.
   c. Thus far during the month of May, the mayor gave five speeches and this was the fifth.
   d. This was the fifth speech the mayor has given during the month of May.

22. The troposphere is the lowest layer of Earth's <u>atmosphere' it extends</u> from ground level to an altitude of seven to ten miles.
   a. atmosphere, it extends
   b. of which it extends
   c. atmosphere. Extending
   d. atmosphere; it extends

23. <u>Along with your membership to our health club or</u> two months of free personal training.
   a. Along with your membership to our health club and
   b. Along with your membership to our health club comes
   c. With your membership to our health club,
   d. In addition to your membership to our health club being

24. <u>To determine the speed of automobiles: radar is often used by the state police.</u>
   a. To determine the speed of automobiles, radar is often used by the state police.
   b. In determining the speed of automobiles, the use of radar by state police is often employed.
   c. To determine the speed of automobiles, the state police often use radar.
   d. Radar by state police in determining the speed of automobiles is often used.

25. Three of the sentences below contain one or more grammatical or spelling errors. Select the answer choice that is correct as is.
   a. Ethics and the law having no true relationship.
   b. There is no true relationship between ethics and the law.
   c. Between ethics and the law, no true relationship.
   d. Ethics and the law is no true relationship.

26. Three of the sentences below contain one or more grammatical or spelling errors. Select the answer choice that is correct as is.
   a. Some people say jury duty is a nuisance that just takes up their precious time and that we don't get paid enough.
   b. Some people say jury duty is a nuisance that just takes up your precious time and that one doesn't get paid enough.
   c. Some people say jury duty is a nuisance that just takes up precious time and that doesn't pay enough.
   d. Some people say jury duty is a nuisance that just takes up our precious time and that they don't get paid enough.

27. Three of the sentences below contain one or more grammatical or spelling errors. Select the answer choice that is correct as is.

   a. The art professor, along with several of her students, is planning to attend the gallery opening tomorrow evening.

   b. The art professor, along with several of her students, are planning to attend the gallery opening tomorrow evening.

   c. The art professor, along with several of her students, plan to attend the gallery opening tomorrow evening.

   d. The art professor, along with several of her students, have planned to attend the gallery opening tomorrow evening.

28. Three of the sentences below contain one or more grammatical or spelling errors. Select the answer choice that is correct as is.

   a. A longer happier life, caused by one's owning a pet.

   b. Owning a pet, for one to live a longer, happier life.

   c. To live a longer, happier life by one's owning a pet.

   d. Owning a pet can help one live a longer, happier life.

29. Three of the sentences below contain one or more grammatical or spelling errors. Select the answer choice that is correct as is.

   a. One of the first modern detectives in literature were created by Edgar Allan Poe.

   b. One of the first modern detectives in literature was created by Edgar Allan Poe.

   c. Edgar Allan Poe having created one of the first modern detectives in literature.

   d. In literature, one of the first modern detectives, created by Edgar Allan Poe.

30. Three of the sentences below contain one or more grammatical or spelling errors. Select the answer choice that is correct as is.

   a. I don't like fish as well as my sister does.

   b. I don't like fish as well as my sister.

   c. Fish isn't liked by me as well as my sister.

   d. My sister likes it, but I don't like fish as well.

31. Identify the sentence that contains a mistake in capitalization, punctuation, grammar, or spelling. If you find no mistakes, select choice **d**.

   a. Our class took a field trip, going to the art museum.

   b. There are rocky cliffs along the coast.

   c. We saw Dr. Mason because our doctor was on vacation.

   d. No mistakes.

32. Identify the sentence that contains a mistake in capitalization, punctuation, grammar, or spelling. If you find no mistakes, select choice **d**.

   a. Make sure your seatbelt is fastened.

   b. I'm afraid of spiders George is too.

   c. Yes, I will bring the dessert.

   d. No mistakes.

33. Identify the sentence that contains a mistake in capitalization, punctuation, grammar, or spelling. If you find no mistakes, select choice **d**.

   a. They traveled south and hiked in the desert.

   b. "Don't shout at me," she yelled back.

   c. Joshua enters lots of contests, therefore he knows he can't win.

   d. No mistakes.

34. Identify the sentence that contains a mistake in capitalization, punctuation, grammar, or spelling. If you find no mistakes, select choice **d.**
  a. Where's my blue jacket?
  b. The prizes were awarded to Juan and me.
  c. After midnight, you will turn into a pumpkin.
  d. No mistakes.

35. Identify the sentence that contains a mistake in capitalization, punctuation, grammar, or spelling. If you find no mistakes, select choice **d.**
  a. When I heard the alarm, I jump out of bed.
  b. Mr. Fox is the president of his own company.
  c. At night, I listened to jazz on the radio.
  d. No mistakes.

36. Identify the sentence that contains a mistake in capitalization, punctuation, grammar, or spelling. If you find no mistakes, select choice **d.**
  a. The muffins cost more than the bread does.
  b. Roberta and I were in the same watercolor class.
  c. The temperature was colder today than it was yesterday.
  d. No mistakes.

37. Look at the four numbered sentences below. Choose the sentence order that would result in the best paragraph.
  (1) During the parole period, he is supervised by a parole officer.
  (2) The parole officer must also be concerned, however, about the safety of the community.
  (3) After a prisoner has served his sentence, he may be paroled to the county where he was tried.
  (4) A parole officer has a certain amount of latitude in supervising her parolees' transition from prison life.
  a. 1, 4, 2, 3
  b. 2, 1, 4, 3
  c. 4, 1, 3, 2
  d. 3, 2, 4, 1

38. Look at the four numbered sentences below. Choose the sentence order that would result in the best paragraph.
  (1) A man in Texas was convicted of stealing the guns belonging to Clayton Moore, TV's Lone Ranger.
  (2) For example, drivers are ordered to place a bumper sticker on their cars that publicize their crimes.
  (3) In addition to a fine and probation, the gun thief was ordered to complete 600 hours of community service cleaning the Houston Police Department's horse stables.
  (4) In recent years, courts have begun handing down criminal sentences that include an element of humiliation.
  a. 1, 4, 2, 3
  b. 2, 1, 4, 3
  c. 4, 1, 3, 2
  d. 3, 2, 4, 1

39. Look at the four numbered sentences below. Choose the sentence order that would result in the best paragraph.
  (1) Visits, especially from family members, can aid in a prisoner's rehabilitation.
  (2) Usually, this means that a prisoner and his visitors may not have physical contact with each other.
  (3) Therefore, they are separated by a pane of glass and must talk by phone.
  (4) However, in order to maintain prison safety, family visits cannot be unrestricted.
  a. 2, 4, 1, 3
  b. 1, 4, 2, 3
  c. 1, 2, 3, 4
  d. 3, 1, 2, 4

40. The following question consists of four numbered sentences. Choose the sentence order
that would result in the best paragraph.
(1) Therefore, persuading another person to
commit a crime by discussing a specific
crime with the intention that the crime be
carried out is considered solicitation.
(2) First, the person must have persuaded
another person to commit a crime.
(3) Second, the person must have been discussing a specific crime and must have had
the intention that the act would be done.
(4) Police officers may become aware of a person who did not actually commit a crime,
but solicited another person to do so.
- **a.** 1, 3, 4, 2
- **b.** 2, 4, 1, 3
- **c.** 4, 2, 1, 3
- **d.** 4, 2, 3, 1

41. Find the quotient of 12,440 and 40.
- **a.** 497,600
- **b.** 12,480
- **c.** 12,400
- **d.** 311

42. $540 \div 6 + 3 \times 24 =$
- **a.** 2,232
- **b.** 1,440
- **c.** 1,260
- **d.** 162

43. 7^3 is equal to
- **a.** 343
- **b.** 49
- **c.** 38
- **d.** 21

44. $376 - 360 + 337 =$
- **a.** 663
- **b.** 553
- **c.** 453
- **d.** 353

45. The fraction $\frac{8}{200}$ is equivalent to which of the
following?
- **a.** $\frac{4}{100}$
- **b.** $\frac{2}{5}$
- **c.** $\frac{3}{4}$
- **d.** $\frac{1}{4}$

46. $\frac{4}{5} + \frac{1}{6} =$
- **a.** $\frac{5}{6}$
- **b.** $\frac{5}{11}$
- **c.** $\frac{7}{15}$
- **d.** $\frac{29}{30}$

47. $(25 + 17)(64 - 49) =$
- **a.** 57
- **b.** 63
- **c.** 570
- **d.** 630

48. In a department store, a woman's handbag was
stolen while she was shopping. The handbag is
worth approximately $150. Inside the handbag
were the following items:
- 1 leather makeup case: $65
- 1 vial of unopened perfume: $75
- 1 pair of earrings: $150
- cash: $178

Officer Beatriz Ceballos is writing the police
report. What should she write as the value of
the stolen cash and property?
- **a.** $468
- **b.** $608
- **c.** $618
- **d.** $718

49. $\frac{17}{20}$ is equivalent to what percent?

a. 17%

b. 65%

c. 85%

d. 90%

50. 184 is evenly divisible by

a. 46

b. 43

c. 41

d. 40

51. If 14 workers can complete a job in 2 days, how long will it take 4 workers to complete the same job? Assume all workers work at the same rate.

a. $\frac{4}{7}$ day

b. 5 days

c. 6 days

d. 7 days

52. If a police car travels at the speed of 62 miles per hour for 15 minutes, how far will it travel? (Distance = Rate × Time)

a. 9.3 miles

b. 15.5 miles

c. 16 miles

d. 24.8 miles

53. If a truck is traveling at a constant speed of 50 miles per hour for a total time of 1 hour and 30 minutes, how many miles does it travel? (Distance = Rate × Time)

a. 75 miles

b. 50 miles

c. 5 miles

d. 130 miles

54. A police uniform requires 4 square yards of cloth. To produce uniforms for 84,720 officers, how much cloth is required?

a. 21,180 square yards

b. 21,880 square yards

c. 338,880 square yards

d. 340,880 square yards

55. A squad car uses 16 gallons of gas to travel 448 miles. How many miles per gallon does the car get?

a. 22 miles per gallon

b. 24 miles per gallon

c. 26 miles per gallon

d. 28 miles per gallon

Directions: Answer the following questions based on the map below. The arrows indicate traffic flow. One arrow indicates a one-way street going in the direction of the arrow; two arrows represent a two-way street. You are not allowed to go the wrong way on a one-way street.

56. Your unit has been called to the scene of a car accident at the Livingston Avenue Mall at the southeast corner of the building. While you are there, dispatch notifies you of an alarm going off in a residence located at the northwest corner of Canyon Drive and Linda Lane. What is the quickest route for your unit to take from the mall to the residence?

  a. Turn north on Amhoy Road, then east on Linda Lane, then north on Canyon Drive.

  b. Turn east on McMahon Street, then north on El Camino, then west on Linda Lane, then north on Orinda Road, then east on Barcelona Boulevard to Canyon Drive, and south on Canyon Drive.

  c. Turn north on Amhoy Road, then east on Barcelona Boulevard, then south on Canyon Drive.

  d. Turn north on Amhoy Road, then east on Bortz Road, then north on Orinda Road, then east on Barcelona Boulevard, and south on Canyon Drive.

57. Your unit is southbound on Canyon Drive and has just crossed Edward Street when a call comes in that someone has been hit by a car at a bus stop located at Livingston Avenue and Bortz Road. What is the quickest route for your unit to take to the bus stop?

  a. Turn west on McMahon Street, then north on Livingston Avenue.

  b. Turn east on McMahon Street, then north on El Camino, then west on Bortz Road.

  c. Turn east on Lake Drive, then north on Canyon Drive, then west on Bortz Road.

  d. Turn east on Lake Drive, then north on El Camino, then west on Linda Lane, then south on Livingston Avenue.

58. State Trooper Ricardo has just come off duty and is driving west on Bortz Road. She makes a right onto James Avenue, then a left onto Linda Lane, then a right onto Livingston, and then a right onto Barcelona Boulevard. What direction is she facing?

  a. east

  b. south

  c. west

  d. north

59. A state trooper is escorting an important public official from the northwest corner of Livingston Avenue and McMahon Street to Town Hall. If the entrance to Town Hall is located on a few feet to the left of the northeast corner of the building, how many turns will the state trooper make, taking the most direct route?

  a. one

  b. two

  c. three

  d. four

60. State Trooper Bassett is driving south on Livingston Avenue. She makes a left onto Lake Drive, then a left onto James Avenue, then a right onto McMahon Street, and then a right onto Orinda Road. What direction is she facing?

  a. east

  b. south

  c. west

  d. north

Directions: Answer the following questions based on the map below. The arrows indicate traffic flow. One arrow indicates a one-way street going in the direction of the arrow; two arrows represent a two-way street. You are not allowed to go the wrong way on a one-way street.

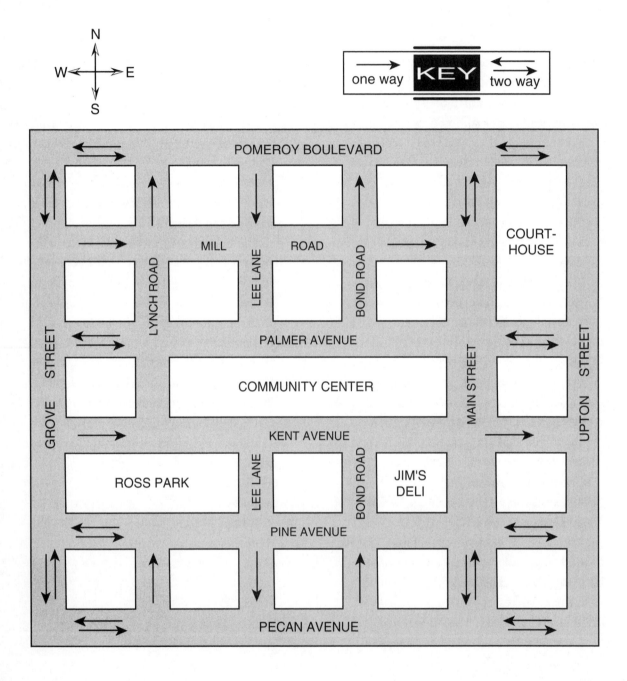

61. Your unit is eastbound on Kent Avenue at Lee Lane when a call comes in from dispatch about an explosion at a residence located at the northeast corner of Lynch Road and Mill Road. What is the quickest route for your unit to take?
- **a.** Continue east on Kent Avenue, then turn north on Main Street to Mill Road, then west on Mill Road to the northeast corner of Lynch Road and Mill Road.
- **b.** Continue east on Kent Avenue, then turn north on Main Street, then east on Pomeroy Boulevard, then south on Lynch Road.
- **c.** Continue east on Kent Avenue, then turn south on Main Street, then west on Pine Avenue, then north on Grove Street, then east on Mill Road to Lynch Road.
- **d.** Continue east on Kent Avenue, then turn north on Main Street, then west on Palmer Avenue, then north on Lynch Road to Mill Road.

62. Officer McElhaney is off duty and driving by the courthouse, northbound on Upton Street. He receives a call on his cell phone about a bomb having gone off at Ross Park on the Grove Street side of the park. He decides he may be able to be of some help. What is the most direct route for McElhaney to take?
- **a.** Continue north on Upton Street, turn west on Pomeroy Boulevard, then south on Main Street, then west on Kent Avenue to Grove Street.
- **b.** Continue north on Upton Street, then turn west on Pomeroy Boulevard, then south on Grove Street to Ross Park.
- **c.** Continue north on Upton Street, then turn west on Pomeroy Boulevard, then south on Main Street, then west on Palmer Avenue, then south on Grove Street to Ross Park.
- **d.** Make a U-turn on Upton Street, then go west on Palmer Avenue, then south on Grove Street to Ross Park.

63. State Trooper Kearney has just had lunch at Jim's Deli and is now heading west on Pine Avenue. She turns left on Lee Lane, then left again onto Pecan Avenue. She turns left on Main Street and finally turns right on Palmer Avenue. What direction is she facing?
- **a.** west
- **b.** south
- **c.** north
- **d.** east

64. State Trooper Santos is driving south on Main Street. He makes a left onto Pine Avenue, then a left onto Upton Street, then a right onto Palmer Avenue, and then a right onto Bond Road. What direction is he facing?
- **a.** east
- **b.** south
- **c.** west
- **d.** north

65. You are dispatched from the courthouse, facing south on Upton Street, to an altercation occurring at the southeast corner of the community center. Which is the most direct legal way to drive there?
- **a.** south to Palmer Avenue and south on Main Street
- **b.** south to Palmer Avenue and west onto Kent Avenue
- **c.** south to Palmer Avenue, west onto Grove Street, and south onto Kent Avenue
- **d.** north to Pomeroy Boulevard, south on Lee Lane, east on Palmer Avenue, and south on Main Street

Directions: Answer the following questions based on the map below. The arrows indicate traffic flow. One arrow indicates a one-way street going in the direction of the arrow and no arrows represent a two-way street. You are not allowed to go the wrong way on a one-way street. Smaller boxes within the building outline indicate building entranceways.

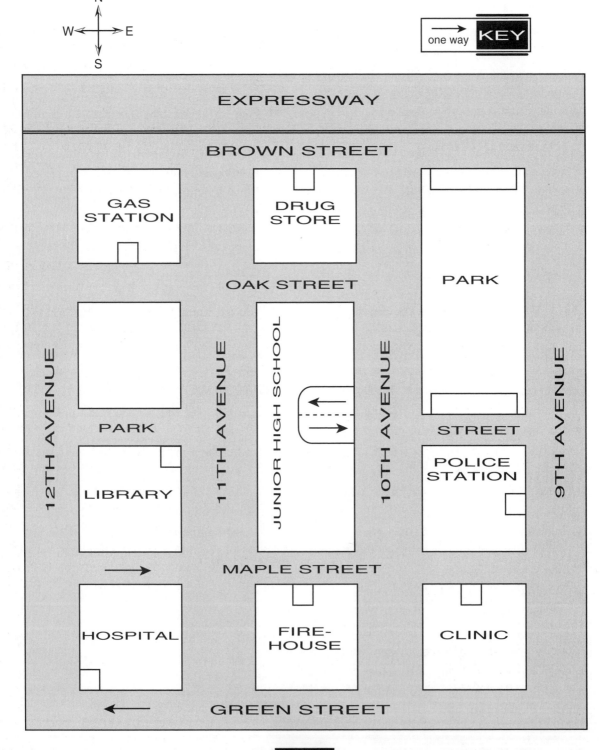

66. There is a vehicular accident at the corner of Brown Street and 9th Avenue, and a fire has started. What is the most direct legal way for the fire engine to travel from the fire station to the accident scene?

  a. east on Maple Street and north on 9th Avenue to the accident

  b. west on Maple Street, north on 12th Avenue, and east on Brown Street to the accident

  c. east on Maple Street and north on 11th Avenue to the accident

  d. west on Maple Street, north on 11th Avenue, and east on Brown Street to the accident

67. What streets run north and south of the park?

  a. Brown Street and Oak Street

  b. Maple Street and Park Street

  c. Brown Street and Park Street

  d. Green Street and Oak Street

68. A civilian leaving the clinic needs to drive to the drugstore. If you were giving her directions from the clinic, what would be the most direct route?

  a. east on Maple Street, north on 9th Avenue, and west on Brown Street to the store entrance

  b. west on Maple Street, north on 10th Avenue, and west on Brown Street to the store entrance

  c. west on Green Street, north on 12th Avenue, and east on Brown Street to the store entrance

  d. east on Oak Street, north on 11th Avenue, and east on Brown Street to the store entrance

69. Someone at the junior high school has been injured and needs to go to the hospital. What directions would you give to the ambulance driver?

  a. Go north on 10th Avenue, west on Brown Street, and south on 12th Avenue to the hospital entrance.

  b. Go south on 10th Avenue and west on Green Street to the hospital entrance.

  c. Go north on 10th Avenue and south on Brown Street to the hospital entrance.

  d. Go south on 10th Avenue, south on Maple Street, and east on Green Street to the hospital entrance.

70. You are leaving work at the police station and need to fill your gas tank before you go home. What is the quickest legal route to the gas station?

  a. south on 9th Avenue, west on Maple Street, north on 11th Avenue, and west on Oak Street to the entrance

  b. north on 9th Avenue and west on Brown Street

  c. south on 9th Avenue, west on Maple Street, north on 12th Avenue, and east on Oak Street to the entrance

  d. north on 9th Avenue, west on Park Street, north on 10th Avenue, and west on Oak Street to the entrance

Directions: You will have ten minutes to read and study the following passage. Then, answer questions 71 through 80 without referring back to the passage.

Often in the course of routine patrol, a police officer needs to briefly detain a person for questioning without an arrest warrant or even probable cause. The officer may also feel that it is necessary to frisk this person for weapons. This type of detention is known as a "Terry Stop," after the U.S. Supreme Court case *Terry vs. State of Ohio*. In that case, the Court determined that a Terry Stop does not violate a citizen's right to be free from unreasonable search and seizure, as long as certain procedures are followed. First, the person must be behaving in some manner that arouses the police officer's suspicion. Second, the officer must believe that swift action is necessary to prevent a crime from being committed or a suspect from escaping. Finally, in order to frisk the individual, the officer must reasonably believe that the person is armed and dangerous. We will now look at each of these elements in more detail.

In determining whether an individual is acting in a suspicious manner, a police officer must rely on his or her training and experience. Circumstances in each case will be different, but an officer must be able to articulate what it was about a person's behavior that aroused suspicion, whether it was one particular action or a series of actions taken together. For example, it may not be unusual for shoppers in a store to wander up and down the aisles looking at merchandise. However, it may be suspicious if a person does this for an inordinate period of time, seems to be checking the locations of surveillance equipment, and is wearing loose clothing that would facilitate shoplifting. Similarly, it is not unusual for a person wearing gym shorts and a T-shirt to be running through a residential neighborhood; however, a person dressed in regular clothes might legitimately be suspect. It is important to note that a person who appears out of place based simply on the manner in which he or she is dressed is not alone cause for suspicion on the part of a police officer.

In addition to the behavior that arouses an officer's attention, the officer must believe that immediate action must be taken to prevent the commission of a crime or a suspect from escaping. In some situations, it may be better to wait to develop probable cause and arrest the person. One important element of this decision is the safety of any other people in the area. In addition, a police officer may determine that his or her immediate action is necessary to avert the commission of a crime, even if no people are in danger. If the suspect appears, for example, to be checking out parked cars for the possibility of stealing one, an officer may well be able to wait until the crime is in progress (thereby having probable cause for an arrest) or even until the crime is actually committed, when patrol cars can be dispatched to arrest the individual. However, a person who appears to be planning a car-jacking should be stopped before the occupants of a car can be hurt. The officer must make a quick decision based on all the circumstances.

Once an officer has detained a suspicious person, the officer must determine if it is necessary to frisk the individual for weapons. Again, an officer should rely on her or his training and experience. If the officer feels that the detainee poses a threat to his or her safety, the suspect should be frisked. For example, although there may certainly be exceptions, a person suspected of shoplifting is not likely to be armed. On the other hand, a person suspected of breaking and entering may very well be carrying a weapon. In addition, the officer should be aware of the behavior of the person once the stop is made. Certain behavior indicates the person is waiting for an opportunity to produce a weapon and threaten the officer's safety. The safety of the officer and any civilians in the area is the most important consideration.

71. According to the reading passage, a Terry Stop is
   a. an arrest for shoplifting.
   b. the brief detention and questioning of a suspicious person.
   c. an officer's frisking a suspect for weapons.
   d. the development of a case that results in an arrest warrant.

72. According to the passage, a Terry Stop includes the frisking of a suspect if
   a. the officer sees evidence of a weapon.
   b. the person is suspected of breaking and entering.
   c. there are civilians in the area.
   d. the officer or others are in danger.

73. An officer on foot patrol notices two people standing on a street corner. The officer observes the two, and after a moment, one of the people walks slowly down the street, looks in the window of a store called McFadden's, walks forward a few feet, and then turns around and returns to the other person. They speak briefly, and then the other person walks down the street, performing the same series of motions. They repeat this ritual five or six times each. The officer would be justified in performing a Terry Stop based on her suspicion that the people
   a. appeared to be carrying weapons.
   b. looked out of place.
   c. might be planning to rob McFadden's.
   d. were obstructing the sidewalk.

74. According to the passage, an officer may choose to conduct a Terry Stop to
   a. discourage loitering.
   b. prevent a crime from being committed or a suspect from escaping.
   c. find out if a person is carrying a concealed weapon.
   d. rule out suspects after a crime has been committed.

75. According to the passage, the determination that a person is suspicious
   a. depends on the circumstances of each situation.
   b. means someone looks out of place.
   c. usually means someone is guilty of planning a crime.
   d. usually indicates a person is carrying a concealed weapon.

76. An officer has stopped a suspicious individual. The suspect seems to be trying to reach for something under her coat. The officer should
   a. call for backup.
   b. arrest the suspect.
   c. frisk the suspect.
   d. handcuff the suspect.

77. An officer observes a person sitting on a bench outside a bank at 4:30 P.M. The officer knows the bank closes at 5:00. The person checks his watch several times and watches customers come and go through the door of the bank. He also makes eye contact with a person driving a blue sedan that appears to be circling the block. Finally, a parking space in front of the bank becomes vacant, and the sedan pulls in. The driver and the man on the bench nod to each other. The officer believes the two are planning to rob the bank just before it closes. What is the first thing the officer should do?
   a. Begin questioning the man on the bench, since it appears he's going to rob the bank.
   b. Begin questioning the driver of the sedan, since it appears she's driving the getaway car.
   c. Go into the bank, warn the employees, and ask all the customers to leave for their own safety.
   d. Call for backup, because it appears the potential robbers are waiting for the bank to close.

78. According to the U.S. Supreme Court, a Terry Stop
   a. is permissible search and seizure.
   b. often occurs in the course of police work.
   c. should be undertaken only when two officers are present.
   d. requires probable cause.

79. According to the passage, persons suspected of shoplifting
   a. should never be frisked, as shoplifters rarely carry weapons.
   b. may legitimately be the subjects of a Terry Stop.
   c. always wear loose clothing and wander in the store a long time.
   d. may be handcuffed immediately for the safety of the civilians in the area.

80. An officer in a squad car is patrolling a wealthy residential neighborhood. She notices one house in which a light will come on in one part of the house for a few minutes, then go off. A moment later, a light will come on in another part of the house, then go off. This happens several times in different parts of the house. The officer also notes that the garage door is standing open and that there are no cars parked there or in the driveway. The officer believes there may be a burglary in progress, and pulls over to observe the house. While she is watching the house, a man wearing torn jeans and a dirty T-shirt walks by the house. According to the passage, the officer should NOT
   a. allow the man to see her, as he may be dangerous.
   b. involve the neighbors by asking them if they have information.
   c. stop the man, as there is no indication he is involved in criminal activity.
   d. radio headquarters until she is absolutely sure a crime is being committed.

81. At 9:30 P.M., while parked at 916 Woodward Avenue, Police Officers Whitebear and Morgan were asked to respond to an anonymous complaint of a disturbance at 826 Rosemary Lane. When they arrived, they found the back door open and the jamb splintered. They drew their weapons, identified themselves, and entered the dwelling, where they found Mr. Darrell Hensley, of 1917 Roosevelt Avenue, sitting on the couch. Mr. Hensley calmly stated he was waiting for his wife. At that point, two children emerged from a hallway: Dustin Hensley, age 7, who lives in the dwelling, and Kirstin Jackson, age 14, Dustin's babysitter, who lives at 916 Ambrose Street. Kirstin stated she and Dustin had been sitting at the kitchen table when the back door was kicked in and Mr. Hensley entered, shouting obscenities and calling for Karen Hensley, Dustin's mother. Kirstin then hid with Dustin in a hallway storage closet. The officers contacted Mrs. Hensley at her place of employment at O'Reilley's Restaurant at 415 Ralston. At 9:55, she returned home and showed an Order of Protection stating that Mr. Hensley was not to have contact with his wife or child. Mr. Hensley was placed under arrest and taken in handcuffs to the station house. Based on Darrell Hensley's behavior when he first arrived at his wife's house, what was his most likely motivation for being there?
   a. to see his child, for a scheduled visitation
   b. to force his wife to speak with him
   c. to have a place to stay that night
   d. to peacefully reconcile with his family

82. An off-duty state trooper was seated in a diner when two armed teenagers entered and robbed the cashier. The officer made no attempt to prevent the robbery or apprehend the teenagers. The state trooper later justified his conduct, stating that an off-duty officer is a private citizen with the same rights and obligations as all private citizens. The state trooper's conduct was

a. correct; the state trooper was out of uniform at the time of the robbery.

b. correct; it would have been a mistake for him to intervene when outnumbered by the armed robbers.

c. incorrect; a state trooper must attempt to prevent crimes and apprehend criminals at all times.

d. incorrect; he should have obtained the necessary information and descriptions after the armed robbers left.

83. During her night patrol, State Trooper Griffin notices a well-dressed man break a car window with a rock, open the door, and get into the car. Of the following, the most essential action for the officer to take is to

a. approach the car and ask the man for proof of ownership.

b. take down the license plate number of the car and a description of the man in case the car is later reported stolen.

c. enter the car and order the man to drive to the nearest police station to explain his actions.

d. approach the car and ask the man to explain his actions.

84. When approaching a suspect to make an arrest, it is least important for a state trooper to prevent a suspect from

a. running away.

b. being armed.

c. spreading a disease.

d. using physical force.

85. While on foot patrol downtown, Officer Gutierrez is approached by Ms. Louise Herald, who says that a man snatched a shopping bag full of gifts from her arm and ran away. Ms. Herald remembers the contents of the shopping bag as follows:

- 1 cashmere sweater valued at $260
- 3 diamond bracelets, each valued at $365
- 1 computer game valued at $78
- 1 cameo brooch valued at $130

Later, Officer Gutierrez receives a call from Ms. Herald, who says she has found the receipts for the stolen merchandise. She says that what she told the officer was correct, except that there were only two diamond bracelets, not three, and that the value of the cashmere sweater was $245. What should Officer Gutierrez write as the total value of the stolen property?

a. $833

b. $1,183

c. $1,198

d. $1,563

86. Officer Kemp has worked more night shifts in a row than Officer Rogers, who has worked five. Officer Miller has worked 15 night shifts in a row, more than Officers Kemp and Rogers combined. Officer Calvin has worked eight night shifts in a row, fewer than Officer Kemp. How many night shifts in a row has Officer Kemp worked?
   a. eight
   b. nine
   c. ten
   d. 11

87. For the past two months, stereo shops all over the city have been hit by burglars in the early morning hours. Sergeant Adams tells Officer Bryant that he should carefully watch the stores in his area that specialize in stereo equipment. Which one of the following situations should Officer Bryant investigate?
   a. a truck with its motor running, backed up to the rear door of the House of Stereos at 1:00 A.M.
   b. a lone man going through a dumpster at the rear of the House of Stereos at 2:00 A.M.
   c. a delivery van marked "House of Stereos" parked in the rear of the store at 2:00 A.M.
   d. two teenage boys intently examining a stereo system in the window of House of Stereos just after midnight

88. Four eyewitnesses saw a vehicle being stolen and noted the license plate number. Each wrote down a different number listed below. Which one is probably right?
   a. KLV 017
   b. XIW 007
   c. XIW 017
   d. XIV 017

Directions: Use the following procedures to answer questions 89 and 90.

An officer responding alone to the scene of a burglar alarm call should do the following:
   ■ Turn off siren and emergency lights as soon as possible to keep from alerting suspects.
   ■ Park the patrol car away from the building.
   ■ Notify the dispatcher of his or her arrival and location.
   ■ Begin checking the outside of the building for signs of entry.
   ■ Notify the dispatcher if signs of entry are discovered.
   ■ Wait for backup if it is available before going inside a building where entry has been made.
   ■ Tell backup officers where to position themselves as they arrive.

89. Officer Kim is dispatched to a burglar alarm call at 100 South Main Street, where the Quik Stop convenience store is located. The store closed at 1 A.M. and it is now 3 A.M. Officer Kim is parked in the parking lot of the pawnshop next door, writing a report, when the call comes out. Officer Kim's next step should be to
   a. walk up to the building from the side so her approach is undetected.
   b. wait for backup before approaching the building.
   c. inform the dispatcher that she has arrived at 100 South Main Street.
   d. check the outside of the building for signs of entry.

90. Officer Smith is sent to 1313 Milbury Way on a residential burglary alarm call at 1 P.M. Traffic is heavy on the way to the call, and he turns on his emergency lights to help clear the way. Officer Smith is notified that no backup is available in his sector. What is the next thing Officer Smith should do?

  a. Park his patrol car a house or two away from 1313 Milbury Way.
  b. Inform the dispatcher when he arrives.
  c. Approach the front door, since any suspects are probably gone by now.
  d. Turn off his emergency lights as soon as he can safely do so.

91. Police officers may find themselves in situations in which using a normal, conversational tone of voice is not enough to get an individual to do what the officer needs done. Which situation below calls for an officer to shout using a firm, authoritative tone of voice?

  a. asking to see a driver's proof of automobile insurance after an accident
  b. advising a new partner of a recently implemented departmental policy
  c. chasing a burglar out of a house
  d. asking a boy why he is not in school on a Monday morning

92. On Monday morning, Officers Rosen and McNalty respond to a call of a burglary that apparently took place over the weekend at Datamation Computer Consultants. The owner of the business says that the following equipment is missing:

  - 3 telephone sets, each valued at $125
  - 2 computers, each valued at $1,300
  - 2 computer monitors, each valued at $950
  - 1 printer valued at $600
  - 1 answering machine valued at $50

  Officer McNalty is preparing a complaint report on the burglary. What should she write as the total value of the missing property?

  a. $3,025
  b. $5,400
  c. $5,525
  d. $6,525

93. In a four-day period—Monday through Thursday—each of the following officers worked only one day, each a different day. Officer Johnson was scheduled to work on Monday, but she traded with Officer Carter, who was originally scheduled to work on Wednesday. Officer Falk traded with Officer Kirk, who was originally scheduled to work on Thursday. After all the switching was done, who worked on Tuesday?

  a. Carter
  b. Falk
  c. Johnson
  d. Kirk

94. Mrs. Oneida called the police to report that a man was looking into her bedroom window last night around 9:45 P.M. Officer Williams talks to residents in the area and finds out that several people have seen a white male dressed in black walking up and down the street at about 10 P.M. for the past week. Officer Williams decides to patrol the area closely and is in the area by 9:30 P.M. Which of the following situations should she investigate?

  a. two teenagers in jeans and dark T-shirts sitting on the curb, smoking cigarettes

  b. a man wearing black jogging shorts and dark shoes stretching his legs in the driveway of a house

  c. a man dressed in dark jeans and a navy blue turtleneck walking rapidly away from some shrubbery at the side of a house

  d. a man in dark clothing attaching a water hose to the faucet on the side of a house

95. Four people witnessed a mugging. Each gave a different description of the mugger. Which description is probably right?

  a. He was average height, thin, and middle-aged.

  b. He was tall, thin, and middle-aged.

  c. He was tall, thin, and young.

  d. He was tall, of average weight, and middle-aged.

96. All police officers are expected to know how to properly package evidence after the decision has been made to collect it. The following steps should be carried out in the order listed:

  1. Place each item in a separate container.

  2. Seal each container in such a way that it cannot be opened without breaking the seal.

  3. The officer collecting the evidence should write his or her name or employee number on the seal.

  4. Place a tag on the container that identifies the case number, the date and time collected, where the item was found, what the item is, who collected it, and what condition the item is in.

  5. Turn the evidence in personally to the Property Room without breaking the chain of custody by allowing someone else to do it.

Officer Jones is the first officer to arrive at the scene of a burglary at Wiggin's Liquor Store. After making sure the scene is secure, he begins to collect evidence. The first item he finds is a screwdriver lying on the sidewalk in front of the glass doors leading into the store. The second item he sees is a small flashlight on the floor inside the building. Officer Jones places the screwdriver in a small plastic bag. What is the next thing he should do?

  a. Lock the screwdriver in the trunk of his car.

  b. Seal the bag with evidence tape so that the bag cannot be opened.

  c. Write the case number and other information about the evidence on the outside of the bag.

  d. Put the flashlight in the bag with the screwdriver.

97. Officers Roberts and Reed are on bicycle patrol in the downtown area. Sergeant McElvey tells them that a white male has been committing robberies along the nearby bike path by stepping out of the bushes and threatening bicyclists with an iron pipe until they give him their bicycles. There have been three separate incidents, and the suspect descriptions are from three different victims.

Robbery #1: Suspect is a white male, 20–25 years old, 5′9″, 145 pounds, with a shaved head, wearing a skull earring in the left ear, floppy white T-shirt, worn light blue jeans, and black combat boots.

Robbery #2: Suspect is a white male, 25–30 years old, dark brown hair in a military-style crew cut, 6′2″, 200 pounds, wearing a white T-shirt with the words "Just Do It" on the back, blue surgical scrub pants, and black combat boots.

Robbery #3: Suspect is a white male, 23 years old, 5′10″, skinny build, no hair, wearing a Grateful Dead T-shirt, blue baggy pants, dark shoes, and one earring.

Three days after Sergeant McElvey told the officers about the robberies, Officer Reed arrested a suspect for attempting to take a woman's mountain bike from her on the bicycle path. The description of the suspect is as follows:

Robbery #4: Suspect is a white male, 22 years old, 140 pounds, 5′10″, with a shaved head and one pierced ear, wearing a plain white T-shirt two sizes too large for him, faded baggy blue jeans, and scuffed black combat boots.

After comparing the suspect description with those in the first three robberies, Officer Reed should consider the arrested man as a suspect in which of the other robberies?
a. Robbery #1, Robbery #2, and Robbery #3
b. Robbery #1, but not Robbery #2 or Robbery #3
c. Robbery #1 and Robbery #3, but not Robbery #2
d. Robbery #1 and Robbery #2, but not Robbery #3

98. Officers are required to immediately report to their supervisor any damage to a patrol car. In which situation below should an officer call the supervisor to report a damaged patrol car?
a. A disgruntled citizen kicks a tire on the patrol car as she walks past it.
b. The driver's door is dented in by an irate man under arrest for public intoxication.
c. The officer bumps a pole while backing out of an alley but finds no dents or scratches on the vehicle.
d. The officer finds a dozen eggs smashed on the windshield.

99. The first officer to respond to the scene of a sexual assault has many responsibilities. The officer should take the following steps in the order listed:

1. Aid the victim if necessary by calling for an ambulance or administering first aid.
2. Try to calm and comfort the victim as much as possible.
3. If the attack is recent, get a suspect description from the victim and radio the dispatcher to put out a be-on-the-lookout broadcast.
4. Find out from the victim where the crime occurred.
5. Determine if there is any physical evidence on the victim that may need to be preserved, such as pieces of the suspect's skin or blood under the victim's fingernails.
6. If possible, have the victim change clothing, and then take the clothing he or she was wearing as evidence.
7. Convince the victim to undergo a medical exam for his or her health and safety and so that evidence may be gathered.

Officer Augustine is at 2101 Reynolds Street talking to Betty Smith, the victim of a sexual assault. Ms. Smith is uninjured and is very calm. She gives Officer Augustine a detailed description of her attacker and says she thinks he may be headed for a nearby tavern. At this point, Officer Augustine should

a. get into his patrol car and drive to the tavern.
b. give the dispatcher the description of the suspect.
c. take the victim straight to the hospital for a medical exam.
d. have the victim change clothing.

100. Fred is a business owner downtown who makes it well known that he hates police officers and thinks they are all corrupt. Fred runs a red light downtown, almost causing a van to hit him, and then pulls over in front of his store, cursing loudly about the other driver's driving skills. Officer Martinez was standing on the corner and watched Fred run the light. What should she do?

a. Write Fred a citation for running a red light.
b. Warn Fred not to run red lights and hope this improves Fred's opinion of police.
c. Suggest to Fred that he take defensive driving classes.
d. Look into having someone retime the lights in the downtown area.

▶ Answers

1. d. Although the last sentence expands on the main idea of the passage, the rest of the passage explains why hearsay evidence is admissible only when it doesn't matter whether or not the statement is true.

2. a. Although this statement may be true, it isn't stated anywhere in the passage.

3. b. The proper use of hearsay evidence is explained by the hypothetical example found in the final sentence of the passage.

4. c. The passage mentions discerning *the truth* and *the truth of a statement* several times.

5. c. Although choices **a** and **b** are also true, they are not the main idea, which should be supported by the whole passage and spelled out in the last sentence.

6. b. This is implied in the next-to-last sentence of the passage.

7. c. See the first sentence of the passage.

8. d. Miranda rights are read only when the suspect is taken into custody. The right to call a lawyer (choice **c**) and the right to a phone call (choice **b**) are included in the Miranda rights.

9. b. See the last sentence of paragraph 1, which discuss the stalking victim's *worst fear.*

10. c. The last two paragraphs of the passage discuss why modern anti-stalking laws are more effective than previous methods, but also how they are flawed. The other answer choices are mentioned in the passage but are not the central argument.

11. d. The victim's knowledge or lack of knowledge about anti-stalking laws is not discussed anywhere in the passage. All the other choices are mentioned in the third paragraph.

12. a. The first passage states that a restraining order is a *civil remedy often ignored by the offender.*

13. c. Nowhere in the passage does it state that a stalker's motive is to rob or steal from his or her victim. All the other choices are mention in the final paragraph.

14. a. See the second paragraph. Choices **b** and **c** apply only to the Orange County women; choice **d** cannot be shown to apply to either example.

15. b. The second and third sentences of the passage state that *officers should keep complete notes detailing any potentially criminal or actionable incidents* and that the officers *may refer to those notes to refresh their memory about particular events.*

16. d. The passage provides information for law enforcement officers; choice **d** is therefore the most logical choice. Choice **a** refers to a memo directed to police officers, but the subject matter is incorrect. The subject matter of choice **b** is also incorrect. The wording and tone of the passage do not seem to be attempting recruitment, as in choice **c**.

17. a. The first very first sentence of the passage states that testimony *is an important part of an officer's job.*

18. a. The discussion of the traits of a person with antisocial personality disorder in the middle of the passage specifies that such a person does not have distortions of thought. The passage speaks of the antisocial person as being *inordinately self-confident* (choice **b**) and of the person's *emotional shallowness* (choices **c** and **d**).

19. d. The third sentence of the passage speaks of *con games.* None of the other professions would suit an impulsive, shallow person who has been in trouble with the law.

20. b. The passage mentions *emotional shallowness.* The other choices hint at the capacity to feel meaningful emotion.

21. d. This is the only choice that does not contain excessive wordiness or a redundancy. In choice **a**, the phrase *the fifth of five* is a redundancy. Choice **b** also repeats by using both *five* and *fifth*. Choice **c**, although constructed differently, makes the same error.

22. d. The correct punctuation between two independent clauses is a semicolon. Choice **a** is wrong because it creates a comma splice. Choice **b** creates faulty subordination. Choice **c** creates a sentence fragment.

23. b. This choice is the only one that is a complete sentence.

24. c. This choice is best because it is written in the active voice, and the sentence is constructed so that all modifiers are appropriately placed.

25. b. Choices **a** and **c** are sentence fragments. Choice **d** represents confused sentence structure as well as a lack of agreement between subject and verb.

26. c. The other choices contain unnecessary shifts in person, from *people* to *their* and *we* in choice **a**, to *your* and *one* in choice **b**, and to *our* and *they* in choice **d**.

27. a. The subject of the sentence *art professor* is singular and takes the singular verb *is planning*.

28. d. This is a complete sentence; the other choices are fragments.

29. b. This is a complete sentence. Choices **c** and **d** are fragments. In choice **a**, the verb does not agree in number with its subject, *one*.

30. a. This sentence is clearest. In choice **b**, the speaker likes his or her sister better than fish. Choice **c** is confusing. Choice **d** has an unclear pronoun: The use of *it* makes it unclear whether fish or the sister is referenced.

31. a. This sentence has faulty subordination; the word *going* should be deleted and the comma should be eliminated.

32. b. This is a run-on sentence.

33. c. The connecting word between the two clauses creates an illogical statement. The word *therefore* should be changed to the word *but*.

34. d. There are no errors.

35. a. This sentence makes an illogical shift from the past to the present tense.

36. d. There are no errors.

37. c. Sentence 4 is the topic sentence. Sentence 1 provides detailed information and sentence 3 provides further detail about the information in sentence 1. Sentence 2, with the word *however*, adds to the information.

38. c. Sentence 4 is the general topic sentence. Sentence 1, with the phrase *for example*, gives a specific case. Sentence 3 gives the details of the example. Sentence 2 provides another more general example.

39. b. Sentence 1 provides a general rule. Sentence 4, with the word *however*, notes an exception to the general rule. Sentence 2, with the word *usually*, gives an example of the exception. Sentence 3 tells how the example is applied in practice.

40. d. Sentence 4 introduces the topic of solicitation and explains how it might come up. Sentence 2 gives the first part of the definition of *solicitation*; sentence 3 gives the second part of the definition. Sentence 1 refers to all the elements mentioned in sentences 2 and 3.

41. d. A quotient results from division. $12,440 \div 40 = 311$.

42. d. Consider **PEMDAS**: *parentheses, exponents, multiplication, division, addition, subtraction*. Here you must solve the division first: $540 \div 6 = 90$. The equation becomes $90 + 3 \times 24$. Again, considering PEMDAS, you know you should calculate the multiplication first. $3 \times 24 = 72$, so the equation reduces to $90 + 72 = 162$.

43. a. $7^3 = 7 \cdot 7 \cdot 7$, which equals $49 \cdot 7 = 343$.

44. d. Do this problem in the order it is presented; first subtract, then add.

45. b. You can reduce this fraction in steps: $\frac{80}{200} \div \frac{20}{20} = \frac{4}{10} \div \frac{2}{2} = \frac{2}{5}$.

46. d. The quickest way to find a common denominator is to multiply the two given denominators. $5 \times 6 = 30$, so the new denominator will be 30. To convert $\frac{4}{5}$ into 30ths, multiply by $\frac{6}{6}$: $\frac{4}{5} \times \frac{6}{6} = \frac{24}{30}$. To convert $\frac{1}{6}$ into 30ths, multiply by $\frac{5}{5}$: $\frac{1}{6} \times \frac{5}{5} = \frac{5}{30}$. Next, add: $\frac{24}{30} + \frac{5}{30} = \frac{29}{30}$.

47. d. Perform the operations in the parentheses first: $25 = 17 = 42$; $64 - 49 = 15$. Then, go on to multiply those numbers as indicated by the two side-by-side parentheses: $42 \times 15 = 630$.

48. c. The values added together total $618. If you chose choice **a**, you forgot to add the value of the handbag ($150) to the total.

49. c. First, set up a proportion: $\frac{17}{20} = \frac{?}{100}$. Cross multiply to get $17 \times 100 = 5 \times ?$, or $1,700 = 20 \times ?$. Divide both sides by 20 to get $? = 85$. Thus, the answer is 85%, choice **c**.

50. a. 46 goes into 184 four times. The other choices cannot be divided evenly into 184.

51. d. Set up a proportion when confronted with this scenario: $\frac{14 \text{ workers}}{2 \text{ days}} = \frac{4 \text{ workers}}{? \text{ days}}$. Notice that the ? in the denominator of the second ratio will necessarily be smaller than the 2 days in the denominator of the first ratio. If 14 workers can complete the job in 2 days, it will take one person 14 times as long to complete the same job: 28 days. It will take 4 people $\frac{1}{4}$ as long to complete this amount of work, or 7 days.

52. b. Solving this problem requires converting 15 minutes to 0.25 hour, which is the time, then using the formula: 62 mph $\times$ 0.25 hour = 15.5 miles, choice **b**.

53. a. The truck travels for 1 hour and 30 minutes, which is 1.5 hours. According to the formula, then, the distance traveled is 1.5 hours times 50 mph, or 75 miles, choice **a**.

54. c. This is a multiplication problem: 84,720 officers $\times$ 4 square yards of cloth equals 338,880 square yards of cloth. If you selected choice **a**, you made a mistake in your division.

55. d. Take the total number of miles and find the average by dividing: $448 \div 16$ gallons = 28 miles per gallon.

56. c. This is the simplest way around the one-way streets and Town Hall. Because Linda Lane is one-way going the wrong way, some backtracking is inevitable. However, the residence is only one block off Barcelona Boulevard, and so turning eastbound on Barcelona requires the least amount of backtracking. Choice **a** directs your unit to turn the wrong way down a one-way street. Choice **b** requires too much backtracking because Barcelona Boulevard is a one-way street going east. Choice **d** requires too many turns and is the least direct route.

57. b. This is the most direct route because it requires the fewest turns. Choice **a** requires your unit to go the wrong way on McMahon Street. Choice **c** is not correct because Canyon Drive is a one-way street going south. Choice **d** is a much longer route.

58. a. If Ricardo turns right onto James Avenue, she will be facing north. A left turn onto Linda Lane turns her west again, and a right turn onto Livingston Avenue turns her north. The final right turn onto Barcelona Boulevard turns her east, choice **a**.

59. c. The state trooper needs to make a right onto Bortz Road, a left onto El Camino, and a left onto Linda Lane. This is the most direct route. If you chose choice **a**, you may have thought the trooper could just make a right onto

Linda Lane, but this is a one-way street heading west. If you chose choice **b**, you may have thought the trooper arrived at the final destination by reaching the northeast corner of Town Hall. However, the entrance is to the left of the northeast corner of the building, so the trooper must make a left onto Linda Lane.

60. b. If State Trooper Bassett turns right onto Orinda Road, he will be facing south.

61. d. This is the most direct route because it does not require any backtracking. Choice **a** is not correct because it would require your unit to go the wrong way on Mill Road. Choice **b** requires your unit to go the wrong way on Lynch Road. Choice **c** is not as direct because it requires your unit to move in the opposite direction from the call.

62. b. This is the fastest route, requiring the fewest turns. Choice **a** is not correct because Kent is a one-way street going east. Choice **c** requires too many turns and is not the most direct route. Choice **d** is not correct because Upton Street is one-way, going north.

63. d. A left turn onto Lee Lane turns Trooper Kearney south. Another left turn onto Pecan Avenue turns her east. A left onto Main Street turns her north and the final right turn onto Palmer turns her back east, choice **d.**

64. d. Bond Road is a one-way northbound street, so if State Trooper Santos turns right onto Bond Road, he will be facing north.

65. a. Choice **b** takes you the wrong way on Kent Avenue. Choices **c** and **d** are not the most direct routes.

66. a. The other routes are impossible or illegal.

67. c. Brown Street and Park Street are the two streets that run north and south of the park.

68. a. The other routes are impossible or illegal.

69. b. The other routes are impossible (choices **c** and **d**) or circuitous (choice **a**).

70. d. Choices **a** and **c** take you the wrong way on Maple Street. Choice **b** will not get you to the entrance of the gas station.

71. b. A Terry Stop is described in the first three sentences of the first paragraph of the passage.

72. d. See the fourth paragraph. If the officer feels that the suspect poses a threat to the officer's safety, the suspect should be frisked.

73. c. Based on the actions described, an officer's training and experience would indicate that the people were planning a robbery.

74. b. See the third-to-last sentence of the first paragraph.

75. a. See the second sentence of the second paragraph.

76. c. See the fourth paragraph.

77. d. See the third paragraph.

78. a. See the third and fourth sentences of the first paragraph.

79. b. Refer to the fourth sentence of the second paragraph.

80. c. See the sixth sentence of the second paragraph.

81. b. You can approach this question by asking why Mr. Hensley has forced open the door and has told police he is waiting for his wife. Choice **a** is incorrect; Mr. Hensley's child hid from him in a closet, and he evidently didn't try to get his son to come out. Choice **c** is incorrect, because Mr. Hensley has a residence of his own at 1917 Roosevelt. Mr. Hensley evidently didn't intend peaceful reconciliation (choice **d**), because he kicked the door in.

82. c. Even when he or she is not on official duty, a state trooper must fulfill the police role if a crime is taking place in his or her presence.

83. a. This is the quickest way to find out if the man is the owner of the car or if he is committing a criminal act.

84. c. The state trooper must be concerned that the suspect might try to escape, be armed, or use physical violence. The state trooper must be least concerned with diseases the suspect may carry, but this is still a valid concern.

85. b. Add the corrected value of the sweater ($245) to the value of the two, not three, bracelets ($730), plus the other two items ($78 and $130).

86. b. Officer Kemp has worked more shifts in a row than Officer Calvin; therefore, Kemp has worked more than eight shifts. The number of Kemp's shifts plus the number of Rogers's shifts (five) cannot equal 15 or more, the number of Miller's shifts. Therefore, Kemp has worked nine shifts in a row (5 + 9 = 14).

87. a. A truck with the motor running, backed up to the rear door of a closed business at 1:00 A.M., is suspicious. Delivery vans owned by businesses are commonly parked on store property after hours (choice **c**). A lone man going through a dumpster would have no way to carry stereo equipment (choice **b**), and it would not be unusual for teenage boys to be looking at a stereo system in the window, even at midnight (choice **d**).

88. c. The elements of the license plate number that most often repeat in the descriptions are XIW and 017. Therefore, the correct license number is most likely XIW 017.

89. c. The officer has already done steps 1 and 2 because she is already at the location. Her next step would be to let the dispatcher know that she is on the scene (step 3).

90. d. Officer Smith should turn off his emergency lights as the first step in answering a burglar alarm call.

91. c. It would not be appropriate to shout in the situations described in choices **a**, **b**, or **d**. An officer would shout at a burglar because the situation calls for identifying himself or herself as a police officer. A loud, authoritative shout in this situation is part of the voice control officers should exercise as the first step in the use of force.

92. c. The total value of all three telephone sets at $125 each is $375. The total value of both computers at $1,300 each is $2,600. The two computer monitors, each valued at $950, have a total value of $1,900. Add those three totals to the printer at $600 and the answering machine at $50 for a grand total of $5,525 for all the stolen property.

93. d. After all the switches were made, Officer Kirk worked on Tuesday. Officer Carter worked on Monday, Officer Johnson on Wednesday, and Officer Falk on Thursday.

94. c. The officer is looking for a suspect dressed in dark clothing who has been seen walking up and down a residential street during a specific time span—a window peeper. Choices **a**, **b**, and **d** suggest normal neighborhood activity because all the people involved are out in the open. The shrubbery the man in choice **c** is walking away from suggests a hiding place near a window.

95. b. Tall, thin, and middle-aged are the elements of the description repeated most often and are therefore the most likely to be accurate.

96. b. Sealing the bag is step 2 on the list of procedures.

97. c. The suspect described in Robbery #2 has a crew-cut hairstyle, is at least five inches taller than the other suspects, and is about 60 pounds heavier. The other three descriptions are much more likely to be of the same man because they all describe a similar build and mention one earring or a pierced ear.

98. b. No damage has been done to the patrol car in choices **a**, **c**, or **d**.

99. b. The officer has already taken care of steps 1 and 2: The victim doesn't need immediate medical help, and she is calm. Step 3 tells the officer to radio the suspect description to the dispatcher so a be-on-the-lookout bulletin can be issued.

100. a. Fred's opinion of police has nothing to do with the situation. Officer Martinez should write the ticket because the situation was dangerous, and that is what she would do under normal circumstances. A warning is not appropriate because a collision was narrowly averted.

CHAPTER
6 ▶ Reading-Based Questions

CHAPTER SUMMARY
State police officers must have the ability to comprehend written materials, to draw logical inferences from the materials, and to apply the information and inferences to problem solving. Some of the written materials that officers encounter are legal statutes and cases, law enforcement training manuals, investigative reports, and written complaints from the public.

Testing whether you can comprehend written materials and draw logical inferences serves a dual purpose. It determines whether you can read sufficiently well to understand information and whether you possess the necessary reasoning ability to perform the functions of a state police officer. In order to pass the exam, you must do well on the reading-based portions of the exam.

Reading questions offer you two advantages as a test taker. First, you do not need any prior knowledge about the topic of the passage. Second, you will be tested only on the information presented in the passage. The disadvantage is that you have to know where and how to find the information you need under certain time constraints and in an unfamiliar text. This somewhat stressful combination makes it easy to choose one of the wrong answer choices, especially since the choices are deliberately designed to mislead you. If you are in a hurry, it is easy to make a mistake.

The reading-based portions of exams usually contain excerpts of text that are a few hundred words in length. Topics can vary widely from popular culture to scientific concepts, but most often, they relate to law-enforcement subjects. Each passage is followed by specific questions based on the text.

As you study for the state trooper exam, understand that your vocabulary skills play a vital role when you have to decipher any written text. Sometimes, just one difficult word can skew your understanding of a sentence.

Two or three unknown words can make a passage difficult, or even impossible, to interpret. It is important to understand that vocabulary and reading comprehension go hand in hand as you continue your test preparation.

The best way to do well is to be very familiar with the kinds of questions that are typically asked, and then to know how to respond to these questions. Questions most frequently ask you to:

- determine the main idea of the passage
- identify a specific fact or detail in the passage
- identify the topic sentence
- discern fact from opinion
- make an inference based on the passage
- define a vocabulary word from the passage

Once you know the kinds of questions that will be asked, you can develop some strategies to help you choose correct answers. To do this, you must be a discriminating reader and know where to look for the information, facts, and details you need to help you choose correctly.

You must be sure to answer reading-based questions on the state trooper exam solely on basis of the information provided in the reading passage. You should not answer the questions based on your opinions or personal knowledge about the subject matter.

▶ Active Reading

People often think of reading as a passive activity. After all, you are just sitting there, looking at words on a page. But reading should actually be an active exercise. When you read, you should *interact* with the text, paying careful attention and being involved as you read. Whenever you read—for a test, for class, for pleasure— use these active reading strategies to improve your reading comprehension.

Skim Ahead and Jump Back

Skimming ahead helps prepare you for your reading task. Before you begin reading, scan the text to see what's ahead. Is the reading broken into sections? What are the main topics of those sections? In what order are they covered? What key words or ideas are boldfaced, bulleted, boxed, or otherwise highlighted?

When you finish reading, jump back. Review the summaries, headings, and highlighted information. (This includes what you highlighted, too.) Jumping back helps you remember the information you just read. You can see how each idea fits into the whole and how ideas and information are connected.

Look up Unfamiliar Vocabulary Words

One of the best ways to build your vocabulary is to *always* look up words you don't know. You need to know what all the words in a sentence mean to fully understand what someone is saying. Remember, a key word or phrase can change the meaning of a whole passage.

So, whenever possible, have a dictionary with you when you read. Circle and look up any unfamiliar words right away. (Circling them makes them easier to find if you lose your place.) Write the meaning of the word in the margin. That way, you won't have to look up the meaning again if you forget it; it will always be there for you to refer to. If you don't own the book, write the vocabulary word and its definition in a notebook.

If you don't have a dictionary with you, try to figure out what the word means. What clues does the author provide in the sentence and surrounding sentences? Mark the page or write down the word somewhere so you can look it up later. See how closely you were able to guess its meaning.

Mark up the Text

As you read, mark up the text (or notepaper if the text doesn't belong to you) by:

- highlighting or underlining key words and ideas
- taking notes
- making notes

One strategy used by many readers is highlighting and underlining. By highlighting or underlining key words and phrases, you can make important details stand out. This helps you quickly find the information later when you need to answer a question or write a summary. To highlight key words and ideas, you must be able to determine which facts and ideas are most important.

Here are three guidelines for highlighting or underlining your text.

1. **Be selective.** If you highlight four sentences in a five-sentence paragraph, this will not help you. The key is to identify what is most important in the paragraph. Ask yourself two questions:
   - What is the main point the author is trying to make—what is the main idea of the paragraph?
   - What information is emphasized or seems to stand out as especially important?
2. **Watch for word clues.** Certain words and phrases indicate that key information will follow. Words and phrases such as *most important, the key is,* and *significantly* are clues to watch out for.
3. **Watch for visual clues.** Key words and ideas are often boldfaced, underlined, or italicized. They may be boxed or repeated in a sidebar as well.

Careful, active reading will help you improve your overall reading comprehension skills and make reading a more pleasant experience. It will also be your best strategy for tackling the reading questions on the state trooper exam.

▶ Practice Questions

For practice, read the following passage and answer the questions that follow.

In order for a defendant to be held criminally responsible for a homicide, his or her conduct must actually contribute to the victim's death. The defendant's conduct does not have to be the sole cause of death; however, the connection between the defendant's conduct and the resulting death must be more than a mere probability that the conduct would cause the result. It must be a sufficiently direct cause that it was reasonably foreseeable that the conduct was likely to lead to the result. Whether the result was reasonably foreseeable is determined by an objective standard, not a subjective, personal view.

Manslaughter and murder are forms of homicide. Manslaughter occurs when a person recklessly causes the death of another person. Murder occurs when a person intending to cause the death of another person engages in conduct that causes such death.

A person acts recklessly with respect to a result defined as an offense when he or she is aware of and consciously disregards a substantial and unjustifiable risk that such result will occur. A person acts intentionally with respect to a result defined as an offense when his or her conscious objective is to cause such result or to engage in such conduct. A person's conduct can be both intentional and reckless when he or she engages in unlawful conduct with the conscious objective of causing a specific result but the conduct also creates a dangerous situation that could cause a different result.

Larry Dewitt had been indicted for several misdemeanor crimes. He jumped bail and a warrant was issued for his arrest. A bail bondsman alerted the police that the defendant had boarded a bus. The police intercepted the bus in a police car.

Realizing that the police had blocked the bus, Dewitt disembarked and began to run away. A police officer pursued him and ordered him to stop, but

Dewitt ran toward an expressway, which was a six-lane highway that had a six-foot-tall chain-link fence in the median. The top of the fence was bordered by a metal wire and was somewhat unstable. After crossing the first three lanes of traffic, Dewitt climbed over the fence and ran across the highway. As the police officer attempted to vault over the fence, it began to bend under his weight. He fell from the fence onto the hood of an oncoming car and was thrown into the air, hitting the ground headfirst. The officer died from the injuries he sustained.

1. It would be most correct to state that the defendant, Dewitt, would be
   a. not guilty of homicide because his conduct was not the sole cause of the death.
   b. not guilty of homicide because the death was caused by the oncoming car, not by Dewitt.
   c. not guilty of homicide because the police officer was negligent and should have known better than to attempt to vault over the fence.
   d. guilty of a form of homicide even though he did not intend to cause the death of the police officer.

2. It would be most correct to state that the defendant, Dewitt, would not be guilty of manslaughter
   a. because the unstable fence contributed to the death, and he was not responsible for the fence.
   b. if he was unaware that the officer was chasing him and that the officer had ordered him to stop.
   c. if he knew the officer was chasing him, but he did not want the officer to get hurt.
   d. if he did not realize or think that his conduct was so dangerous.

3. It would be most correct to state that the defendant, Dewitt, would be guilty of
   a. murder if he intended to engage in the conduct of escaping but did not intend to cause the death of the officer.
   b. murder if he recklessly caused the death of the officer.
   c. manslaughter only if he was armed as he fled.
   d. manslaughter if he intended only to engage in escaping but he was aware of the danger in the situation.

4. It would be most correct to state that the defendant, Dewitt, could be
   a. not guilty of murder if he tried to warn the officer about the unstable fence.
   b. guilty of murder if he knew that the fence was unstable and purposely led the officer to the fence, hoping the officer would fall.
   c. guilty of murder even if he tried to warn the officer about the unstable fence.
   d. guilty of murder even if he did not intentionally cause the death of the officer.

5. It would be most correct to state that
   a. a person acts intentionally when he or she is aware of a substantial and unjustifiable risk but consciously disregards the risk.
   b. a person acts recklessly when he or she fails to perceive that his or her conduct creates a substantial and unjustifiable risk of injury and causes such injury.
   c. although another person caused the death of the officer and could be charged with manslaughter for the death, Dewitt also could be guilty of manslaughter for creating the risk.
   d. Dewitt could not be guilty of either murder or manslaughter if the driver of the car that struck the officer had been recklessly speeding above the speed limit.

6. If the officer had not been killed by the car on the expressway, but had safely arrested Dewitt and begun to drive him to the police station, it would be most incorrect to state that the defendant, Dewitt,

   a. could not be charged with murder if the officer was struck by another vehicle while driving with activated lights and siren and died in the collision.

   b. could not be charged with manslaughter if the officer was struck by another vehicle while driving with activated lights and siren and died in the collision.

   c. could not be charged with manslaughter if the officer had safely arrived at the police station and, while removing Dewitt from the police car, had slipped on the sidewalk, hit his head, and died from the injury sustained.

   d. could not be charged with manslaughter if as the officer drove to the police station, Dewitt tried to climb out the car window, causing the officer to swerve, lose control of the vehicle, and be killed in a collision.

▶ Answers

1. d. This is most correct because he could be guilty of manslaughter based on his reckless conduct. He was aware that he was being pursued by the police, that entering the expressway would create a substantial and unjustifiable risk, and he disregarded the risk. It was reasonably foreseeable that a car would strike the officer. Choice **a** is incorrect because his conduct does not have to be the sole cause of death but is sufficient causation if it contributes to the death. Choice **b** is incorrect because the defendant's conduct unjustifiably set in motion the events leading to the officer being struck by the car. Choice **c**

is incorrect for the same reasons as choice **b** and because it was reasonably foreseeable that accidents, injuries, or deaths could result from the defendant's unjustifiable conduct.

2. b. This is most correct because for his conduct to be considered reckless, the defendant must be aware of a risk and consciously disregard it. Choice **a** is incorrect because his conduct does not have to be the sole cause of death but is sufficient causation if it contributes to the death. Choice **c** is incorrect because he was reckless in that he consciously disregarded the substantial and unjustifiable risk. Choice **d** is incorrect because the standard for determining whether a result was reasonably foreseeable is an objective standard, not a subjective, personal standard.

3. d. This is most correct because his intentional conduct in escaping also recklessly created the substantial and unjustifiable risks associated with crossing the expressway, and the latter is legally sufficient to support a conviction for manslaughter. Choice **a** is incorrect because he could not be guilty of murder, which would have required the higher mental culpability of intending to cause the death of the officer. Choice **b** is incorrect for the same reasons as choice **a**. Choice **c** is incorrect because for manslaughter, there is no requirement that the defendant must be armed.

4. a. Choice **a** is most correct because his warning to the officer about the unstable fence shows that he did not intend for the officer to be killed, and intent is required for murder. Choice **b** is incorrect because, although the defendant's conduct was culpable and intentional, his intention was only to cause the officer to fall, not to cause his death. For murder, the intent must be to cause death, not a lesser physical injury. Choice **c** is incorrect because it is the opposite conclusion from choice **a**. By trying to warn the officer, the defendant showed that he did not intend to cause his death, and therefore could not be guilty of intentional murder. Choice **d** is incorrect because based on the information provided by the question, an element of murder is the intention to cause the death of another.

5. c. This is most correct because the defendant's conduct unjustifiably set in motion the events leading to the officer being struck by the car. The fact that another person could also be charged in the death does not exonerate the defendant. Choice **a** is incorrect because the answer describes reckless conduct, not intentional conduct. Choice **b** is incorrect because for his conduct to be considered reckless, the defendant must be aware of the risks and disregard them. In choice **b**, the person did not perceive the risk and was unaware, which could be negligent but not reckless conduct. Choice **d** is incorrect for the same reasons that choice **c** is correct. If both the defendant and the driver of the car contributed to the death by sufficiently direct causation, they can both be guilty of crimes for their individual conduct.

6. d. This is the most incorrect statement. The defendant's conduct created a substantial and unjustifiable risk that defendant was aware of and disregarded. Therefore, he could be guilty of reckless manslaughter. Choices **a** and **b** are both true statements because the defendant's act of running away was not a sufficiently direct cause of this unrelated accident. As the passage states, "the connection between the defendant's conduct and the resulting death must be more than a mere probability that the conduct would cause the result. It must be a sufficiently direct cause that it was reasonably foreseeable that the conduct was likely to lead to the result." Choice **c** is true for the same reasons as choices **a** and **b**. The fact that the defendant had jumped bail and caused the officer to arrest him was not a sufficiently direct cause of the officer slipping on the sidewalk while making a routine arrest. The officer slipped on the sidewalk for reasons insufficiently related to the defendant's conduct of running across the expressway.

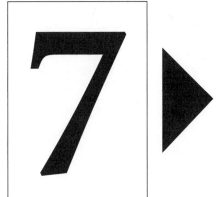

7 ▶ Writing and Information Ordering

CHAPTER SUMMARY

Police officers must frequently write reports and complete forms that ask for more than box-checking. Initial incident reports must be clear so that you can understand your own report later, so that supervisors, detectives, or investigators can also understand what happened, and so that later in the process, the attorneys working on a case will be able to determine what occurred and be able to question you intelligently about the facts of the case.

There are many types of situations in which your reports will become public documents. Your credibility and the credibility of your agency will be determined by your reports. If there are spelling or grammar errors, slang expressions, or factual errors, your words will not carry much weight.

Writing questions on a state trooper exam test your ability to use correct spelling, punctuation, grammar, and vocabulary to relay information in written format. Information ordering questions test your ability to present information not only in a written format, but also in a logical manner so that a reader can understand what happened in a particular situation.

In order to communicate with others and get your point across in writing, using words and punctuation correctly is necessary. Maybe you're one of the millions of people who, as a student in elementary or high school, found memorizing grammar rules tedious. Maybe you were confused by all of the exceptions to those rules. The good news is that grammar and writing skills can be developed with practice.

► Mechanics: Capitalization and Punctuation

Because every sentence begins with a capital letter, the how-to's of capitalization seem like a logical place to begin learning about language mechanics. The following checklist will help you identify when capitalization should be used.

Capitalization Checklist

- the first word of every sentence
  Yes, we do carry that model stereo system.
- the first word of a quoted sentence (not just a quoted phrase)
  And with great flourish, he sang, "O beautiful for spacious skies, for amber waves of grain!"
- the specific name of a person (and his or her title), a place, or a thing (otherwise known as *proper nouns*). Proper nouns include specific locations and geographic regions; political, social, and athletic organizations and agencies; historical events, documents and periods; nationalities and their languages; religions, their members, and their deities; brand or trade names; and holidays.
- the abbreviations for proper nouns. Government agencies are probably the most frequently abbreviated. Remember to capitalize each letter.
  CIA employees represent a broad mix of academic backgrounds and experience
- adjectives (descriptive words) derived from proper nouns
  the American flag
- the pronoun *I*
- the most important words in a title
  Last *March, I endured a 20-hour public reading of Moby Dick.*

Punctuation Checklist

Proper punctuation is the difference between your audience understanding your writing and losing the meaning behind what you are trying to convey. The following checklist explains major punctuation marks and when they should be used.

Periods

- at the end of a declarative sentence (sentence that makes a statement)
  Today, I took a walk to nowhere.
- at the end of a command or request
  Turn left at the light.
- at the end of an indirect question
  Jane asked if I knew where she had left her keys.
- before a decimal number
  Statisticians claim that the average family raises 2.5 children.
- between dollars and cents
  I remember when $1.50 could buy a meal.
- after an initial in a person's name
  You are Sir James W. Dewault, are you not?
- after an abbreviation
  On Jan. 12, I take the state trooper exam.

Question Marks

- at the end of a question
  Why do you look so sad?
- inside a quotation mark, when the quote is a question
  She asked, "Why do you look so sad?"

Exclamation Points

- at the end of a word, phrase, or sentence filled with emotion
  That building is on fire!
- inside a quotation mark, when the quote is an exclamation
  The woman screamed, "That building is on fire!"

Quotation Marks

- when directly quoting dialogue, not when paraphrasing
  Hamlet says, "To be, or not to be. That is the question."
- for titles of chapters, articles, short stories, poems, songs, or periodicals
  My favorite short story is "Flowers for Algernon."

Semicolons

- between two independent clauses (an *independent clause* is a complete thought. It has a subject and a predicate.)
  Edward joined the basketball team; remarkably, the 5′ 4″ young man excelled at the sport.
- between elements in a series that uses commas
  The possible dates for the exam are Thursday, June 5; Saturday, June 7; or Monday, June 9.

Colons

- between two complete ideas when the second idea explains the first
  Keri pushed her dinner away: She had eaten on the car ride home.
- before a list
  On test day, you should bring three forms of identification: your license, your Social Security card, and your birth certificate.
- between titles and subtitles
  Measurement: Translating into Metric
- between volumes and page numbers
  Marvel Comics 21:24
- between Bible chapters and verses
  Job 4:12
- between hours and minutes
  It's 2:00 A.M.—time to sleep.

Apostrophes

- where letters or numbers have been deleted, as in a contraction
  I looked at my father and whispered, "It's [It is] okay to cry every so often."
- at the end of a name to indicate possession
  Jane's father sprained his ankle during practice.

Commas

- between items in dates and addresses
  Michael arrived at Ellis Island, New York, on February 14, 1924.
- between words in a list
  The university hired a woman to direct the offices of the bursar, financial aid, and the registrar.
- between equally important adjectives (be careful not to separate adjectives that describe each other)
  The reporter spoke with several intense, talented high school athletes.
- after a tag that precedes a direct quote
  David whined, "I am famished."
- in a quote that precedes a tag and is not a question or an exclamation
  "I am famished," whined David.
- around nonessential clauses, parenthetical phrases, and appositives (a *nonessential* or *nonrestrictive* clause is a word or group of words that are not necessary for the sentence's completion; a parenthetical phrase interrupts the flow of a sentence; and an appositive is a word or group of words that rename the noun preceding them)
  Matt's mother, Janie (appositive), who has trouble with directions (nonessential clause), had to ask for help.
- after introductory words, phrases and clauses
  Hoping for the best, we checked our luggage.
- before conjunctions (words that link two independent clauses together)
  Drew wanted to experience ballroom dancing before his wedding, so he signed up for lessons at a local hall.

▶ Sentence Structure

Every sentence must have at least a subject and a predicate. The *subject* is the focus of the sentence; it is the *who* or the *what* of the sentence. The *predicate* describes the subject; it explains what the subject is or what the subject is doing. The completed idea is called a *clause*, and it is the building block of all sentences.

Important Terms to Know

independent clause	a clause that expresses a complete thought. (Example: *Monica walked on the grass*.)
dependent (subordinate) clause	a clause that does not express a complete thought. (Example: *Though it was wet*)
essential clause	a dependent clause that is necessary to the basic meaning of the completed sentence. (Example: Women *who are pregnant* can crave salty or sweet foods.)
nonessential clause	a dependent clause that is not necessary to the basic meaning of the completed sentence. (Example: Elmo, *who growls whenever the phone rings*, tried to attack the vacuum cleaner.)
phrase	a group of words that lacks either a subject or a predicate. (Example: *In early spring*, I notice a change in people's attitudes.)
appositive	a phrase that makes a preceding noun or pronoun clearer or more definite by explaining or identifying it. (Example: Candice's grandfather brought her favorite desserts, *rice pudding and fruit salad*.)
fragment	a phrase punctuated like a sentence even though it does not express a complete thought. (Example: Timothy saw the car. *And ran*.)
coordinating conjunction	a word that, when preceded by a comma or a semicolon, joins two independent and equal clauses. (Examples: *and*, *but*, *so*, *or*, *for*, *nor*, *yet*)
subordinating conjunction	a word that makes a clause a dependent clause. (Examples: *after*, *although*, *as*, *because*, *before*, *if*, *once*, *since*, *than*, *that*, *though*, *unless*, *until*, *when*, *whenever*, *where*, *wherever*, *while*)
conjunctive adverb	a word that introduces a relationship between two independent clauses. (Examples: *accordingly*, *besides*, *consequently*, *furthermore*, *hence*, *however*, *instead*, *moreover*, *nevertheless*, *otherwise*, *then*, *therefore*, *thus*)

Rule for Writing Correct Sentences

To construct a sentence:

- Always have at least one independent clause in the sentence.
- Join two independent clauses with a semicolon or a comma and a conjunction.
  Chaucer was a narrator, and he was a pilgrim in his Canterbury Tales.

- Do not run two or more independent clauses together without punctuation; that error is appropriately called a *run-on*.
  Incorrect: *Chaucer was a narrator he was a pilgrim in his* Canterbury Tales.
- Do not separate two independent clauses with just a comma; that error is called a *comma splice*.
  Incorrect: *Chaucer was a narrator, he was a pilgrim in his* Canterbury Tales.

- Do not use a conjunctive adverb (the words *accordingly, besides, consequently, furthermore, hence, however, instead, moreover, nevertheless, otherwise, then, therefore, thus*) like a conjunction.
  Incorrect: *Chaucer was a narrator, moreover he was a pilgrim in his* Canterbury Tales.
- Use a comma after a conjunctive adverb when it follows a semicolon.
- Use a comma after introductory words, phrases, and clauses.
- Use commas around nonessential clauses. Do not use commas around essential clauses.
- Use commas around appositives.
- Use commas around parenthetical elements (a word or group of words that interrupt a sentence's flow).
  Mrs. Moses, that mean old crone, yelled at little Paula for laughing too loud!

Agreement

Agreement is a very important step in constructing a coherent sentence. There are three basic types of agreement: subject-verb agreement, tense agreement, and antecedent-pronoun agreement.

Subject-Verb Agreement

- If the subject is singular, the verb is singular; if the subject is plural, the verb is plural.
  Mrs. Hendrickson feeds the birds every day.
  Or: *The Hendricksons feed the birds every day.*
- Subjects joined by *and* are plural and receive a plural verb.
  Jolie and Lara swim together every Thursday.
- Subjects joined by *or* or *nor* adopt the singularity or plurality of the last subject; accordingly, the verb matches the last subject.
  Either that cat or those dogs have been eating my snacks!

Pronoun-Antecedent Agreement

- *Each, either, neither, anybody, anyone, everybody, everyone, no one, nobody, one, somebody,* and *someone* are singular pronouns and receive singular verbs.
- *Both, few, many,* and *several* are plural pronouns and receive plural verbs.
- *All, any, most, none,* and *some* can be singular or plural pronouns, depending on their use. These pronouns can receive plural or singular verbs.
- Do not be confused by words or phrases that follow a subject that are not the subject.
  One of the chairs is damaged.

Tense Agreement

- Maintain one tense in a sentence: past or present.
  Incorrect: *In the game of hide and seek, Bobby chased Mary and tag her from behind.*
  Correct: *In the game of hide and seek, Bobby chased Mary and tagged her from behind.*
  Incorrect: *Dusk had just settled when I see a fawn timidly step onto the beach.*
  Correct: *Dusk had just settled when I saw a fawn timidly step onto the beach.*

Pronouns

Pronouns substitute for nouns. Instead of saying, "Because Janie was late, Janie hopped on Janie's moped, and Janie raced to the wedding," you would say, "Because Janie was late, *she* hopped on *her* moped, and *she* raced to the wedding."

Often, certain pronouns and contractions are confused. "The file cabinet drawer snagged on an overstuffed folder; *it's* now stuck just before *its* halfway point." *It's* is a contraction meaning *it is,* while *its* is a possessive pronoun meaning *the drawer's* halfway point. The only visual difference between the two is an apostrophe neatly inserted between the *t* and the *s* in the contraction.

antecedent

In the sentence "Because Janie was late, she hopped on her moped, and she raced to the wedding," *Janie* is the specific noun that *she* and *her* replace, so *Janie* is the antecedent. The presence of the antecedent in a sentence is as important as the pronouns that substitute for it.

contractions

When two words are made into one by omitting letters and using an apostrophe to highlight the omission—that's a contraction.

subjective, objective, and possessive cases

Persons or things (nouns) acting on other things are subjects. Pronouns that refer to these subjects are in the subjective case (*I, you, he, she, we, they, who*). Persons or things acted upon (in other words, they are not performing the action) are objects. Pronouns that refer to these objects are in the objective case (*me, you, him, her, us, them, whom*). Subjects or objects that claim ownership of something are possessors. Pronouns that claim their possessions are in the possessive case (*my, your, his, her, our, your, whose*).

- Avoid ambiguous pronoun references. The antecedent that a pronoun refers to must be clearly stated and in close proximity to its pronoun. If more subjects than one are present, indicate which subject is the antecedent.
  When Katherine and Melissa left for England, she promised to write me about all their adventures. Who is *she*? Katherine or Melissa?
- Pronouns should agree in number with their antecedents. Singular antecedents use singular pronouns, and plural antecedents use plural pronouns.
- Compound antecedents joined by *and* use plural pronouns.
  A horse and a donkey make a mule.
- Even though the horse and the donkey are singular subjects, together they create one plural subject.
- Compound antecedents joined by *or* or *nor* use pronouns that agree with the nearest antecedent.
  Neither my cat nor my four dogs are as difficult to maintain as my one pet fish.
- Collective nouns use singular pronouns unless it is obvious that every person or thing in the group acts individually.

The company mandated a universal naptime for all its employees. They felt workers could sustain productivity longer into the afternoon if they rested in the early afternoon.

Unless it is a one-person operation, a company usually employs many people. However, it is treated like a singular noun. In the first sentence the singular pronoun *it* substitutes for *company*. In the second sentence, individuals in the company feel separately, and so the plural pronoun *they* replaces the subject.

- Persons receive the pronouns *who, whom,* or *whose,* not *that* or *which.*
- Pronouns preceding or following *infinitive verbs* (the plain form of a verb preceded by *to*) take the objective case.
  Billie Jean begged him to play catch, but he did not want to play ball with her at that moment.

In the first clause, *him* is the subject; in the second clause, *her* is an object. Despite their difference, both take the objective case because of the infinitive *to play.*

Modifiers

Adjectives and adverbs modify subjects and/or their actions in a sentence. In the sentence, "The orange striped cat leapt nimbly across the dresser," adjectives and adverbs specify what kind of cat (an *orange striped cat*) and how that cat leapt (*nimbly*).

A modifier describes or limits another word. *Lily* is a subject. Add the word *tiger* before *lily* and the subject is modified: It is now a specific type of lily. *Pushed* is an action word. Add *shyly* and the action is limited: It is now a gentler action. Put the subject, its action, and the modifiers altogether and the sentence reads: *Unlike its fierce namesake, the tiger lily pushed its head shyly through the soil.*

Types of modifiers:

- *Adjectives* modify nouns or pronouns. (Hint: An adjective answers one of three questions: which one, what kind, or how many?)
- *Adverbs* modify verbs, adjectives, other adverbs, or whole groups of words. (Hint: An adverb answers one of four questions: where, when, how or to what extent?)
- *Comparatives* are adjectives and adverbs used to compare two things.
- *Superlatives* are adjectives and adverbs used to compare more than two things.

Follow these guidelines:

- Always identify whether a modifier describes or limits a sentence's subject or its action.
- Use *good* and *bad* to describe nouns.
- Use *well* and *badly* to describe verbs, except when *well* means "fit" or "healthy." When *well* describes a state of being, it is an adjective.
  With repetition, you will soon write well.
  Well describes how the subject writes; it is an adverb.
  After two months of physical therapy, Bob was well.
  Well describes Bob's state of being; it is an adjective.

- Use an adjective after a *linking verb*. The following words are linking verbs when they express a state of being: *look, sound, smell, feel, taste, appear, seem, become, grow, turn, prove, remain,* and *stay*.
  Howard leaned over and surreptitiously smelled Lee; she smelled sweet. Surreptitiously describes how Howard sniffed at the other person; in this case, it is an adverb because it describes the act of smelling. *Sweet* describes Lee; the word *smell* links the adjective back to the subject.
- Use the adjective *fewer* to describe plural nouns and the adjective *less* to describe singular nouns.
- Use the word *number* to describe plural nouns and the word *amount* to describe singular nouns.
- Add *-er* to a modifier or place the word *more* or *less* before the modifier to compare two things. This creates a comparison. (Hint: One to two syllable modifiers usually receive the suffix *-er*; more than two syllable modifiers use *more* or *less* before them.)
- Add *-est* to a modifier or place the word *most* or *least* before the modifier to indicate the extreme degree of a thing. (*Hint*: One to two syllable modifiers receive *-est*; modifiers with more than two syllables use *most* or *least* before them.)
- Avoid double comparatives and double superlatives. Adding the suffix *-er* or *-est* to a modifier and preceding the modifier with *more* or *most* is redundant.
  Lindsey amazed the class with her grammatical skills; she was the most smartest person they had ever seen.
  Lindsey is already *the smartest. Most* also means smartest—the phrase *most smartest* is redundant.
- Avoid double negatives unless you mean to express the positive.
  Tom hardly did not feel tense whenever he approached grammar.
  Hardly and *did not* cancel each other out. The sentence should read: *Tom felt tense whenever approaching grammar.*

- Avoid illogical comparisons. Some words already indicate an extreme degree; as with double comparatives and double superlatives, adding the word *more* or *most* before such words is redundant.
  Some women believe Brad Pitt is more perfect than Matt Damon.
  There are not degrees of perfection; one is either perfect or not perfect. However, one can more nearly approach perfection than someone else.

▶ Paragraph Development

Paragraphs are groups of related sentences that form complete units. They usually support the main ideas of an essay, article, or story; however, every paragraph has an identity and an idea of its own. A paragraph is like a miniature essay.

The following guidelines will help you organize your paragraphs. Because paragraphs and essays are similar in structure, these guidelines can be applied to the organization of an entire essay.

- Write a paragraph to explore a single idea using a topic sentence near the beginning of the paragraph.
- Maintain *paragraph unity*, the logical development of a single idea in a group of related sentences, by using:
  - *a consistent organizing strategy*. Paragraphs not only present ideas, they also group information in order to develop ideas. Organizing strategies arrange that information into logical and easy-to-anticipate patterns. These patterns can be top-to-bottom, left-to-right, near-to-far, then-to-now, beginning-to-ending, general-to-specific, least-important-to-most-important, least-familiar-to-most-familiar, or simplest-to-most-complex. Other strategies use stories, descriptions, examples, definitions, categorizations, comparisons and contrasts, or causes and effects to logically organize information. As you become more proficient at writing, you will probably incorporate more than one strategy in a paragraph.
  - *parallelisms*. By arranging sentences in identical patterns, a writer can convey that two different things are equally important. Patterning sentence structure is called parallelism.
    Bob quickly ran to the store; Alex also quickly ran to the store. It was a race to see who was fastest.
  - *repeated words or word groups*. Though similar to parallelisms, repeated word groups can occur anywhere in a sentence.
    *Humans **still** worship trees. Rain or shine, they **still** marvel at the solstice.*
  - *transitional phrases* or *words* to connect sentences and/or ideas
    ***First**, Katie gathered the ingredients. **Then**, she assembled the meal.*

▶ Practice Questions

For writing and information ordering practice, answer the questions below.

1. Identify the sentence that contains a mistake in capitalization, punctuation, grammar, or spelling. If you find no mistakes, select choice **d**.
   a. He shouted from the window, but we couldn't hear him.
   b. NASA was launching its first space shuttle of the year.
   c. The boys' wore identical sweaters.
   d. no mistakes

2. Choose the correct verb form.
The volunteers from the fire department
_____ quickly and extinguished a fire
on North Country Road.
   a. will respond
   b. responded
   c. will have responded
   d. have responded

3. Three of the sentences below contain one or
more grammatical or spelling errors. Select the
answer choice that is correct as is.
   a. The longtime residents in the community
   were proud of there school district.
   b. The longtime residents in the community
   were proud of their school district.
   c. The longtime residents in the community
   was proud of their school district.
   d. The longtime residents in the community,
   were proud of their school district.

Choose the answer choice that best rephrases the
given sentence.

4. There wasn't nothing that could have been easier.
   a. Nothing could have been easier.
   b. There was nothing that could have been
   more easier.
   c. There wasn't nothing that could have been
   easier.
   d. Nothing couldn't have been more easy.

5. Look at the three numbered sentences below.
Choose the sentence order that would result in
the best paragraph.
   (1) The idea communicated may even be purely
   whimsical, in which case the artist might
   start out with symbols developed from a
   bird's tracks or a child's toy.
   (2) Native American art often incorporates a
   language of abstract visual symbols.
   (3) The artist gives a poetic message to the
   viewer, communicating the beauty of an
   idea through religious symbols or by repro-
   ducing a design from nature—such as rain
   on leaves or sunshine on water.
   a. 3, 1, 2
   b. 2, 3, 1
   c. 2, 1, 3
   d. 1, 3, 2

▶ Answers

1. c. The word *boys'* should not show possession; no apostrophe is needed.

2. b. This sentence is in the past tense.

3. b. This sentence uses the correct form of *their*, the correct verb, and the correct punctuation. The word *there* is used incorrectly in choice **a**. Choice **c** uses verb tense incorrectly. Choice **d** is an example of comma misuse.

4. a. This is the correct choice because the sentence does not contain a double negative. The other choices either use two negative words within a single sentence or use an incorrect comparative form of *easy*.

5. b. Sentence 2 is the topic sentence, introducing the subject. Sentence 3 expands the topic, and Sentence 1 gives more definition to the Native American art form.

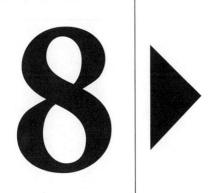

8 ▶ Mathematics

CHAPTER SUMMARY

While a state trooper may rarely be called upon to solve complex calculus problems, knowledge of basic arithmetic and some algebra and geometry are important abilities that are tested on the written exam. Officers will often have to calculate the value of items, determine fees or bonds, or estimate distances traveled or distances from a particular point to another.

Questions in the mathematics section tend to be straightforward; each question will provide you with all the information you need to answer it. Your first step, as with all questions, is to read the question carefully to determine the fact pattern and what you are being asked to calculate. You must next determine the correct arithmetic operation (addition, subtraction, division, multiplication) that is needed to solve the problem. Sometimes, you may have to apply more than one operation to get to your final answer.

Many of the math questions may also test your reading skills, because you will be given a situation that will require you to understand what took place and then to perform some mathematical computations that have to do with distance traveled, items reported missing, travel expense vouchers, or situations that a trooper could reasonably be expected to face.

▶ Math Strategies

It is best not to work in your head. Use scratch paper to take notes, draw pictures, and calculate. Although you might think that you can solve math questions more quickly in your head, that's a good way to make mistakes. Instead, write out each step.

Before you begin to make your calculations, read a math question in chunks rather than straight through from beginning to end. As you read each chunk, stop to think about what it means. Then, make notes or draw a picture to represent that chunk. When you get to the actual question, circle it. This will keep you more focused as you solve the problem.

Glance at the answer choices for clues. If they are fractions, you should do your work in fractions; if they are decimals, you should work in decimals.

Develop a plan of attack to help you solve the problem. When you get your answer, reread the circled question to make sure you have answered it. This helps avoid the careless mistake of answering the wrong question.

Always check your work after you get an answer. You may have a false sense of security when you get an answer that matches one of the multiple-choice answers. Remember to:

- Ask yourself if your answer is reasonable, if it makes sense.
- Plug your answer back into the problem.
- Do the question a second time, using a different method if you have time.
- Approximate when appropriate. For example:
  $5.98 + $8.97 is a little less than $15.
  (Add: $6 + $9)
  .9876 × 5.0342 is close to 5. (Multiply: 1 × 5)
- Skip questions that you find difficult and come back to them later. Mark them so you can find them quickly.

▶ Working Backward

You can frequently solve a word problem by plugging the answer choices into the question to see which one works. The process is faster than you might think, because you may have to substitute only one or two answers to find the right one. This approach works only when all of the answer choices are numbers or when you are asked to find a simple number, not a sum, product, difference, or ratio.

Here's what to do:

1. Look at all the answer choices and begin with the one in the middle of the range. For example, if the answers are 14, 8, 2, 20, and 25, begin by plugging 14 into the problem.
2. If your choice doesn't work, eliminate it. Determine if you need a bigger or a smaller answer.
3. Plug in one of the remaining choices.
4. If none of the answers works, you may have made a careless error. Begin again or look for your mistake.

Example: Juan sold $\frac{1}{3}$ of the books in the store during the morning shift. On the evening shift, Marcella sold $\frac{3}{4}$ of the remaining stock, which left 10 books. How many books were there to begin with?
  a. 60
  b. 80
  c. 90
  d. 120

Starting with the middle answer, let's assume there were 90 books to begin with:

Because Juan sold $\frac{1}{3}$ of them, that means he sold 30 ($\frac{1}{3} \times 90 = 30$), leaving 60 of them (90 − 30 = 60). Marcella then sold $\frac{3}{4}$ of the 60 books, or 45 of them ($\frac{3}{4} \times 60 = 45$). That leaves 15 books (60 − 45 = 15).

The problem states that there were 10 books left. That indicates that we started with too big a number. Thus, 90 and 120 are both wrong! With only two choices left, let's use common sense to decide which one to try. The next lower answer is only a little smaller than 90 and may not be small enough. So, let's try 60:

Because Juan sold $\frac{1}{3}$ of them, that means he sold 20 ($\frac{1}{3} \times 60 = 20$), leaving 40 of them (60 − 20 = 40). Marcella then sold $\frac{3}{4}$ of the 40 books, or 30 of them ($\frac{3}{4} \times 40 = 30$). That leaves 10 books (40 − 30 = 10).

The correct answer is **a**.

▶ Practice Questions

For math practice, answer the following questions.

1. (14 × 7) + 12 =
   a. 98
   b. 266
   c. 110
   d. 100

2. A dealer buys a car from the manufacturer for $13,000. If the dealer wants to earn a profit of 20% based on the cost, at what price should she sell the car?
   a. $16,250
   b. $15,600
   c. $15,200
   d. $10,833

3. Officer Mehta arrived at work at 8:14 A.M. and Officer Kersh arrived at 9:12 A.M. How long had Officer Mehta been at work when Officer Kersh got there?
   a. 1 hour 8 minutes
   b. 1 hour 2 minutes
   c. 58 minutes
   d. 30 minutes

4. Guests in a hotel have been charged $168.50 for their stay. When the guests reviewed their bill, they noticed that there was an overcharge of $13.20. When the mistake is corrected, what will the new bill be?
   a. $142.10
   b. $155.30
   c. $168.50
   d. $181.70

5. Todd gets time and a half for hours worked over his required 40 hours per week. What is his regular hourly wage if he made a total of $725 for a 52-hour work week?
   a. $12.10
   b. $12.50
   c. $18.13
   d. $18.75

▶ Answers

1. c. Perform the operations in the parentheses first: $14 \times 7 = 98$. Then, add 12 to get the answer.

2. b. $13,000 × (100% + 20% markup = 120% or 1.20) = $15,600.

3. c. Between 8:14 and 9:00, 46 minutes elapse, and between 9:00 and 9:12, 12 minutes elapse, so this is a simple addition problem: $46 + 12 = 58$.

4. b. The guests are refunded $13.20, which means it must be subtracted from their bill ($168.50 − 13.20 = 155.30$); $155.30 is the new charge.

5. b. Todd's regular rate is x and his overtime rate is $1.5x$. He worked a total of 52 hours, so he worked his regular 40 hours and also 12 hours of overtime ($52 − 40 = 12$). The money he earned from the regular week is time × rate, which is represented by $40x$ ($40 \times x = 40x$). The money he earned from overtime work is also time × rate, which is $18x$ ($12 \times 1.5x = 18x$). His regular salary plus overtime gives the total and can be written as $40x + 18x = 725$. Solve for x:

$$58x = 725$$
$$\frac{58x}{58} = \frac{725}{58}$$
$$x = 12.5$$

So Todd's regular hourly wage is $12.50 per hour.

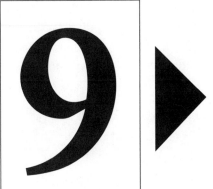

Spatial and Directional Orientation

CHAPTER SUMMARY

State police officers must have the ability to orient themselves in spatial and directional contexts in order to carry out their functions efficiently and effectively. They must also have the ability to communicate spatial and directional information to others in order to coordinate their activities. Map reading is essential for determining spatial relationships and for determining the best or shortest routes from one point to another.

When studying for the state trooper exam, you should familiarize yourselves with various types of maps. An important key to looking at a map is to understand that a map does not have to be read from left to right as though reading a page of written text. A map can be turned to the most convenient position to solve the directional problem. Before answering the questions, study the map carefully to see whether there are directional arrows (north, south, east, or west) and where they are located on the map. This will help you orient yourself and prepare yourself for questions that may be based solely on directions or getting from one point on the map to another. Also, get a sense of what the map conveys; not all maps contain only highway routes. Does the map show streets and avenues, railroad tracks or routes, or cities and towns in relationship to one another?

The key to answer spatial and directional orientation questions is to take your time. If you hurry through a question, you may misread the question or the answer choices.

▶ Finding the Shortest Route

Some questions may ask you to identify the shortest legal route on a map. The best approach to this type of question is to study your map and get your bearings. Read the question, then turn the map and figure out what looks like the best route to you. (Do not look at the answer choices before figuring out the route you would take.) Start with the first answer choice and study the route turn by turn. If none of the choices looks like the route you came up with after reading the question first, then you may need to reconsider your route. If this is the case, then you'll also need to start over and consider all the answer choices with a fresh eye.

▶ Finding the Direction

Some questions may ask you to identify the directional relationships of two or more locations. These questions may be based on a map, or they may just be written descriptions. Again, trace your path after reading the question. Then, look through the answer choices until you find the one that matches your decision.

Tips for Map-Reading Questions

1. Read carefully and follow all directions.
2. Feel free to move the map around during the test to face the direction you find comfortable.
3. Trace your path lightly on the map with your pencil. Make sure you erase all marks as you complete each question so that you don't confuse yourself for the next question.

▶ Practice Questions

Directions: Answer the following questions based on the map below.

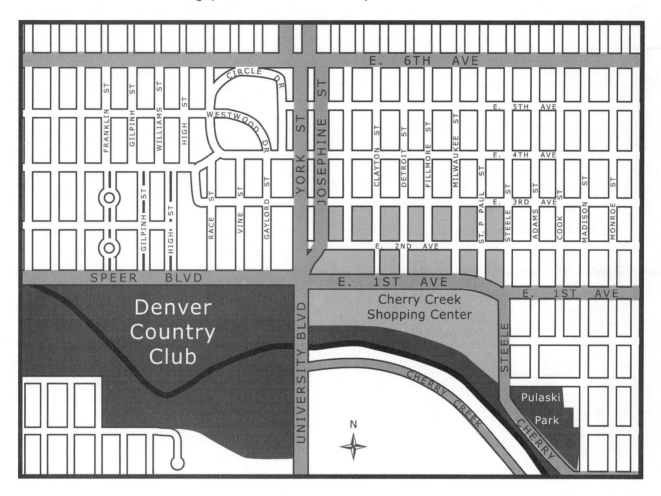

1. Starting from the Denver Country Club, Cherry Creek runs in what direction?
  a. northwest
  b. southeast
  c. northeast
  d. southwest

2. Pulaski Park is located _____ of Cherry Creek Shopping Center and _____ of Cherry Creek.
  a. northwest, northeast
  b. southeast, northeast
  c. northeast, southeast
  d. southwest, southeast

3. Third Avenue intersects with Gilpin Street _____ of Cherry Creek Shopping Center.
   a. northeast
   b. southeast
   c. northwest
   d. southwest

4. The only marked avenue(s) north of the Denver Country Club that run(s) directly north/south is (are)
   a. Gilpin and High Streets.
   b. Franklin, Gilpin, and High Streets.
   c. Franklin Street.
   d. Franklin and Race Street.

5. North of 4th Avenue, Gilpin and High Streets
   a. are closer together than they are south of 4th Avenue.
   b. are separated by Williams Street.
   c. cease to be shown on the map.
   d. are no longer parallel.

6. The southernmost border of the area known as Cherry Creek North is
   a. Speer Boulevard.
   b. East Third Avenue.
   c. East First Avenue.
   d. Steel Street.

▶ **Answers**

1. d. Southwest is the only correct choice based on the directional coordinate you are given.

2. b. The words *southeast* and *northeast* correctly complete this statement.

3. c. It is the only correct choice based on the directional coordinate given.

4. c. Only Franklin runs due north/south; the other streets have twists and turns along their routes.

5. b. Williams Street begins at 4th Avenue and runs north between Gilpin and High Streets.

6. c. Speer Boulevard changes its name to East First Avenue at University Boulevard; East Third Avenue is the northern border, and Steel Street is the eastern border, of Cherry Creek North.

10 ▶ Memory and Observation

CHAPTER SUMMARY

Undoubtedly, one of the most essential skills for a state police officer is to be able to commit to memory the details of an observation. During an incident, an officer must have keen observation skills and must be able to store and utilize information to effectively handle problems. Moreover, reports prepared after an incident must be as accurate as possible, and to achieve this, an officer must have the ability to make accurate observations and to recall correctly the observed information.

In court and in other situations requiring testimony, it is imperative that an officer can remember accurately what he or she observed before, during, and after the incident that is the subject of the testimony. If an officer demonstrates poor observation and memory abilities, cases may be lost, criminals may unjustly escape proper justice, and the reputation and credibility of the officer and his or her department may be impugned.

Exam questions use a variety of methods to test your observation and memory skills. You may be shown drawings or photographs of street scenes for a brief period of time, then answer questions about what you observed. Often, exams will utilize wanted posters of suspects with their pedigree information. You will be asked to recall the suspect's description and the pedigree information.

Some questions test your memory skills by having you read a lengthy, detailed block of text within a set amount of time (five to ten minutes is common). You are asked to answer multiple-choice questions on the material without being able to refer back to the passage.

► Memorization Tips

Memorization is much easier if you approach the task with the expectation that you *will* remember what you see or read. When you run through practice questions in this book, prepare your mind before you start. Tell yourself over and over that you will remember what you see or read. Your performance level will rise to meet your expectations.

Yes, it's easy for your brain to seize up in a stressful testing situation. But if you've programmed yourself to stay calm, stay alert, and execute your plan, you'll remember the details when you need them. Your goal is to retain the information long enough to get through this test.

► Observation Tips

Some people are naturally observant. However, it's never too late to sharpen or acquire strong observation skills.

Newspaper photos make great observation tools. News photos are action-oriented and often have more than one person in the scene. Sit down in a quiet place, clear your mind, remind yourself for several minutes that you will retain all the details you need when you study the picture, and then turn to the picture and study it for about five minutes. At the end of the time, turn the picture over, get a piece of paper and pencil, then write down all the details you can think of in the picture. Do this as much as possible before the test day.

You can tone your observation skills on the way to work or school, too. Instead of sitting in your car waiting for a light to change, look around and say what you see aloud. If you're on a bus or train, you can say these things to yourself silently. Not only are you practicing a basic skill you will need to become an excellent police officer, but you are also training your mind to succeed at whatever memory question the test maker throws your way.

► Practice Questions

Study the illustration on p. 97. You will have five minutes. Then, answer questions 1 through 5 based upon the illustration you have just studied. Do not refer back to the illustration when answering these questions.

ITEMS TAKEN FROM DEFENDANT TRACY MUTZ

FIVE 5¢ CENTS

$ FIVE DOLLARS $

TWENTY FIVE 25¢ CENTS

pill

Driver's License
Jamall Tione
Eyes: BRN
Height: 5'9
#9280329304

perfume

ITEMS TAKEN FROM DEFENDANT JEFFREY CLEVELAND

TWENTY FIVE 25¢ CENTS

Film

$ TEN DOLLARS $

TWENTY FIVE 25¢ CENTS

Credit Card
XXXXXXXXX4598

1. Together, Tracy Mutz and Jeffrey Cleveland possessed
   a. no keys.
   b. one key.
   c. two keys.
   d. three keys.

2. One of the defendants had a driver's license in his or her possession. What was the name on the license?
   a. Jeffrey Cleveland
   b. Jamall Tione
   c. Tracy Mutz
   d. Jeffrey Mutz

3. Which defendant has a razor?
   a. Tracy Mutz
   b. Jeffrey Cleveland
   c. neither of them
   d. both of them

4. How much money did Jeffrey Cleveland have in his possession?
   a. $0.50
   b. $1.50
   c. $5.30
   d. $10.50

5. One of the defendants had a credit card in his or her possession. What are the last four digits of the credit card?
   a. 4698
   b. 4589
   c. 4598
   d. 8954

▶ **Answers**

1. **b.** Jeffrey Cleveland did not possess any keys, and Tracy Mutz had only one key.
2. **b.** Tracy Mutz had a driver's license for Jamall Tione among her items.
3. **a.** Tracy Mutz has a razor; Jeffrey Cleveland does not.
4. **d.** If you selected choice **a**, you may have forgotten to include the $10 bill with the change. If you selected choice **b**, you may have mistaken the $10 bill for a $1 bill. Choice **c** shows how much money Tracy Mutz had on her.
5. **c.** All the answer choices contain the correct numbers, but only choice **c** has the digits in the correct order. To help you recall this type of information, it might be useful to break the four digits into 2 two-digit numbers, 45 and 98. The, you can think "four is followed by five" and "nine is preceded by eight."

11 ▶ Problem Solving

CHAPTER SUMMARY

State troopers are called to solve problems that other people cannot. In fact, many times when people call the police, they are in distress and unsure of what to do. They rely on the police to solve their problems for them. The variety and types of situations police officers may confront are unlimited, and most often, there are no books or training manuals that can instruct them as to what exact steps they should take in the unique situation they face. Training, practice, and experience can all help you to develop good problem-solving skills, but natural common sense is the indispensable ingredient.

T o succeed as a state trooper, you must possess common sense, problem-solving skills, good reasoning ability, good judgment, and sensitivity to human and cultural conditions. Most problem-solving questions on the state trooper exam involve reasoning, judgment, and sensitivity. Major portions of state police exams are devoted to testing a candidate's abilities in these areas.

▶ Safety First

In every action an officer takes, the safety and well-being of everyone involved is priority number one. Protecting life is an officer's first responsibility.

When you look at a test question, remember that troopers have the importance of safety drilled into them from day one at the academy. Is it safer to have the man stand in the street to explain how an accident happened, or is it better to have him move to the sidewalk? Is it safer for you to stand in front of a door or to the side of a door before knocking? Is it safer for bystanders if you pursue the speeder through downtown traffic or let her go?

The safety issue may not surface in every question, but when it does, be aware that safety is a police officer's highest priority.

▶ Use of Force

The smallest amount possible is the right amount of force. Common sense is important in this area. Expect to see questions asking you what the proper amount of force is for an officer to use when physical control is necessary, and what kind of force is appropriate out of the choices you see.

▶ Improving Your Problem-Solving Skills

In times of stress, people are more likely to carry out a task if they've practiced it—mentally or physically. If you've thought about a situation and you've arrived at a conclusion about what you would do under the given circumstances, then you've given your brain a plan for the situation if it actually comes up. Maybe you've heard someone say, "I didn't know what to do. I just froze." Most likely, he or she didn't have a plan to follow.

Train yourself to play the game "what if." Do it in various public places. Ask yourself, "If I were a state trooper, what would I do if . . ." This simple game could program your brain to respond promptly to these types of problem-solving questions.

Tips for Answering Problem-Solving Questions

- Read carefully, but don't read anything into the situation that isn't there.
- Read through all the options before you choose an answer.
- Find information that supports your answer, if possible.
- Think like a state trooper. Safety first: Use the least possible force.
- Use your common sense.
- Stay calm and work methodically.

▶ Practice Questions

For practice with problem-solving questions, answer the questions below.

Use the passage below to answer practice questions 1 through 3.

Officers who use pepper spray to disperse a crowd should do the following:

1. Warn other officers that pepper spray is about to be deployed.
2. Order the crowd to disperse.
3. Take a position upwind of the crowd.
4. Direct the spray into the crowd while continuing to order them to disperse.
5. Provide first aid to anyone who is overcome by the spray.

1. Officers Brady, Dion, and Rodriguez are called to the scene of a large fight in front of Omar's Grill. When they arrive, they see a group of approximately 15 adult males bunched up in the parking lot, punching each other. Officer Dion pulls out his canister of pepper spray. What should he do next?
   a. Order the crowd to stop fighting.
   b. Warn the other two officers that he's about to spray the crowd.
   c. Warn the crowd that he has pepper spray.
   d. Stand downwind of the crowd before spraying.

2. Officers Perez and Navarro arrive at City Hall to find a mob rocking Mayor Dickson's car back and forth in the street. Officer Navarro shouts to Officer Perez that she is going to use her pepper spray. What should she do next?
   a. Stand downwind of the crowd.
   b. Shout to the crowd to disperse.
   c. Warn the crowd that pepper spray is about to be deployed.
   d. Stand upwind of the crowd before using the spray.

3. A large crowd has formed at the city council chambers to protest a new city ordinance against sleeping in public. The crowd is angry and has begun to throw rocks at the building. Officers Jenson and Morin arrive, followed by Officer Jacobs, who is shouting for them to look out because he is about to spray. He orders the crowd to disperse. What should he do next?
   a. Stand downwind of the other two officers.
   b. Warn the crowd he is about to spray.
   c. Position himself upwind of the crowd.
   d. Spray the crowd.

4. Officer Yang has noticed an increase in gang graffiti in his area. Store owners are complaining about the damage and have asked him to keep a closer eye out for this problem. Which situation below should Officer Yang investigate?
   a. Two teenagers are leaning against a park wall completely covered with gang-related graffiti.
   b. Four teenagers are leaning against the clean white wall of a neighborhood grocery store. One teenager has a spray paint can hanging out of the rear pocket of his baggy pants.
   c. Three teenagers are riding bicycles in a grocery store parking lot late at night.
   d. Six teenagers are walking along the sidewalk bouncing a basketball and yelling at passing cars while making gang signs with their hands.

5. Merchants in the South Oaks Shopping Mall are upset by a recent rash of purse-snatchings in their parking lot. Officer Crandall is closely patrolling the mall area, including the vacant lot behind the stores. Which situation below would Officer Crandall most likely investigate?
   a. a car horn honking continuously in the mall parking lot
   b. a car in the mall parking lot with four flat tires and a broken windshield
   c. a woman's voice raised in anger in the mall parking lot
   d. a man running through the vacant lot with a bulky object under his sweatshirt

6. Officers Taylor, Hudson, Xavier, and Muller are on the security detail for the governor's visit. Taylor is in front of the stage, Hudson is behind the stage, Xavier is near the exit door and Muller is at the back of the auditorium. If Hudson switches places with Xavier and Xavier then switches places with Muller, where is Muller?

   a. near the exit
   b. in front of the stage
   c. behind the stage
   d. at the back of the auditorium

▶ Answers

1. b. According to Step 1, the officer should warn the other officers before he takes further action. The officer does want the crowd to stop fighting and will order them to do so (choice **a**), but he must first warn the other two officers that he plans to use his pepper spray. Choice **c** is not listed as a step, and choice **d** is not a good answer because the officer will always want to be upwind of pepper spray, not downwind.

2. b. The officer has already warned her partner that she is about to use the spray. Her next step will be to order the crowd to disperse.

3. c. Officer Jacobs's next step after ordering the crowd to disperse is to position himself upwind of the crowd so that the spray will not come back on him or his partners.

4. b. Seeing a teenager with a spray paint can is the most suspicious of the incidents described since Officer Yang is looking for graffiti artists. Spray paint is not an item most people carry around with them and is suspicious given the circumstances.

5. d. Seeing a man running through the vacant lot with a bulky item under his shirt should make the officer suspicious. A purse-snatcher would very likely choose to run through the vacant lot to get away from the area and would very likely want to hide an object as obvious as a woman's purse from view. Choice **a** is not particularly suspicious given that most car alarms activate the car horn, and car alarms frequently go off in parking lots. In choice **b**, a car with flat tires and a broken windshield may indicate criminal mischief, but it isn't necessarily linked to the purse-snatchings. In choice **c**, a woman's voice raised in anger would be a plausible thing to hear following a purse-snatching, but it's not nearly as suspicious as the situation in choice **d**.

6. c. After all the switches are made, Muller is behind the stage, Hudson is near the exit, Xavier is at the back of the auditorium, and Taylor is in front of the stage.

12 ▶ State Trooper Practice Test 2

CHAPTER SUMMARY

This is the second practice exam in the book based on the most commonly tested areas on the state trooper exam.

The practice test consists of 100 multiple-choice questions in the following areas: reading comprehension, writing and information ordering, mathematics, spatial and directional orientation, memory, and observation, and problem solving. Give yourself two hours to take this practice test.

State Trooper Practice Test 2

1.	ⓐ ⓑ ⓒ ⓓ	36.	ⓐ ⓑ ⓒ ⓓ	71.	ⓐ ⓑ ⓒ ⓓ
2.	ⓐ ⓑ ⓒ ⓓ	37.	ⓐ ⓑ ⓒ ⓓ	72.	ⓐ ⓑ ⓒ ⓓ
3.	ⓐ ⓑ ⓒ ⓓ	38.	ⓐ ⓑ ⓒ ⓓ	73.	ⓐ ⓑ ⓒ ⓓ
4.	ⓐ ⓑ ⓒ ⓓ	39.	ⓐ ⓑ ⓒ ⓓ	74.	ⓐ ⓑ ⓒ ⓓ
5.	ⓐ ⓑ ⓒ ⓓ	40.	ⓐ ⓑ ⓒ ⓓ	75.	ⓐ ⓑ ⓒ ⓓ
6.	ⓐ ⓑ ⓒ ⓓ	41.	ⓐ ⓑ ⓒ ⓓ	76.	ⓐ ⓑ ⓒ ⓓ
7.	ⓐ ⓑ ⓒ ⓓ	42.	ⓐ ⓑ ⓒ ⓓ	77.	ⓐ ⓑ ⓒ ⓓ
8.	ⓐ ⓑ ⓒ ⓓ	43.	ⓐ ⓑ ⓒ ⓓ	78.	ⓐ ⓑ ⓒ ⓓ
9.	ⓐ ⓑ ⓒ ⓓ	44.	ⓐ ⓑ ⓒ ⓓ	79.	ⓐ ⓑ ⓒ ⓓ
10.	ⓐ ⓑ ⓒ ⓓ	45.	ⓐ ⓑ ⓒ ⓓ	80.	ⓐ ⓑ ⓒ ⓓ
11.	ⓐ ⓑ ⓒ ⓓ	46.	ⓐ ⓑ ⓒ ⓓ	81.	ⓐ ⓑ ⓒ ⓓ
12.	ⓐ ⓑ ⓒ ⓓ	47.	ⓐ ⓑ ⓒ ⓓ	82.	ⓐ ⓑ ⓒ ⓓ
13.	ⓐ ⓑ ⓒ ⓓ	48.	ⓐ ⓑ ⓒ ⓓ	83.	ⓐ ⓑ ⓒ ⓓ
14.	ⓐ ⓑ ⓒ ⓓ	49.	ⓐ ⓑ ⓒ ⓓ	84.	ⓐ ⓑ ⓒ ⓓ
15.	ⓐ ⓑ ⓒ ⓓ	50.	ⓐ ⓑ ⓒ ⓓ	85.	ⓐ ⓑ ⓒ ⓓ
16.	ⓐ ⓑ ⓒ ⓓ	51.	ⓐ ⓑ ⓒ ⓓ	86.	ⓐ ⓑ ⓒ ⓓ
17.	ⓐ ⓑ ⓒ ⓓ	52.	ⓐ ⓑ ⓒ ⓓ	87.	ⓐ ⓑ ⓒ ⓓ
18.	ⓐ ⓑ ⓒ ⓓ	53.	ⓐ ⓑ ⓒ ⓓ	88.	ⓐ ⓑ ⓒ ⓓ
19.	ⓐ ⓑ ⓒ ⓓ	54.	ⓐ ⓑ ⓒ ⓓ	89.	ⓐ ⓑ ⓒ ⓓ
20.	ⓐ ⓑ ⓒ ⓓ	55.	ⓐ ⓑ ⓒ ⓓ	90.	ⓐ ⓑ ⓒ ⓓ
21.	ⓐ ⓑ ⓒ ⓓ	56.	ⓐ ⓑ ⓒ ⓓ	91.	ⓐ ⓑ ⓒ ⓓ
22.	ⓐ ⓑ ⓒ ⓓ	57.	ⓐ ⓑ ⓒ ⓓ	92.	ⓐ ⓑ ⓒ ⓓ
23.	ⓐ ⓑ ⓒ ⓓ	58.	ⓐ ⓑ ⓒ ⓓ	93.	ⓐ ⓑ ⓒ ⓓ
24.	ⓐ ⓑ ⓒ ⓓ	59.	ⓐ ⓑ ⓒ ⓓ	94.	ⓐ ⓑ ⓒ ⓓ
25.	ⓐ ⓑ ⓒ ⓓ	60.	ⓐ ⓑ ⓒ ⓓ	95.	ⓐ ⓑ ⓒ ⓓ
26.	ⓐ ⓑ ⓒ ⓓ	61.	ⓐ ⓑ ⓒ ⓓ	96.	ⓐ ⓑ ⓒ ⓓ
27.	ⓐ ⓑ ⓒ ⓓ	62.	ⓐ ⓑ ⓒ ⓓ	97.	ⓐ ⓑ ⓒ ⓓ
28.	ⓐ ⓑ ⓒ ⓓ	63.	ⓐ ⓑ ⓒ ⓓ	98.	ⓐ ⓑ ⓒ ⓓ
29.	ⓐ ⓑ ⓒ ⓓ	64.	ⓐ ⓑ ⓒ ⓓ	99.	ⓐ ⓑ ⓒ ⓓ
30.	ⓐ ⓑ ⓒ ⓓ	65.	ⓐ ⓑ ⓒ ⓓ	100.	ⓐ ⓑ ⓒ ⓓ
31.	ⓐ ⓑ ⓒ ⓓ	66.	ⓐ ⓑ ⓒ ⓓ		
32.	ⓐ ⓑ ⓒ ⓓ	67.	ⓐ ⓑ ⓒ ⓓ		
33.	ⓐ ⓑ ⓒ ⓓ	68.	ⓐ ⓑ ⓒ ⓓ		
34.	ⓐ ⓑ ⓒ ⓓ	69.	ⓐ ⓑ ⓒ ⓓ		
35.	ⓐ ⓑ ⓒ ⓓ	70.	ⓐ ⓑ ⓒ ⓓ		

▶ State Trooper Practice Test 2

Directions: Read the following passage, then answer questions 1 through 4.

Evidence concerning the character of a witness must be limited to questions of truthfulness. The credibility of a witness can be attacked by any party, and by evidence of a prior conviction for a felony, so long as the relevance of the conviction to the question of truthfulness is deemed by the court to outweigh the prejudicial damage caused to the witness. If, for example, the witness is guilty of some crime that the jury might find repugnant but that is not relevant to the witness's credibility, this would be deemed unacceptably prejudicial. The elements of credibility that can be impeached are perception, memory, clarity, and sincerity. Police officers should not base an arrest on the testimony of an untruthful or otherwise unreliable witness—for example, a witness who is mentally unstable, senile, or intoxicated. Officers should recognize that a case based on the testimony of a witness with prior felony convictions is vulnerable to dismissal.

1. What is the primary purpose of the passage?
   a. to review the criteria for impeaching the credibility of a witness
   b. to argue for the importance of determining the credibility of a witness before arresting a suspect
   c. to raise questions concerning the reliability of witnesses with prior convictions
   d. to teach police officers proper witness interrogation techniques

2. Which of the following would NOT be admissible to impeach the credibility of a witness?
   a. proof of a felony conviction
   b. a psychiatric evaluation
   c. a neighbor's claim that the witness is a liar
   d. a claim that the witness is prone to spousal abuse

3. According to the passage, why shouldn't the police base their case on the testimony of an untruthful witness?
   a. The accused might be innocent.
   b. The case might be dismissed.
   c. The police will be embarrassed in court.
   d. The police will be vulnerable to a lawsuit.

4. Which of the following witnesses would be least likely to be vulnerable to having his or her credibility impeached, according to the criteria set forth in the passage?
   a. a nearsighted person who wasn't wearing glasses
   b. an alcoholic
   c. a petty thief
   d. a person with a psychiatric history

Directions: Read the following passage, then answer questions 5 through 10.

At 8:16 A.M., a police operator received a report of a car accident on Morton Avenue near Farley Street from Helen Moreno of 1523 Morton Avenue. The caller said she had just arrived home when she heard the collision from her living room. Officer Rayburn arrived on the scene at 8:19. He saw that three vehicles, including an armored truck, were involved and that the driver of the green sedan was unconscious. He called for an ambulance and backup. He then checked the injured driver, saw that he was not bleeding, and covered him with a blanket provided by Mrs. Moreno. Martin Wilcox, of 1526 Morton, who was a passenger in the green sedan, identified the driver as Henry Woolf, also of 1526 Morton. Mrs. Moreno identified the third vehicle involved in the accident, a blue convertible, as her car.

The ambulance arrived at 8:24. At 8:25, four officers, including Lieutenant Watts, arrived. Lieutenant Watts assigned Officers Rayburn and Stein to blocking off both streets and controlling traffic, Officer Washington to security on the armored truck, and Officer Parisi to examining the skid marks on Farley Street. Mr. Wilcox told Lieutenant Watts that Woolf had stopped at the "T" intersection, then turned left onto Morton. Wilcox said the driver's side was struck almost immediately by the truck, which was skidding down Morton. The impact caused the Woolf vehicle to strike Mrs. Moreno's convertible. Frank Burroughs, the driver of the armored truck, told Officer Washington that he was due at Security Bank at 8:10 and that his brakes had failed. After checking with Lieutenant Watts and Officer Parisi, Officer Washington cited Burroughs for speeding, failing to obey a stop sign, and giving false information.

5. Who was the first person to view the accident scene?
   a. Lieutenant Watts
   b. Officer Washington
   c. Officer Rayburn
   d. the police operator

6. Which of the following can be concluded about the Morton Avenue-Farley Street intersection?
   a. There were at least two stop signs there.
   b. Farley Street is a one-way street.
   c. Morton Avenue runs north and south.
   d. No cars were parked near the intersection.

7. Which of the following best represents the order in which the accident occurred?
   a. The Woolf vehicle struck the Moreno vehicle, which struck the armored vehicle.
   b. The armored vehicle struck the Woolf vehicle, which struck the Moreno vehicle.
   c. The Moreno vehicle struck the armored vehicle, which struck the Woolf vehicle.
   d. The armored vehicle struck the Moreno vehicle, which struck the Woolf vehicle.

8. Who examined evidence relating to Frank Burroughs's claim that his brakes failed?
   a. Officer Rayburn
   b. Officer Stein
   c. Officer Washington
   d. Officer Parisi

9. Which vehicle had been traveling on Farley Street?
   a. the green sedan
   b. the blue convertible
   c. the armored truck
   d. the ambulance

10. Which of the following can be concluded about Helen Moreno's vehicle?
   a. It was parked on a steep incline.
   b. It was parked across the street from the Moreno residence.
   c. It was unoccupied at the time of the accident.
   d. It was struck by the armored truck.

Directions: Read the following passage, then answer questions 11 through 13.

Detectives who routinely investigate violent crimes can't help but become somewhat jaded. Paradoxically, the victims and witnesses with whom they work closely are often in a highly vulnerable and emotional state. The emotional fallout from a sexual assault, for example, can be complex and long lasting. Detectives must be trained to handle people in emotional distress and must be sensitive to the fact that for the victim, the crime is not routine. At the same time, detectives must recognize the limits of their role and resist the temptation to act as therapists or social workers, instead referring victims to the proper agencies.

11. What is the main idea of the passage?
  a. The best detectives do not become emotionally hardened by their jobs.
  b. Victims of violent crime should be referred to therapists and social workers.
  c. Detectives should be sensitive to the emotional state of victims of violent crime.
  d. Detectives should be particularly careful in dealing with victims of sexual assault.

12. According to the passage, what is *paradoxical* about the detective's relationship to the victim?
  a. Detectives know less about the experience of violent crime than do victims.
  b. What for the detective is routine is a unique and profound experience for the victim.
  c. Detectives must be sensitive to victims' needs but can't be social workers or psychologists.
  d. Not only must detectives solve crimes, but they must also handle the victims with care.

13. According to the passage, detectives who investigate violent crimes should NOT
  a. refer victims to appropriate support services.
  b. be aware of the psychological consequences of being victimized.
  c. become jaded.
  d. become too personally involved with victims' problems.

Directions: Read the following passage, then answer questions 14 through 16.

Following a recent series of arson fires in public-housing buildings, the mayor of a large U.S. city has decided to expand the city's Community Patrol, made up of 18- to 21-year-olds, to about 400 people. The Community Patrol is an important part of the city's efforts to at least reduce the number of these crimes.

In addition to the expanded patrol, the city also plans to reduce the seriousness of these fires, which are most often started in stairwells, by stripping the paint from the stairwell walls. Fed by the thick layers of oil-based paint, these arson fires race up the stairwells at an alarming speed.

Although the city attempted to control the speed of these fires by covering walls with a flame retardant, it is now clear that the retardant failed to work in almost all cases. In the most recent fire, the flames raced up ten stories after the old paint under the newly applied fire retardant ignited. Because the retardant failed to stop the flames, the city decided to stop applying it and will now strip the stairwells down to the bare walls.

14. One of the main points of the passage is that flame retardants
  a. reduce the number of arson fires in large cities.
  b. are being stripped from walls by the Community Patrol.
  c. have not prevented stairwell fires from spreading.
  d. have increased the speed of flames in stairwell fires.

15. The passage indicates stairwell fires spread extremely rapidly because
   a. the stairwells have no ventilation from the outdoors.
   b. arsonists set the fires in several locations at once.
   c. the stairwell walls are old and often bare.
   d. the flames are fed by the oil-based paint on the walls.

16. The city has decided to stop using flame retardants because the retardants
   a. have failed to control the speed of stairwell fires.
   b. send toxic fumes and gases into the buildings.
   c. are thick and have a flammable oil base.
   d. increase the speed at which flames travel up stairs.

Directions: Read the following passage, then answer questions 17 through 20.

At 1:30 A.M., while parked at 917 Crescent, Police Officers Lin and Lawton were asked to respond to a call from Tucker's Tavern at 714 Clarinda. At 1:42 A.M., when the officers arrived, they found paramedics attempting to revive 18-year-old Brent Morrow, who lay unconscious on the floor. A patron of the tavern, Edward Pickens, stated that at around 12:10 A.M., Mr. Morrow's two companions had playfully challenged Mr. Morrow to "chug" a pint of whiskey and that Mr. Morrow had done so in approximately 15 minutes. Mr. Pickens thought the two should be arrested. Mr. Morrow's companions, Jeremy Roland and Casey Edwards, denied Mr. Pickens' statement. The bartender, Raymond Evans, stated that he had not served Mr. Morrow and that Tucker's Tavern does not sell whiskey by the pint. At 1:50 A.M., paramedics took Mr. Morrow to University Hospital, where he remains unconscious. No arrests were made. An investigation is pending.

17. Which of the following persons most likely called police to Tucker's Tavern?
   a. Raymond Evans
   b. Brent Morrow
   c. Jeremy Roland
   d. Edward Pickens

18. What was the main reason Brent Morrow was removed from Tucker's Tavern?
   a. He was drunk.
   b. He was underage.
   c. He was ill.
   d. He was a university student.

19. At about what time did Brent Morrow finish chugging the pint of whiskey?
   a. 12:25 A.M.
   b. 1:30 A.M.
   c. 1:42 A.M.
   d. 1:50 A.M.

20. According to the passage, which of the following statements is accurate?
   a. Jeremy Roland and Casey Edwards were arrested.
   b. Brent Morrow was treated and released from University Hospital.
   c. Police Officers Lin and Lawton were parked at 917 Crescent at 1:30 A.M.
   d. Paramedics did not attempt to revive Brent Morrow until after 2:00 A.M.

Directions: For questions 21 through 25, choose the answer choice that best rephrases the underlined portion of the given sentence.

21. <u>If someone be looking</u> for the best car loan, you should compare interest rates at several banks.
   a. If someone is looking
   b. When one is looking
   c. If you are looking
   d. To have a person look

22. A corporation created by the federal government during the Great Depression, the Tennessee Valley Authority (TVA) is responsible for <u>flood control must generate electric power, and soil conservation.</u>
   a. flood control, must generate electric power, and soil conservation.
   b. flood control, generating electric power, and for soil conservation.
   c. controlling floods, generating electric power, and soil conservation.
   d. flood control, the generation of electric power, and soil conservation.

23. With her book *Coming of Age in Samoa*, anthropologist Margaret Mead emphasized the role of culture, <u>in shaping human behavior over biology.</u>
   a. rather than biology, in shaping human behavior.
   b. rather than biology with shaping human behavior.
   c. somewhat better than biology to shape human behavior.
   d. in shaping human behavior, and not biology.

24. We loved our trip to the <u>desert where you could see</u> the tall cactus, the blooming flowers, and the little desert animals.
   a. desert in that you saw
   b. desert; you could see
   c. desert; where we saw
   d. desert; we saw

25. The news reporter who <u>covers the story, suddenly became ill, and they called me</u> to take her place.
   a. had been covering the story suddenly became ill, and I was called
   b. was covering the story suddenly becomes ill, and they called me
   c. is covering the story suddenly becomes ill, and I was called
   d. would have been covering the story suddenly became ill, and I am called

26. Three of the sentences below contain one or more grammatical or spelling errors. Select the answer choice that is correct as is.
   a. After renting him the room, Alvin discovered Mr. Morris owned a cat.
   b. After renting him the room, a cat was discovered to belong to Mr. Morris.
   c. A cat belonging to Mr. Morris was discovered by Alvin after renting him a room.
   d. After renting him a room, Mr. Morris was discovered by Alvin to own a cat.

27. Three of the sentences below contain one or more grammatical or spelling errors. Select the answer choice that is correct as is.
   a. We ate the popcorn and watch the movie.
   b. While watching the movie, the popcorn was eaten.
   c. Popcorn, while watching the movie, was eaten.
   d. We ate the popcorn while we watched the movie.

28. Three of the sentences below contain one or more grammatical or spelling errors. Select the answer choice that is correct as is.
  a. Officer DeAngelo phoned his partner every day when he was in the hospital.
  b. When his partner was in the hospital, Officer DeAngelo phoned him every day.
  c. When in the hospital, a phone call was made every day by Officer DeAngelo to his partner.
  d. His partner received a phone call from Officer DeAngelo every day while he was in the hospital.

29. Three of the sentences below contain one or more grammatical or spelling errors. Select the answer choice that is correct as is.
  a. Some of the case transcripts I have to type are very long, but that doesn't bother one if the cases are interesting.
  b. Some of the case transcripts I have to type are very long, but that doesn't bother you if the cases are interesting.
  c. Some of the case transcripts I have to type are very long, but it doesn't bother a person if the cases are interesting.
  d. Some of the case transcripts I have to type are very long, but that doesn't bother me if the cases are interesting.

30. Three of the sentences below contain one or more grammatical or spelling errors. Select the answer choice that is correct as is.
  a. For three weeks, the Merryville Fire Chief received taunting calls from an arsonist, who would not say where he intended to set the next fire.
  b. The Merryville Fire Chief received taunting calls from an arsonist, but he would not say where he intended to set the next fire, for three weeks.
  c. He would not say where he intended to set the next fire, but for three weeks the Merryville Fire Chief received taunting calls from an arsonist.
  d. The Merryville Police Chief received taunting calls from an arsonist for three weeks, not saying where he intended to set the next fire.

31. Identify the sentence that contains a mistake in capitalization, punctuation, grammar, or spelling. If you find no mistakes, select choice **d.**
  a. Science and math are my two best subjects.
  b. We met senator Moynihan at a conference last June.
  c. Did you see the movie *Babe*?
  d. no mistakes

32. Identify the sentence that contains a mistake in capitalization, punctuation, grammar, or spelling. If you find no mistakes, select choice **d.**
  a. "I'll come and stay with you, grandma," I said.
  b. "Don't ever tell a lie," he warned.
  c. "Why won't you play with us?" he asked.
  d. no mistakes

33. Identify the sentence that contains a mistake in capitalization, punctuation, grammar, or spelling. If you find no mistakes, select choice **d**.
  a. He's the best dancer in the school.
  b. We were planning to go, but the meeting was canceled.
  c. "Okay," she said, I'll go with you."
  d. no mistakes

34. Identify the sentence that contains a mistake in capitalization, punctuation, grammar, or spelling. If you find no mistakes, select choice **d**.
  a. I have learned to appreciate Mozart's music.
  b. My cousin Veronica is studying to be a Veterinarian.
  c. Mr. Shanahan is taller than Professor Martin.
  d. no mistakes

35. Identify the sentence that contains a mistake in capitalization, punctuation, grammar, or spelling. If you find no mistakes, select choice **d**.
  a. The industrial revolution began in Europe.
  b. Is Labor Day a national holiday?
  c. General Patton was a four-star general.
  d. no mistakes

36. Identify the sentence that contains a mistake in capitalization, punctuation, grammar, or spelling. If you find no mistakes, select choice **d**.
  a. Of the four of us, I am the tallest.
  b. Wilson's brother is a chemical engineer.
  c. That fine circus elephant now belongs to my sister and I.
  d. no mistakes

37. Look at the three numbered sentences below. Choose the sentence order that would result in the best paragraph.
  (1) From these teenagers, Philip learned compassion for the poor; from him, they learned that a good deed can pay off big-time.
  (2) After the hit man nearly succeeded in killing him, Philip, dazed and gravely injured, wandered into a bad part of town and was rescued by a couple of homeless teenagers.
  (3) Philip Barnes, a wealthy, 60-year-old CEO of a megaconglomerate, was a happy man until he learned that his wife and business partner had hired a hit man to do away with him.
  a. 1, 2, 3
  b. 2, 3, 1
  c. 3, 1, 2
  d. 3, 2, 1

38. Look at the three numbered sentences below. Choose the sentence order that would result in the best paragraph.
  (1) The reason for so many injuries and fatalities is that a vehicle can generate heat of up to 1,500° F.
  (2) Firefighters know that the dangers of motor-vehicle fires are too often overlooked.
  (3) In the United States, one out of five fires involves motor vehicles, resulting each year in 600 deaths, 2,600 civilian injuries, and 1,200 injuries to firefighters.
  a. 1, 2, 3
  b. 1, 3, 2
  c. 2, 3, 1
  d. 3, 2, 1

39. Look at the four numbered sentences below. Choose the sentence order that would result in the best paragraph.

(1) The course titles will be Yoga for Teenagers; Hip Hop Dance: Learning the Latest Moves; and Creative Journaling for Teens: Discovering the Writer Within.

(2) The latter course will not be held at the Allendale Cultural Center.

(3) The Allendale Cultural Center has expanded its arts programming to include classes for young adults.

(4) It will meet at the Allendale Public Library.

a. 2, 4, 1, 3
b. 1, 4, 2, 3
c. 1, 2, 3, 4
d. 3, 1, 2, 4

40. Look at the three numbered sentences below. Choose the sentence order that would result in the best paragraph.

(1) But to keep the Peace Corps dynamic with fresh ideas, no staff member can work for the agency for more than five years.

(2) People who work for the Peace Corps do so because they want to.

(3) One of the missions of the Peace Corps is to help the people of interested countries meet their need for trained men and women.

a. 1, 2, 3
b. 3, 2, 1
c. 2, 3, 1
d. 3, 1, 2

41. If a squad car travels at the speed of 54 mph for 30 minutes, how far will it travel?
(Distance = Rate × Time)

a. 108 miles
b. 1.8 miles
c. 1,620 miles
d. 27 miles

42. A train must travel to a certain town in 6 days. The town is 3,450 miles away. How many miles must the train average each day to reach its destination?

a. 500 miles
b. 525 miles
c. 550 miles
d. 575 miles

43. State Trooper Jancieski drives 2,052 miles in 6 days, stopping at two towns each day. How many miles does she average between stops?

a. 300 miles
b. 400 miles
c. 500 miles
d. 900 miles

44. A police car uses 18 gallons of gas to travel 414 miles. How many miles per gallon does the car get?

a. 21 miles per gallon
b. 24 miles per gallon
c. 23 miles per gallon
d. 28 miles per gallon

45. The cost of a list of supplies for a police station is as follows: $19.98, $52.20, $12.64, and $7.79. What is the total cost?

a. $91.30
b. $92.61
c. $93.60
d. $93.61

46. A police station receives an emergency call on August 3 at 10:42 P.M. and another emergency call at 1:19 A.M. on August 4. How much time has elapsed between emergency calls?

a. 1 hour 37 minutes
b. 2 hours 23 minutes
c. 2 hours 37 minutes
d. 3 hours 23 minutes

47. State Trooper Green earns $26,000 a year. If he receives a 4.5% salary increase, how much will he earn?
  a. $26,450
  b. $27,170
  c. $27,260
  d. $29,200

48. If it takes four state troopers 1 hour and 45 minutes to perform a particular job, how long would it take one state trooper working at the same rate to perform the same task alone?
  a. 4.5 hours
  b. 5 hours
  c. 7 hours
  d. 7.5 hours

49. $7,777 - 3,443 + 1,173 =$
  a. 5,507
  b. 5,407
  c. 5, 307
  d. 5,207

50. What is the value of $43,254 \div 8$, rounded to the nearest whole number?
  a. 5,000
  b. 5,400
  c. 5,406
  d. 5,407

51. Which of the following choices is divisible by both 7 and 8?
  a. 42
  b. 78
  c. 112
  d. 128

52. If one gallon of water weighs 8.35 pounds, a 25-gallon container of water would most nearly weigh
  a. 173 pounds.
  b. 200 pounds.
  c. 209 pounds.
  d. 215 pounds.

53. $292 \times 50 =$
  a. 14,600
  b. 14,500
  c. 10,500
  d. 1,450

54. $12(84 - 5) - (3 \times 54) =$
  a. 786
  b. 796
  c. 841
  d. 55,080

55. A police department is selling tickets to a fund-raiser event. If 35 officers sell 6 tickets each, how many tickets were sold all together?
  a. 6
  b. 41
  c. 180
  d. 210

Directions: Answer the following questions based on the map below. The arrows indicate traffic flow. One arrow indicates a one-way street going in the direction of the arrow; two arrows represent a two-way street. You are not allowed to go the wrong way on a one-way street.

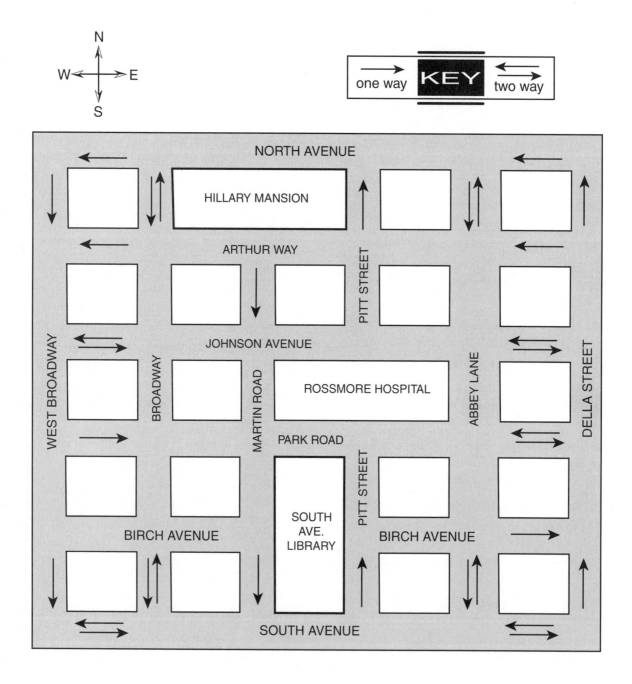

56. Officer Lazere is spending her lunch break at the South Avenue Library, which faces South Avenue. She gets a call of a burglary at the Hillary Mansion, the entrance to which faces North Avenue. What is Officer Lazere's most direct route to the Hillary Mansion?
   a. Go east on South Avenue, then north on Abbey Lane to North Avenue, then west on North Avenue to the Hillary Mansion.
   b. Go east on South Avenue, then north on Pitt Street, then west on North Avenue to the Hillary Mansion.
   c. Go west on South Avenue, then north on West Broadway, then east on North Avenue to the Hillary Mansion.
   d. Go west on South Avenue, then north on Broadway to North Avenue, then east on North Avenue to the Hillary Mansion.

57. Officer Lew is southbound on Martin Road, and has just crossed Park Road. Dispatch assigns a family disturbance call to him and sends him to a residence at the corner of Arthur Way and Della Street. What is Officer Lew's most direct route to the residence?
   a. Make a U-turn on Martin Road and go north on Martin Road to Arthur Way and then east on Arthur Way to the residence.
   b. Continue south on Martin Road and then go east on South Avenue, then north on Pitt Street, then east on Park Road, then north on Abbey Lane, and then east on Arthur Way to the residence.
   c. Continue south on Martin Road and then go east on South Avenue and then north on Della Street to the residence.
   d. Continue south on Martin Road and then go east on Birch Avenue and then north on Della Street to the residence.

58. Officer Berger is heading west on Johnson Avenue. She makes a right turn on Broadway, a left turn on Arthur Way, a left turn onto West Broadway, and finally a left turn onto Birch Avenue. Which way is Officer Berger facing?
   a. east
   b. south
   c. west
   d. north

59. There is a report of a driver going the wrong way on Birch Avenue. If the report is true, which way is this car traveling?
   a. north
   b. south
   c. west
   d. east

60. State Trooper Balisky is heading south on Abbey Lane. At Johnson Avenue, he makes a right. He drives three blocks and makes another right. From there, he drives one block and parks. Where is he?
   a. at the southwest corner of the Hillary Mansion
   b. at the northwest corner of the Hillary Mansion
   c. at the northeast corner of the Rossmore Hospital
   d. at the southeast corner of the Rossmore Hospital

Directions: Answer the following questions based on the map below. The arrows indicate traffic flow. One arrow indicates a one-way street going in the direction of the arrow; no arrows represent a two-way street. You are not allowed to go the wrong way on a one-way street. Smaller boxes within the building outline indicate building entranceways.

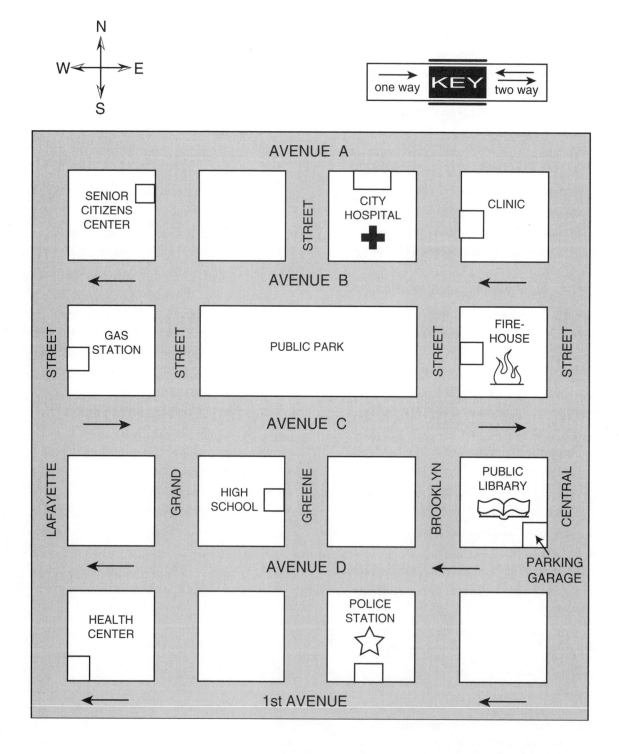

61. While you are on foot patrol, an elderly man stops you in front of the firehouse and asks you to help him find the senior citizens' center. You should tell him to
- **a.** walk across the street to the senior citizens' center.
- **b.** walk south to Avenue C, make a right, and walk west on Avenue C, make a right on Grand Street and walk up to the senior citizens' center.
- **c.** walk north to Avenue B and then west on Avenue B to the end of the park, make a right and go one block.
- **d.** walk north to Avenue B and then west on Avenue B to Lafayette Street, make a right, and go one block.

62. The head librarian needs gasoline for his automobile. He is leaving the Avenue D garage exit from the library. His quickest legal route is to go
- **a.** north on Central Street to Avenue C and west on Avenue C to the gas station.
- **b.** west on Brooklyn Street to Avenue B and north on Avenue B to the gas station.
- **c.** west on Avenue D to Grand Street and north on Grand Street to the gas station.
- **d.** west on Avenue D to Lafayette Street and north on Lafayette Street to the gas station.

63. You are dispatched from the police station to an altercation occurring at the northwest corner of the public park. Which is the most direct legal way to drive there?
- **a.** east to Central Street, north on Central Street to Avenue B, and west on Avenue B to Grand Street
- **b.** west to Grand Street and north on Grand Street to Avenue B
- **c.** east to Brooklyn Street, north on Brooklyn Street to Avenue B, and west on Avenue B to Grand Street
- **d.** west to Greene Street, north on Greene Street to Avenue C, and east on Avenue C to Brooklyn Street

64. Your spouse is a nurse at the city hospital and goes to the public library every Monday as a volunteer. What would be the shortest legal route from the hospital to the library?
- **a.** west on Avenue A, south on Lafayette Street, east on Avenue C, and south on Central Street to the library entrance
- **b.** east on Avenue B and south on Central Street to the library entrance
- **c.** west on Avenue A, south on Lafayette Street, and east on Avenue D to the library entrance
- **d.** east on Avenue A and south on Central Street to the library entrance

65. After responding to a call at the firehouse, you are ready to drive back to the police station for the end of your shift. What is the quickest legal route?
   a. south on Brooklyn Street and west on 1st Avenue to the police station
   b. north on Brooklyn Street, west on Avenue A, south on Lafayette Street, and east on 1st Avenue to the police station
   c. north on Brooklyn Street and east on 1st Avenue to the police station
   d. south on Brooklyn Street, west on Avenue C, south on Grand Street, and east on 1st Avenue to the police station

66. Your unit has been called to the scene of a car accident at the senior citizens' center at the southwest corner of the building. While there, dispatch notifies you of an alarm going off at the high school. What is the quickest route for your unit to take from the center to the high school?
   a. Turn south on Lafayette Street, east on Avenue D, then north on Greene Street.
   b. Turn north on Lafayette Street, east on Avenue A, south on Brooklyn Street, west on Avenue D, then north on Greene Street.
   c. Turn south on Lafayette Street, east on Avenue C, then south on Greene Street.
   d. Turn south on Lafayette Street, east on Avenue D, north on Grand Street, west on Avenue C, then south on Greene Street.

67. State Trooper Livingston has just come off duty and is driving west on Avenue A. He makes a right onto Greene Street, then a right onto Avenue B, then a left onto Grand Street, and then a right onto Avenue D. What direction is he facing?
   a. east
   b. south
   c. west
   d. north

68. A woman faints in the public park at the intersection of Greene Street and Avenue C. If she wants to seek medical attention, which route would be the quickest?
   a. east on Avenue C, then north on Central Street, then west on Avenue B, and north on Brooklyn Street to the clinic
   b. east on Avenue C, then north on Brooklyn Street to the clinic
   c. south on Greene Street, then west on Avenue D, then south on Lafayette Street to the health center
   d. west on Avenue C, then south on Lafayette Street to the health center

69. A state trooper is escorting a pregnant woman from the corner of Central Street and Avenue D to the city hospital. What is the most direct legal route for the trooper to take?

   a. north on Central Street, then west on Avenue B, then north on Greene Street, then east on Avenue A

   b. north on Central Street, then west on Avenue B, then north on Grand Street, then east on Avenue A

   c. north on Central Street, then west on Avenue B, then north on Greene Street, then west on Avenue A

   d. north on Central Street, then west on Avenue A, then south on Brooklyn Street

70. A teenager volunteers at the senior citizens' center after school on Wednesdays. If he is trying to get from the high school to the senior citizens' center, how many turns will the teenager make, taking the most direct route?

   a. 2

   b. 3

   c. 4

   d. 5

Directions: You will be given ten minutes to study the four wanted posters below. Try to remember as many details as you can. You may not take any notes at this time. Then, answer questions 71 through 80 without referring back to the wanted posters.

WANTED FOR ASSAULT

NAME:	James Beckham
AGE:	31
HEIGHT:	5'11"
WEIGHT:	215
RACE:	Caucasian
HAIR COLOR:	blonde
EYE COLOR:	green
IDENTIFYING MARKS:	piercing in left ear, tattoo of woman's face on left shoulder
NOTE:	carries a gun and must be considered dangerous; has a heroin habit

WANTED FOR ARMED ROBBERY

NAME:	Manuel Martinez
AGE:	34
HEIGHT:	5'8"
WEIGHT:	198
RACE:	Hispanic
HAIR COLOR:	black
EYE COLOR:	brown
IDENTIFYING MARKS:	tattoo on left shoulder that says "Mother"; scar on right shoulder from previous gunshot wound
NOTE:	has family in the Dominican Republic

WANTED FOR RAPE

NAME:	David Torsiello
AGE:	43
HEIGHT:	5'9"
WEIGHT:	180
RACE:	Caucasian
HAIR COLOR:	brown
EYE COLOR:	brown
IDENTIFYING MARKS:	missing right eye from industrial accident; often wears a patch over right eye
NOTE:	carries a hunting knife; tends to confront victims outside their residences and force them inside

WANTED FOR MURDER

NAME:	Fernando Gomez
AGE:	32
HEIGHT:	5'7"
WEIGHT:	178
RACE:	Hispanic
HAIR COLOR:	brown
EYE COLOR:	brown
IDENTIFYING MARKS:	scar on upper thigh, tattoo of Mexican flag on upper right arm; lost thumb in a car accident
NOTE:	last seen in stolen black 1998 Nissan Altima

71. Which suspect was involved in an industrial accident?

a.

b.

c.

d.

72. Which suspect might flee the country for the Dominican Republic?

a.

b.

c.

d.

73. Which suspect has green eyes?

a.

b.

c.

d.

74. An officer observes a suspect lurking outside an apartment building as a woman returns home from her night shift. Which suspect has a history of such behavior?

a.

b.

c.

d.

75. Which suspect is not in his thirties?

a.

b.

c.

d.

76. Which suspect can you assume is of Mexican heritage?

a.

b.

c.

d.

77. What is an identifiable mark of this suspect?

a. tattoo of woman's face on left shoulder
b. scar on upper thigh
c. tattoo on left shoulder that says "Mother"
d. scar on right shoulder

78. The suspect wanted for _____ is missing a finger.
a. rape
b. assault
c. armed robbery
d. murder

79. Which suspect has a drug habit?

a.

b.

c.

d.

80. Suspect Fernando Gomez was last seen in what kind of stolen car?
 a. black 1999 Nissan Altima
 b. black 1998 Nissan Altima
 c. black 1998 Nissan Pathfinder
 d. blue 1998 Nissan Altima

Directions: Read the following passage, then answer questions 81 through 87.

First Bank has recently had a problem with teller drawers coming up short. Banks anticipate a certain amount of this kind of loss, so bank officials were not overly concerned until they began to notice a pattern. Every two or three days, for a period of six months, the cash at teller station 3 would be short; occasionally, another drawer would be short. Vice President Ralph Jensen reported the pattern and authorities were called. There are a total of 12 teller stations, but it is rare that all 12 are open at once. The number of stations that is open depends on the number of tellers working and the amount of business being transacted.

During the course of the investigation, the following statements were made:

1. Vice President Jensen stated that he personally tallied the drawer totals at the end of each business day; on days when he did not work, the tallies were done by Vice President Cruz.
2. Gloria Dennis, the teller supervisor, said that she usually opened teller stations in order; that is, station 1 would be opened first, station 2 second, and so on. Each teller is assigned to a station for the shift, but they cover for each other on breaks.
3. Dennis also stated that there is an average of five stations open at any given time, but sometimes as few as two stations are open.
4. Teller Dave Feller said that the tellers came and went from work at staggered times and that more than half of the tellers only worked part-time.
5. Teller Marilyn Nguyen said that Felicia Ralston, another teller, had recently gotten divorced and complained that her ex-husband was not paying child support.
6. Vice President Enrique Cruz stated that the tallies had never been short on the days he did them.
7. Teller Felicia Ralston said that recently a new customer, John Mitchell, had been coming in every few days and often only wanted change for a large bill. Ralston thought he might be a drug dealer.
8. Teller Mike Richards said that, although tellers were not assigned to particular stations all the time, each teller had a favorite station and Dennis normally let them work at those stations. Richards said that both Ralston and Nguyen liked station 3.
9. Head of Personnel Heidi Sargent checked the records and said that tellers Nguyen, Ralston, Richards, Ford, Beloit, and Rawlings were all working on days when station 3 came up short. In addition, Gloria Dennis and Ralph Jensen worked all of those days. Teller Feller worked all but two of those days.
10. Teller Sarah Beloit said that she saw Vice President Jensen and Teller Richards have lunch together once or twice a week for the last six months.

81. Which of the following statements could be an attempt by one teller to divert suspicion to another teller?
 a. Statements 1 and 4
 b. Statements 3 and 6
 c. Statements 7 and 10
 d. Statements 5 and 8

82. Which of the following statements casts suspicion on Ralph Jensen?
 a. Statements 6 and 10
 b. Statements 1 and 6
 c. Statements 1 and 9
 d. Statements 6 and 9

83. Which of the following statements is hearsay?
  a. Statement 10
  b. Statement 8
  c. Statement 7
  d. Statement 5

84. Which of the following statements indicates that the drawer shortage might not be a case of employee theft?
  a. Statement 7
  b. Statement 9
  c. Statement 3
  d. Statement 5

85. Which of the following statements may offer a motive for the theft?
  a. Statement 4
  b. Statement 6
  c. Statement 5
  d. Statement 7

86. Which of the following statements could lead to the conclusion that there is more than one thief?
  a. Statement 7
  b. Statement 5
  c. Statement 8
  d. Statement 10

87. Which of the following statements provides the strongest alibi?
  a. Statement 7
  b. Statement 9
  c. Statement 5
  d. Statement 3

Directions: Read the following passage, then answer questions 88 through 96.

Wendell March called the local police and said he had evidence that Denise Walker, another student, was spending counterfeit money. Upon questioning, Wendell said he had seen Denise at school carrying several hundred dollars. When he asked her where she got it, she said from her brother, Herb. Later, Wendell heard her tell another student that the money was not real and that there was a great deal more of it. Local police called the Secret Service. During the course of the investigation, the following statements were made:

1. Student Buffy Slater said that Denise had a lot of new clothes lately.
2. Student Todd Carlson said that Wendell asked Denise out three times, but she always turned him down.
3. Margy Adams, cashier at the Sound Wave, said Denise had purchased several new CDs in the past week, always paying cash.
4. Principal Mark Po said that Denise's brother Herb had been a troublemaker who consistently made poor grades, was expelled from school, and had never graduated.
5. Teacher Robert Moss said that Wendell had seemed troubled lately and he heard Wendell's parents were getting divorced.
6. Counselor Rachel Foster said that Herb Walker was a genius, with an IQ over 150, and was an excellent artist.
7. Denise Walker said that her father had recently gotten a promotion at the paper factory where he worked and her mother had just gone back to work as a bookkeeper.
8. Heather Mason, Denise's friend, said that Denise had recently had a lot more money to spend when they went to the mall.
9. Herb Walker said that he suspected Denise might be dealing drugs.
10. April Givins said she was Wendell's girlfriend and had been for two years.

88. Which statement might be an attempt to divert the investigation?
   a. Statement 9
   b. Statement 10
   c. Statement 5
   d. Statement 6

89. Which two statements appear to corroborate each other?
   a. Statements 2 and 5
   b. Statements 4 and 6
   c. Statements 3 and 8
   d. Statements 7 and 9

90. Which statement along with statement 2 is most damaging to Wendell March?
   a. Statement 4
   b. Statement 7
   c. Statement 10
   d. Statement 5

91. Which statement is purely circumstantial evidence?
   a. Statement 10
   b. Statement 4
   c. Statement 1
   d. Statement 7

92. Which statement leads one to be suspicious of information given by Herb Walker?
   a. Statement 4
   b. Statement 6
   c. Statement 7
   d. Statement 9

93. Which statement indicates the allegations against Denise Walker may not be true?
   a. Statement 9
   b. Statement 8
   c. Statement 5
   d. Statement 7

94. Which statement is most damaging to Herb Walker?

    a. Statement 3

    b. Statement 7

    c. Statement 9

    d. Statement 6

95. Which statement indicates that Wendell March has a motive to lie?

    a. Statement 2

    b. Statement 5

    c. Statement 7

    d. Statement 8

96. Which two statements seem to be contradictory?

    a. Statements 1 and 7

    b. Statements 4 and 6

    c. Statements 7 and 9

    d. Statements 5 and 10

97. Abraham has been arrested one more time than Jolson. Kirk has been arrested one less time than Jolson and one more time than Sanchez. Jolson has been arrested seven times. How many times has Sanchez been arrested?

    a. six times

    b. five times

    c. four times

    d. eight times

Directions: Read the following passage, then answer question 98.

Officers responding alone to the scene of a burglar alarm should do the following in the order given:

1. Turn off siren and emergency lights as soon as possible to keep from alerting suspect.
2. Park the patrol car away from the building.
3. Notify the dispatcher of their arrival and location.
4. Begin checking the outside of the building for signs of entry.
5. Notify the dispatcher if signs of entry are discovered.
6. Wait for backup if it is available before going inside a building where entry has been made.
7. Tell backup officers where to position themselves when they arrive.

98. Officer Smith is sent to 1313 Milbury Way on a residential burglar alarm call at 1 P.M. Traffic is heavy on the way to the call, and he turns on his emergency lights to help clear the way. Officer Smith is notified that no backup is available in his sector. What is the next thing Officer Smith should do?

    a. Park his car a house or two away from 1313 Milbury Way.

    b. Inform the dispatcher when he arrives.

    c. Approach the front door, since any suspects are probably gone by now.

    d. Turn off his emergency lights as soon as he can safely do so.

99. The owner of the Sun Times car dealership tells Officer Chervenack that someone is stealing running boards and other parts from the vans he has parked in the south lot sometime after 10:30 P.M. Officer Chervenack decides to patrol the area carefully. Which of the following situations should she investigate?

a. After midnight, a male in his early twenties is walking up and down rows of new pickups parked near the edge of the dealership.

b. After midnight, a panel truck pulls out of the vacant lot next to the dealership near where the vans are lined up.

c. After midnight, two youths in baggy pants and T-shirts are rollerblading in and out of the new cars on the Sun Times lot.

d. After midnight, a station wagon drives into the lot and stops near the door to the main show room. A man gets out and unloads a mop, a bucket, and a broom.

100. Winslow Elementary School is having a criminal mischief problem. Windows are being broken out at the school between 7:00 P.M. and 6:00 A.M. Officer Link has talked to the school principal and is keeping a closer eye on the school. Which of the following situations should he investigate?

a. At 1:00 A.M., Officer Link watches a man carrying a grocery sack cut through the school yard and come out on the other side of the school grounds. The officer can see a loaf of bread protruding out of the sack.

b. At 11:00 P.M., a car pulls up in the school parking lot. Officer Link sees the driver turn on the cabin light and unfold a map.

c. Around 11:30 P.M., Officer Link passes the school and sees two figures come out from behind one of the classroom buildings. They stop when they see him and then start walking, each in a different direction.

d. At 9:00 P.M., several teenagers skateboard into the parking lot, set up a small wooden ramp, and practice skateboarding tricks.

▶ Answers

1. a. The overall subject of the passage concerns the criteria for using information about a witness to cast doubt on his or her testimony.

2. d. An accusation of spousal abuse would be prejudicial, but it would not be relevant to the question of the witness's truthfulness.

3. b. The last two sentences state that *police officers should not base an arrest on the testimony of an untruthful or otherwise unreliable witness*, such as a witness with a prior felony conviction, because *a case based on the testimony of a witness with prior felony convictions is vulnerable to dismissal.*

4. c. Petty theft is not a felony; therefore, a petty thief would be the least likely of the choices to be vulnerable to having his or her credibility impeached, according to the criteria set forth in the passage.

5. c. Officer Rayburn was on the scene first. The other officers arrived later, and the police operator was never on the scene.

6. a. The Woolf vehicle had stopped at the "T" intersection before turning on to Morton, so there must have been a stop sign on Farley. Burroughs was cited for failing to obey a stop sign on Morton.

7. b. Mr. Wilcox told Lieutenant Watts that the armored truck struck the car he was riding in, driven by Mr. Woolf, and that the Woolf vehicle subsequently hit Mrs. Moreno's car.

8. d. Officer Parisi examined skid marks, which show that the armored truck was braking.

9. a. The green sedan, with Mr. Woolf driving, had been driving down Farley before turning on to Morton at the "T" intersection.

10. c. Mrs. Moreno was in her house at the time of the accident, so you can conclude that her car was unoccupied.

11. c. This answer encompasses most of the information in the passage. Choice **a** is incorrect because the first sentence suggests that becoming hardened is unavoidable. Choices **b** and **d** are mentioned in the passage but are too narrow to be the main idea.

12. b. See the first two sentences of the passage.

13. c. The passage claims that becoming jaded is inevitable.

14. c. The passage is mainly about how the flame retardant failed to work.

15. d. See the last sentence of the second paragraph.

16. a. See the first sentence of the third paragraph: *. . . it is now clear that the retardant failed to work in almost all cases.*

17. d. The passage states that Mr. Pickens thought Mr. Morrow's companions should be arrested. Mr. Morrow himself is unconscious. Mr. Evans and Mr. Roland would probably be afraid of being blamed for Mr. Morrow's condition.

18. c. Mr. Morrow chugged a pint of whiskey in 15 minutes and is comatose. He needed medical attention.

19. a. According to Mr. Pickens, Mr. Morrow began to chug the whiskey at 12:10 and did so in about 15 minutes.

20. c. The officers were parked at this location when they were instructed to respond to a call from Tucker's Tavern. All the other choices are inaccurate according to facts in the passage.

21. c. This choice is best because it is the only one in which there is no shift in person: *If you are looking . . . , you should compare . . .* All the other choices shift from third person (*someone, one, a person*) to second person (*you*).

22. d. The series of items in the underlined portion of the sentence should be parallel. Only choice **d** has the appropriate parallel construction. Because all three elements in the series follow *is responsible for*, choice **a** is clearly incorrect because the verb *must generate* breaks the parallel flow of the series. In choice **b**, the word *for* breaks the parallel flow. In choice **c**, the series changes and the first two elements, *controlling floods* and *generating electric power*, are parallel, but the third element, *soil conservation*, is not.

23. a. This sentence requires that the comparison between *culture* and *biology* be logical and clear. Choice **b** is wrong because the use of the preposition *with* is confusing and does not observe standard usage conventions. The phrase *somewhat better* in choice **c** makes no sense. Choice **d** results in an unclear comparison.

24. d. Choice **d** is correctly punctuated with a semicolon between two independent clauses, and there is no shift in person. Choices **a**, **b**, and **c** are incorrect because the sentence shifts from the first person (*we*) to the second person (*you*). Choice **c** uses a semicolon when no punctuation is necessary.

25. a. When constructing sentences, unnecessary shifts in verb tenses should be avoided. Choice **a** is best because all three verbs in the sentence indicate that the action occurred in the past (*had been covering, became,* and *was called*). In choice **b**, there is a shift to the present (*becomes*). Choice **c** begins in the present (*is covering, becomes*), then shifts to the past (*called*). Choice **d** makes two tense shifts.

26. a. In choice **b**, the cat seems to be renting the room. In choice **c**, it's unclear whether *he* refers to the cat or to Mr. Morris. Choice **d** implies that Mr. Morris rented a room to himself.

27. d. In choice **a**, the lack of agreement in tense makes the sentence unclear as to time; choice **b** doesn't make it clear who ate the popcorn; choice **c** implies that the popcorn watched the movie.

28. b. In the other choices, the pronoun reference is ambiguous; it is unclear who is in the hospital.

29. d. The other answers contain unnecessary shifts in person from *I* to *one, you,* and *a person*.

30. a. The other choices are unclear because they are awkwardly constructed, obscuring who intends to set the fire.

31. b. *Senator* should be capitalized because it refers to a particular senator.

32. a. *Grandma* is used as a proper name and should be capitalized.

33. c. To set off the dialogue, there should be quotation marks before the contraction *I'll*.

34. b. *Veterinarian* is not a proper noun and should not be capitalized.

35. a. *Industrial Revolution* is a proper noun and should be capitalized.

36. c. The word *I* should be replaced with the word *me*, because the pronoun is the object, not the subject.

37. d. This is the correct chronological order of the events described in the paragraph.

38. c. Sentence 2 gives an overview of what the paragraph is about. Sentence 3 gives specific reasons why sentence 2 is correct. Sentence 1 gives the reason why sentence 3 is correct.

39. d. Sentence 3 states the main topic about the Allendale Cultural Center. Sentence 1 adds information to the main topic of dentence 3. Sentence 2 states an exception to the first two statements, while sentence 4 adds information to sentence 2.

40. b. Sentence 3 is the topic sentence, and states the purpose of the Peace Corps. Sentence 2 describes the kind of people who join the

Peace Corps. Sentence 3 gives a stipulation for the people who join.

41. d. Solving this problem requires converting 30 minutes to 0.5 hour, which is the time, then using the formula: 54 mph × 0.5 hour = 27 miles, choice **d**.

42. d. To find the average, divide the total number of miles, 3,450, by 6 days.

43. a. This is a two-step division problem: 2,052 miles ÷ 6 days = 342 miles per day, and 342 miles per day ÷ 2 stops = 171 miles between stops.

44. c. Take the total number of miles and find the average by dividing: 414 ÷ 18 gallons = 23 miles per gallon.

45. b. You need to add all the numbers together to solve this problem.

46. c. Subtraction and addition will solve this problem. From 10:42 to 12:42, two hours have elapsed. From 12:42 to 1:00, another 18 minutes has elapsed (60 − 42 = 18). Then from 1:00 to 1:19, there is another 19 minutes. 2 hours + 18 minutes + 19 minutes = 2 hours and 37 minutes, choice **c**.

47. b. There are three steps involved in solving this problem. First, convert 4.5% to a decimal: 0.045. Multiply that by $26,000 to find out how much the salary increases. Finally, add the result ($1,170) to the original salary of $26,000 to find out the new salary, $27,170.

48. c. To solve the problem, first you have to convert the total time to minutes (105 minutes), then multiply by 4 (420 minutes), then convert the answer back to hours by dividing by 60 minutes to arrive at the final answer (7 hours). Or, you can multiply hours by 4 to arrive at the same answer.

49. a. Do this problem in the order it is presented; first subtract, then add.

50. d. 43,254 ÷ 8 is equal to 5,406.75. Rounded to the nearest whole number, this is equal to 5,407.

51. c. 112 is divisible by both 7 and 8 because each can divide into 112 without a remainder. 112 ÷ 7 = 16 and 112 ÷ 8 = 14. Choice **a** is divisible only by 7, choice **b** is not divisible by either, and choice **d** is divisible only by 8.

52. c. To solve the problem, take the weight of one gallon of water (8.35) and multiply it by the number of gallons (25): 8.35 × 25 = 208.7. Now, round to the nearest unit to get 209 pounds.

53. a. The correct answer to this multiplication problem is 14,600. An incorrect answer is likely an error in computation, particularly in not carrying digits to the next place.

54. a. Perform the operations in the parentheses first: 84 − 5 = 79 from the first set and 3 × 54 = 162 from the second set. The expression is now 12(79) − 162. Multiply 12 by 79 to get 948 and then subtract: 948 − 162 = 786.

55. d. Multiply the number of officers (35) by the number of tickets (6). 35 × 6 = 210.

56. a. This the most direct route to the Hillary Mansion and requires the fewest changes in direction. Choice **b** requires the officer to drive through the Rossmore Hospital. Choice **c** takes the officer the wrong way up West Broadway. Choice **d** takes the officer the wrong way on North Avenue.

57. c. This route requires the fewest number of turns. Choice **a** is wrong because Martin Road is a one-way street. Choice **b** requires a number of turns and goes the wrong way on Arthur Way. Choice **d** requires the officer to drive through the South Avenue library.

58. a. A right turn on Broadway turns Officer Berger north. The left turn on Arthur Way turns her back west, the left turn on West

Broadway turns her south, and the left turn onto Birch Avenue turns her east.

59. c. Because Birch Street is one-way going west to east, the car must be headed west.

60. a. If Officer Balisky turns right onto Johnson Avenue, he is heading west. If he then goes three blocks and turns right, he is then heading north on Broadway. One block from there is the southwest corner of the mansion.

61. c. Choice **a** takes the man to the park, not to the senior citizens' center. Choice **b** takes the man too far south. Choice **d** takes him to Lafayette Street, but the entrance to the senior citizens' center is on Grand Street.

62. d. Choice a takes the librarian the wrong way on Avenue C. Choice **b** shows the wrong directions for the streets—Brooklyn Street runs north-south, and Avenue B runs east-west. Choice **c** leaves the librarian one block east of the gas station.

63. b. Choices **a** and **c** take you the wrong way on 1st Avenue. Choice **d** will get you to the southeast, not the northwest, corner of the park.

64. d. Choice **a** is less direct. Choice **b** does not start from the hospital, and involves going the wrong way on Avenue B. Choice **c** is indirect and involves going the wrong way on Avenue D.

65. a. Choice **b** is less direct and involves going the wrong way on 1st Avenue. Choice **c** will lead you away from 1st Avenue, not toward it. Choice **d** takes you the wrong way on Avenue C and 1st Avenue.

66. c. Choices **a** and **d** direct your unit to turn the wrong way down a one-way street. Choice **b** requires too much backtracking because Barcelona Boulevard is a one-way street going east. Choice **b** requires too many turns and is the least direct route.

67. c. The final right turn onto Avenue D turns Trooper Livingston west.

68. b. Choice **a** is not the most direct route. Choice **c** is incorrect, because the clinic is closer than the health center. Choice **d** goes down a one-way street in the wrong direction.

69. a. Choice **b** is not the shortest route to take. Choices **c** and **d** do not take the trooper to the city hospital.

70. a. The teenager can head south on Greene Street, turning right onto Avenue D and right onto Grand Street.

71. c. This suspect lost his eye in an industrial accident. Another suspect lost his thumb, but that was the result of a car accident.

72. b. Manuel Martinez has family in the Dominican Republic.

73. a. Only James Beckham has green eyes.

74. c. David Torsiello is wanted for rape and has confronted victims outside their residences before forcing them inside.

75. c. Suspect David Torsiello is 43 years old.

76. d. Fernando Gomez has a tattoo of the Mexican flag, so you can assume that he is of Mexican heritage.

77. a. James Beckham has a tattoo of a woman's face on his left shoulder.

78. d. Fernando Gomez, who is wanted for murder, is missing his thumb from a car accident.

79. a. James Beckham has a heroin habit.

80. b. Fernando Gomez was last seen in a stolen black 1998 Nissan Altima.

81. d. Statements 5 and 8 contain information provided by tellers that indicates motive or opportunity for other tellers to have embezzled the money.

82. b. The fact that only Jensen and Cruz ever tally the drawer totals, coupled with the fact that the drawers were never short when Cruz performed the tally, casts suspicion on Jensen.

83. d. Statement 5 is a statement made without personal knowledge, simply repeating what others said.

84. a. Statement 7 presents the possibility that a bank customer had been coming in every few days and often he wanted only change for a large bill.

85. c. Statement 5 indicates an employee is having financial problem and that is a motive for theft. Even though a statement is hearsay, it can still be helpful to an investigation.

86. d. Statement 10 notes that a person who is a suspect, Jensen, is meeting regularly with a person who has access to the teller drawers, Teller Richards. This may indicate that the two are involved in the theft together.

87. b. Statement 9 lists the tellers who worked on days the drawers were short. Any teller who worked none or only some of those days would have a strong alibi.

88. a. Statement 9 is as attempt by Herb Walker to divert the investigation from counterfeiting to drugs, as well as from himself to his sister, by alleging his sister is a drug dealer.

89. c. Statements 3 and 8 are statements from different people alleging that Denise has access to cash.

90. d. Statement 2 indicates both a motive for trying to get Denise in trouble by making a false report and a reason why Wendell might be distraught; Statement 5 presents an additional reason for Wendell's distress and an observation of it.

91. c. Circumstantial evidence is evidence from which the presence of a principle fact of the case can be inferred. From the fact of Denise's new clothes, one can infer she has access to money to buy clothes.

92. a. Statement 4 reports past misbehavior by Herb that could indicate that he might not tell the truth.

93. d. Statement 7 provides an explanation for why Denise may have more money than usual.

94. d. Statement 6 tells investigators that Herb Walker has the ability to be a counterfeiter.

95. a. Denise's rejection of Wendell might be a motive for his calling the police and lying about her.

96. b. Statements 4 and 6 seem to be contradictory. One does not normally expect high school students with high IQs to be troublemakers who drop out (or are expelled) from school.

97. b. Sanchez has been arrested five times. Jolson has been arrested seven times, and Kirk has been arrested one less time (six). Sanchez has been arrested one less time than Kirk.

98. d. Officer Smith should turn off his emergency lights as the first step in answering a burglar alarm call.

99. b. A panel truck pulling out of a vacant lot near a car dealership that has suffered a rash of theft of auto parts is suspicious. The truck would be able to hold plenty of auto parts. The two rollerbladers in choice **c** aren't likely to be able to carry off a new running board without attracting attention. The male in his early twenties in choice **a** appears to be doing what a lot of people do late at night, which is look at new cars without having to worry about sales personnel. It is not unusual for cleanup crews to arrive late at night after everyone has gone, as in choice **d**.

100. c. The odd behavior and the location of the two figures should cause the officer to investigate, given the problems the school has been having.

13 ▶ State Trooper Practice Test 3

CHAPTER SUMMARY

This is the third practice test in the book based on the most commonly tested areas on the state trooper exam.

The practice test consists of 100 multiple-choice questions in the following areas: reading comprehension, writing and information ordering, mathematics, spatial and directional orientation, memory and observation, and problem solving. You should give yourself two hours to take this practice test.

State Trooper Practice Test 3

#					#					#				
1.	a	b	c	d	36.	a	b	c	d	71.	a	b	c	d
2.	a	b	c	d	37.	a	b	c	d	72.	a	b	c	d
3.	a	b	c	d	38.	a	b	c	d	73.	a	b	c	d
4.	a	b	c	d	39.	a	b	c	d	74.	a	b	c	d
5.	a	b	c	d	40.	a	b	c	d	75.	a	b	c	d
6.	a	b	c	d	41.	a	b	c	d	76.	a	b	c	d
7.	a	b	c	d	42.	a	b	c	d	77.	a	b	c	d
8.	a	b	c	d	43.	a	b	c	d	78.	a	b	c	d
9.	a	b	c	d	44.	a	b	c	d	79.	a	b	c	d
10.	a	b	c	d	45.	a	b	c	d	80.	a	b	c	d
11.	a	b	c	d	46.	a	b	c	d	81.	a	b	c	d
12.	a	b	c	d	47.	a	b	c	d	82.	a	b	c	d
13.	a	b	c	d	48.	a	b	c	d	83.	a	b	c	d
14.	a	b	c	d	49.	a	b	c	d	84.	a	b	c	d
15.	a	b	c	d	50.	a	b	c	d	85.	a	b	c	d
16.	a	b	c	d	51.	a	b	c	d	86.	a	b	c	d
17.	a	b	c	d	52.	a	b	c	d	87.	a	b	c	d
18.	a	b	c	d	53.	a	b	c	d	88.	a	b	c	d
19.	a	b	c	d	54.	a	b	c	d	89.	a	b	c	d
20.	a	b	c	d	55.	a	b	c	d	90.	a	b	c	d
21.	a	b	c	d	56.	a	b	c	d	91.	a	b	c	d
22.	a	b	c	d	57.	a	b	c	d	92.	a	b	c	d
23.	a	b	c	d	58.	a	b	c	d	93.	a	b	c	d
24.	a	b	c	d	59.	a	b	c	d	94.	a	b	c	d
25.	a	b	c	d	60.	a	b	c	d	95.	a	b	c	d
26.	a	b	c	d	61.	a	b	c	d	96.	a	b	c	d
27.	a	b	c	d	62.	a	b	c	d	97.	a	b	c	d
28.	a	b	c	d	63.	a	b	c	d	98.	a	b	c	d
29.	a	b	c	d	64.	a	b	c	d	99.	a	b	c	d
30.	a	b	c	d	65.	a	b	c	d	100.	a	b	c	d
31.	a	b	c	d	66.	a	b	c	d					
32.	a	b	c	d	67.	a	b	c	d					
33.	a	b	c	d	68.	a	b	c	d					
34.	a	b	c	d	69.	a	b	c	d					
35.	a	b	c	d	70.	a	b	c	d					

▶ State Trooper Practice Test 3

Directions: Read the following passage, then answer questions 1 through 5.

At 12:45 A.M. on October 15, while parked at 1910 Fairlane, Police Officers Flores and Steinbrenner were asked to respond to a disturbance at 1809 Clarkson. When they arrived at the one-story dwelling, the complainant, Alan Weber, who resides next door at 1807 Clarkson, told them that he had been kept awake for two hours by the sound of yelling and breaking glass. He said the occupant of 1809 Clarkson, a Mr. Everett Hayes, lived alone. The officers approached 1809 Clarkson and heard yelling coming from inside. When the officers knocked on the door, Mr. Hayes answered promptly and said, "It's about time you got here." Inside, broken furniture was strewn about. Mr. Hayes stated he had been protecting himself from persons who lived inside the woodwork of his home. He went willingly with the officers to Fairfield County Hospital at 1010 Market, where he was admitted to the psychiatric unit for observation. No arrests were made.

1. Which of the following is most likely a fact?
   a. Alan Weber had been kept awake by noise.
   b. Mr. Hayes had been making noise for two hours.
   c. Mr. Hayes had always been crazy.
   d. The police heard Mr. Hayes shouting inside his house.

2. The call to the police was most likely made from which of the following addresses?
   a. 1910 Fairlane
   b. 1809 Clarkson
   c. 1807 Clarkson
   d. 1010 Market

3. Based on the passage, what was the most likely reason the police were called?
   a. A neighbor was bothered by the noise coming from Mr. Hayes's home.
   b. A neighbor was worried for Mr. Hayes's safety.
   c. A neighbor was worried for the safety of Mr. Hayes's family.
   d. A neighbor was curious about Mr. Hayes's personal life.

4. What was Mr. Hayes's demeanor when the police arrived at his door?
   a. He seemed surprised.
   b. He seemed to have been expecting them.
   c. He seemed frightened and distrustful.
   d. He seemed angered by their presence.

5. Based on the passage, what reason would Mr. Hayes himself most likely give for the commotion at his house?
   a. He was acting in self-defense.
   b. He was mentally ill.
   c. He was cleaning the woodwork.
   d. He broke a glass.

6. Which of the following statements is accurate according to the passage?
   a. Police Officer Flores responded to a disturbance at 1809 Clarkson alone.
   b. 1809 Clarkson was a three-story residence.
   c. Everett Hayes left his residence unwillingly with the officers.
   d. Everett Hayes was not arrested as a result of this incident.

Directions: Read the following passage, then answer questions 7 through 11.

In order for our society to make decisions about the kinds of punishments we will impose on convicted criminals, we must understand why we punish criminals. Some people argue that retribution is the purpose of punishment and that, therefore, the punishment must in some direct way fit the crime. This view is based on the belief that a person who commits a crime deserves to be punished. Because the punishment must fit the specific crime, the theory of retribution allows a sentencing judge to consider the circumstances of each crime, criminal, and victim in imposing a sentence.

Another view, the deterrence theory, promotes punishment in order to discourage commission of future crimes. In this view, punishment need not relate directly to the crime committed, because the point is to deter both a specific criminal and the general public from committing crimes in the future. However, punishment must necessarily be uniformly and consistently applied, in order for the members of the public to understand how they would be punished if they committed a crime. Laws setting sentencing guidelines are based on the deterrence theory and do not allow a judge to consider the specifics of a particular crime in sentencing a convicted criminal.

7. According to the passage, punishment
   a. is rarely an effective deterrent to future crimes.
   b. must fit the crime in question.
   c. is imposed solely at the discretion of a judge.
   d. may be imposed for differing reasons.

8. The retribution theory of punishment
   a. is no longer considered valid.
   b. holds that punishment must fit the crime committed.
   c. applies only to violent crimes.
   d. allows a jury to recommend the sentence that should be imposed.

9. The passage suggests that a person who believes that the death penalty results in fewer murders most likely also believes in
   a. the deterrence theory.
   b. the retribution theory.
   c. giving judges considerable discretion in imposing sentences.
   d. the integrity of the criminal justice system.

10. Which of the following would be a good title for this passage?
   a. "Sentencing Reform: A Modest Proposal"
   b. "More Criminals Are Doing Time"
   c. "Punishment: Deterrent or Retribution?"
   d. "Why I Favor Uniform Sentencing Guidelines"

11. A person who believes in the deterrence theory would probably also support
   a. nonunanimous jury verdicts.
   b. early release of prisoners because of prison overcrowding.
   c. a broad definition of the insanity defense.
   d. allowing television broadcasts of court proceedings.

Directions: Read the following passage, then answer questions 12 through 16.

At 12:15 A.M., while riding the uptown-bound 12 train, Transit Officers Cobb and Wilson received a report of a disturbance in the fourth car of a downtown-bound 12 train. That train was held at the Fourth Street station until the arrival of the officers, who found complainant Alan Sterns tending his injured eye. Mr. Sterns told Officer Wilson that he had been attacked by Caroline Simpson when he attempted to move her bags, after politely asking her to do so, in order to make room to sit down. He said Ms. Simpson poked him in the eye and then threatened him with a switchblade. Ms. Simpson told Officer Cobb that she had been harassed by Mr. Sterns and struck him in self-defense. The officers asked Mr. Sterns, Ms. Simpson, and witnesses Lisa Walker and Lois Casey to step off the train, and proceeded to question them on the platform. Ms. Walker, whose view of the incident had been partially obstructed by a metal pole, stated that Mr. Sterns had raised his arm only after being struck, but she was not sure whether the gesture was threatening or defensive. Ms. Casey, who sat on the other side of Ms. Simpson, maintained that Mr. Sterns was only protecting himself and had behaved in a polite manner. Ms. Simpson was placed under arrest for carrying a concealed weapon.

12. Where did the assault occur?
   a. on a subway platform
   b. on the fourth car of the uptown-bound 12 train
   c. at the Fourth Street station
   d. on the fourth car of the downtown-bound 12 train

13. Which of the following actions caused the arrest?
   a. injuring the complainant's eye
   b. threatening the complainant
   c. carrying a switchblade
   d. disturbing the peace

14. The complainant's last name is
   a. Sterns.
   b. Simpson.
   c. Walker.
   d. Cobb.

15. Where was Ms. Casey sitting?
   a. beside the complainant
   b. across the car, behind a metal pole
   c. between the complainant and the accused
   d. beside the accused

16. According to the complainant, he was struck because
   a. he handled the woman's property.
   b. he asked the woman to move her bags.
   c. he politely asked the woman to move over.
   d. he appeared to raise his arm in a threatening manner.

Directions: Read the following passage, then answer questions 17 through 20.

The rules for obtaining evidence, set down in state and federal law, usually come to our attention when they work to the advantage of defendants in court, but these laws were not created with the courtroom in mind. They were formulated with the pragmatic intent of shaping police procedure before the arrest, in order to ensure justice, thoroughness, and the preservation of civil liberties. A good police officer must be as well schooled in the rules for properly obtaining evidence as is a defense lawyer, or risk losing a conviction. When a case is thrown out of court or a defendant is released because of these evidentiary "technicalities," we are often angered and mystified, but we are not always aware of how these rules of evidence shape police procedure in positive ways every day.

17. The main idea of this passage is that
- **a.** the rules of evidence protect the rights of defendants at trial.
- **b.** police officers should know the rules of evidence.
- **c.** rules of evidence help shape police procedure.
- **d.** the rules of evidence have more positive than negative effects.

18. According to the passage, rules of evidence are designed to ensure all of the following EXCEPT
- **a.** meticulousness in gathering evidence.
- **b.** proof of guilt.
- **c.** protection of individual rights.
- **d.** fairness of treatment.

19. According to the passage, why should a police officer know the rules of evidence?
- **a.** The rules protect the rights of crime victims.
- **b.** The public does not appreciate the importance of rules.
- **c.** An officer must follow the rules to obtain a conviction.
- **d.** Following the rules protects officers from accusations of misconduct.

20. In saying that the intent of rules of evidence is *pragmatic*, the author most likely means that
- **a.** the focus of the rules is on police procedures in the field rather than on legal maneuvers in court.
- **b.** the practical nature of the rules enables lawyers to use them in court to protect defendants.
- **c.** the framers of these rules designed them to maintain idealistic standards of fairness.
- **d.** the rules are often misused in court because of their limited scope.

Directions: For questions 21 through 25, choose the answer choice that best rephrases the underlined portion of the given sentence.

21. The <u>people that are at the back of the line</u> should move to the front.
- **a.** people, who are at the back of the line
- **b.** people who are at the back of the line
- **c.** people, that are at the back of the line,
- **d.** people who, are at the back of the line,

22. The students asked whether I thought there would be a woman <u>president within the next decade?</u>
- **a.** president within the next decade!
- **b.** president, within the next decade.
- **c.** president within the next decade.
- **d.** president, within the next decade?

23. This is the first time you have ever been to a major league baseball <u>game isn't it?</u>
   a. game, isn't it?
   b. game, is'nt it?
   c. game, isn't it.
   d. game isn't it.

24. Chicken <u>pox a virus</u> is very contagious.
   a. pox, a virus,
   b. pox, a virus
   c. pox, a virus—
   d. pox a virus,

25. I was born on <u>May 17, 1962 in Corvallis, Oregon.</u>
   a. May 17 1962 in Corvallis, Oregon.
   b. May 17 1962, in Corvallis Oregon.
   c. May 17, 1962 in Corvallis Oregon.
   d. May 17, 1962, in Corvallis, Oregon.

26. Look at the four numbered sentences below. Choose the sentence order that would result in the best paragraph.
   (1) Leaving us behind in a bitter cloud of exhaust, the bus would cough and jolt down the narrow main street of Crossland.
   (2) Then, even before the bus got moving, she'd look away, ahead toward her real life.
   (3) But I could always imagine the way it would be once it got out on the open highway, gathered speed, and took Grandma back to a life as exotic to me as the deserts of Egypt.
   (4) When Grandma's visit was over, we'd take her down to the Greyhound station, watch her hand her ticket to the uniformed driver, disappear inside, and reappear to wave good-bye—her expression obscured by the bus's grimy window.
   a. 4, 2, 1, 3
   b. 4, 1, 3, 2
   c. 1, 3, 4, 2
   d. 1, 2, 3, 4

27. Look at the four numbered sentences below. Choose the sentence order that would result in the best paragraph.
   (1) The Fifth Amendment of the U.S. Constitution guarantees citizens freedom from double jeopardy in criminal proceedings.
   (2) It also means a person cannot be tried for a crime for which he or she has already been convicted; that is to say, a person convicted by a state court cannot be tried for the same offense in, for example, federal court.
   (3) Finally, a person cannot be punished more than once for the same crime.
   (4) This means that a person cannot be tried for a crime for which he or she has already been acquitted.
   a. 1, 4, 2, 3
   b. 1, 2, 4, 3
   c. 3, 2, 1, 4
   d. 3, 4, 2, 1

28. Look at the four numbered sentences below. Choose the sentence order that would result in the best paragraph.
   (1) If this is true, something must have happened to Mars billions of years ago that stripped away the planet's atmosphere.
   (2) These images also implied that Mars once had an atmosphere that was thick enough to trap the sun's heat.
   (3) Close-up images of Mars by the *Mariner* 9 probe indicated networks of valleys that looked like the stream beds on Earth.
   a. 2, 3, 1
   b. 3, 1, 2
   c. 3, 2, 1
   d. 1, 3, 2

29. Look at the four numbered sentences below. Choose the sentence order that would result in the best paragraph.

(1) Every spring the softball field became his favorite destination, and he had taken his son Arnie there when he was small to teach him how to pitch.

(2) He walked home, as usual, through the park and, as usual, passed by the softball field.

(3) This memory made him feel sad and guilty.

(4) Arnie hadn't been in the least interested in softball, and so after two or three lessons he had given up the idea.

a. 2, 1, 4, 3
b. 3, 2, 1, 4
c. 4, 3, 1, 2
d. 2, 3, 4, 1

30. Three of the sentences below contain one or more grammatical or spelling errors. Select the answer choice that is correct as is.

a. Bus operators will wait there until the police arrive, will allow passengers off the bus at this point, and no passengers will be allowed on until the situation is resolved.

b. Bus operators will wait there until the police arrive, will allow passengers off the bus at this point, and, until the situation is resolved, no passengers are allowed on.

c. Bus operators will wait there until the police arrive, will allow passengers off the bus at this point, and will not allow passengers on until the situation is resolved.

d. Bus operators will wait there until the police arrive, will allow passengers off the bus at this point, and no passengers will be allowed on until the situation is resolved.

31. Three of the sentences below contain one or more grammatical or spelling errors. Select the answer choice that is correct as is.

a. Herbert was enjoying the cool bright fall afternoon. Walking down the street red and yellow leaves crunched satisfyingly under his new school shoes.

b. Herbert was enjoying the cool, bright fall afternoon. He was walking down the street, red and yellow leaves crunched satisfyingly under his new school shoes.

c. Herbert was enjoying the cool, bright fall afternoon. Walking down the street, he crunched red and yellow leaves satisfyingly under his new school shoes.

d. Herbert was enjoying the cool, bright fall afternoon. Walking down the street, red and yellow leaves were crunched satisfyingly under his new school shoes.

32. Three of the sentences below contain one or more grammatical or spelling errors. Select the answer choice that is correct as is.

a. Some people say jury duty is a nuisance that just takes up their precious time and that we don't get paid enough.

b. Some people say jury duty is a nuisance that just takes up your precious time and that one doesn't get paid enough.

c. Some people say jury duty is a nuisance that just takes up one's precious time and that one doesn't get paid enough.

d. Some people say jury duty is a nuisance that just takes up our precious time and that they don't get paid enough.

33. Three of the sentences below contain one or more grammatical or spelling errors. Select the answer choice that is correct as is.
- **a.** The TV show *Columbo* is said to have been inspired in part of the classic Russian novel *Crime and Punishment.*
- **b.** The TV show *Columbo* is said to have been inspired in part by the classic Russian novel *Crime and Punishment.*
- **c.** The TV show *Columbo* is said to have been inspired in part off of the classic Russian novel *Crime and Punishment.*
- **d.** The TV show *Columbo* is said to have been inspired in part from the classic Russian novel *Crime and Punishment.*

34. Identify the sentence that contains a mistake in capitalization, punctuation, grammar, or spelling. If you find no mistakes, select choice **d.**
- **a.** We searched every inch of the room.
- **b.** The words in this document does not make sense.
- **c.** We always have chicken for Sunday dinner.
- **d.** no mistakes

35. Identify the sentence that contains a mistake in capitalization, punctuation, grammar, or spelling. If you find no mistakes, select choice **d.**
- **a.** Either Cassie nor I heard the door open.
- **b.** How many people signed the Declaration of Independence?
- **c.** Draw up a plan before you make your decision.
- **d.** no mistakes

36. Identify the sentence that contains a mistake in capitalization, punctuation, grammar, or spelling. If you find no mistakes, select choice **d.**
- **a.** "Meet me at six o'clock," she said.
- **b.** Tired of running, she slowed her pace to a fast walk.
- **c.** Gabriel and me will attend the geography bee.
- **d.** no mistakes

37. Identify the sentence that contains a mistake in capitalization, punctuation, grammar, or spelling. If you find no mistakes, select choice **d.**
- **a.** The lost dog wandered sad through the streets.
- **b.** Frustrated, Boris threw his pencil across the room.
- **c.** We'll stop at their house first.
- **d.** no mistakes

38. Identify the sentence that contains a mistake in capitalization, punctuation, grammar, or spelling.
- **a.** The memo was distributed on Friday.
- **b.** Although the managers and the support staff had been called.
- **c.** The company was being acquired by a large corporation.
- **d.** Be sure to attend the meeting.

39. Identify the sentence that contains a mistake in capitalization, punctuation, grammar, or spelling.
- **a.** There is only one store that sells that brand.
- **b.** Why are the girls on the team so excited?
- **c.** Here are the shoes I wanted to show you.
- **d.** What is the causes of her constant complaints?

40. Identify the sentence that contains a mistake in capitalization, punctuation, grammar, or spelling.
   a. Anne will head out first, and Nick will follow her.
   b. Maya Angelou, a famous poet, has directed a movie.
   c. The clerk asked for my address and phone number.
   d. Cod liver oil is the most awfulest drink.

41. Dorothy is standing directly under a plane that is 300 meters above her. She sees another plane flying straight behind the first. It is 500 meters away from her, and she has not moved. How far apart are the planes from each other?
   a. 40 meters
   b. 400 meters
   c. 4,000 meters
   d. 40,000 meters

42. Police confiscated 6,000 kg of marijuana in a drug bust. The marijuana was packaged in 5-kg bags. How many bags of marijuana did the police confiscate?
   a. 1,200 bags
   b. 600 bags
   c. 300 bags
   d. 20 bags

43. 1 hour 20 minutes + 3 hours 30 minutes =
   a. 4 hours
   b. 4 hours 20 minutes
   c. 4 hours 50 minutes
   d. 5 hours

44. Fire departments commonly use the following formula to find out how far from a wall to place the base of a ladder:

(Length of ladder ÷ 5) + 2 = distance from the wall.

Using this formula, if the base of a ladder is placed 10 feet from a wall, how tall is the ladder?
   a. 48 feet
   b. 72 feet
   c. 40 feet
   d. 100 feet

45. Sipora drove to Stephanie's house at a constant rate of 45 mph. If Stephanie's house is 220 miles away from Sipora's and Sipora wants to get home in exactly 4 hours, how fast should she drive?
   a. 50 mph
   b. 55 mph
   c. 60 mph
   d. 65 mph

46. What is another way to write 2.75×100^2?
   a. 275
   b. 2,750
   c. 27,500
   d. 270,000

47. Which of the following means $5n + 7 = 17$?
   a. 7 more than 5 times a number is 17
   b. 5 more than 7 times a number is 17
   c. 7 less than 5 times a number is 17
   d. 12 times a number is 17

48. A trash container, when empty, weighs 27 pounds. If this container is filled with a load of trash that weighs 108 pounds, what is the total weight of the container and its contents?
- **a.** 81 pounds
- **b.** 135 pounds
- **c.** 145 pounds
- **d.** 185 pounds

49. What is the value of y when $x = 3$ and $y = 5 + 4x$?
- **a.** 6
- **b.** 9
- **c.** 12
- **d.** 17

50. What two numbers should come next in the following series?
8, 22, 12, 16, 22, 20, 24, . . .
- **a.** 28, 32
- **b.** 28, 22
- **c.** 22, 28
- **d.** 22, 26

51. $6 + (-10) =$
- **a.** 16
- **b.** −16
- **c.** 8
- **d.** −8

52. The city's bus system carries 1,200,000 people each day. How many people does the bus system carry each year? (1 year = 365 days)
- **a.** 3,288 people
- **b.** 32,880 people
- **c.** 43,800,000 people
- **d.** 438,000,000 people

53. $37 \times 60 \times 3 =$
- **a.** 3,660
- **b.** 4,990
- **c.** 5,760
- **d.** 6,660

54. Mark's temperature at 9 A.M. was 97.2 degrees. At 4 P.M., his temperature was 99 degrees. By how many degrees did his temperature rise?
- **a.** 0.8
- **b.** 1.8
- **c.** 2.2
- **d.** 2.8

55. Which of the following expressions is equal to 40,503?
- **a.** 400 + 50 + 3
- **b.** 4,000 + 500 + 3
- **c.** 40,000 + 50 + 3
- **d.** 40,000 + 500 + 3

56. State Trooper Fitzgerald is driving east on Amsterdam Avenue. She makes a U-turn and then turns left. What direction is she now heading?
- **a.** north
- **b.** south
- **c.** east
- **d.** west

57. State Trooper Munoz is pursuing a Honda that was involved in a robbery and is now heading north on Route 80. The Honda notices that it is being followed and quickly makes a left turn, then another left turn. The Honda runs a red light and is hit on its right side by a car entering the intersection. The car that hit the Honda was heading in what direction?
- **a.** north
- **b.** south
- **c.** east
- **d.** west

58. An ambulance is traveling southwest on the parkway. Traffic is merging into the ambulance's lane from the left. The merging traffic is heading in what direction?
   a. north
   b. south
   c. east
   d. west

59. State Trooper Ahmed is driving south on Prospect Avenue during his nightshift. He makes a right turn and notices a late model Ford heading toward him. What direction is the Ford heading?
   a. north
   b. south
   c. east
   d. west

60. State Trooper Troncellito is patrolling a southbound highway, when he sees smoke to his left. If she wishes to go investigate the cause of the smoke, she should turn into the next exit to the
   a. north.
   b. south.
   c. east.
   d. west.

61. State Trooper Howard Smith travels west one block on Elm Street. He turns left onto Beaver Street for one block, turns right onto Providence Avenue for one block, then right for one block onto Michigan Avenue. Finally, State Trooper Smith makes a left and is heading
   a. west on Providence Avenue.
   b. north on Beaver Street.
   c. east on Elm Street.
   d. west on Elm Street.

62. An SUV is driving north on route 287. At the junction of route 287 and Smithfield Road, the SUV turns and proceeds west on Smithfield Road. At the first intersection, the SUV yields to a police car crossing Smithfield Road and entering the intersection from the right. The police car is heading in what direction?
   a. north
   b. south
   c. east
   d. west

Directions: Answer questions 63–66 based on the map below. The arrows indicate traffic flow. One arrow indicates a one-way street going in the direction of the arrow; two arrows represent a two-way street. You are not allowed to go the wrong way on a one-way street.

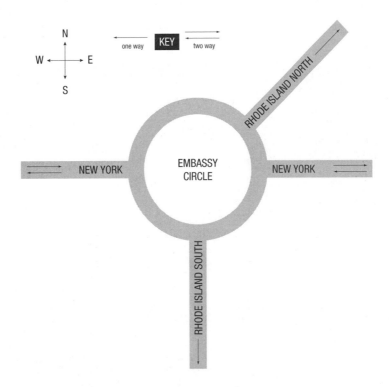

63. If a police vehicle traveling from the east wanted to go west on New York Avenue, it would need to travel around the circle
  a. north and east.
  b. north and west.
  c. south and east.
  d. south and west.

64. Your unit is driving east on New York Avenue and needs to enter Rhode Island Avenue South. You should travel
  a. northeast.
  b. northwest.
  c. southeast.
  d. southwest.

65. If State Trooper William Gates is traveling from east to west in the traffic circle, he must
  a. drive completely around the traffic circle.
  b. drive north around the traffic circle.
  c. drive south around the traffic circle.
  d. none of the above

66. Rhode Island Avenue runs
  a. from north to south.
  b. from south to north.
  c. south and northeast.
  d. south to northeast.

Directions: Answer questions 67 through 70 based on the map below.

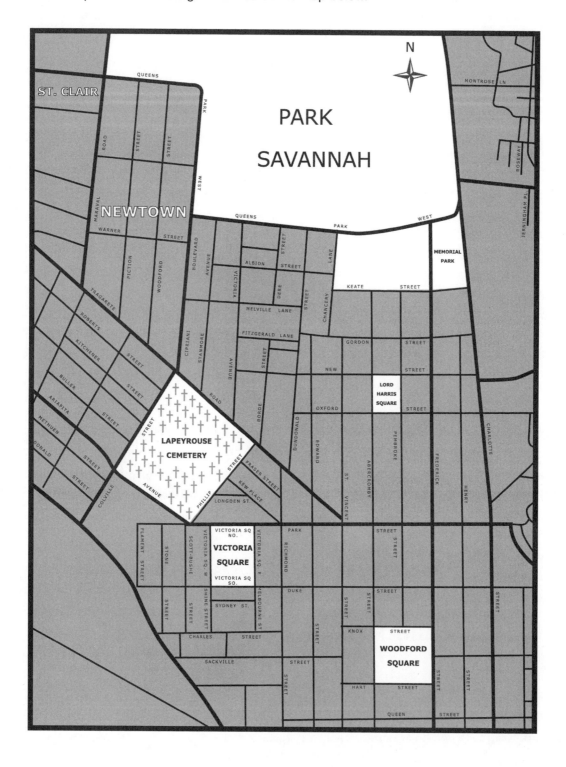

67. Presuming you are at the northeast corner of Woodford Square and want to walk the shortest distance to the closest corner of Victoria Square, your path would be to walk

a. north to Duke Street and west to the intersection of Victoria Square South and Victoria Square East.

b. south to Sackville Street and east until you come to Victoria Square.

c. north to Duke Street and west to the intersection of Victoria Square South and Victoria Square East.

d. north to Park Street and east to the intersection of Victoria Square North and Park Street.

68. Lapeyrouse Cemetery is in what direction from Victoria Square?

a. northeast

b. southeast

c. southwest

d. northwest

69. The Newtown section is located in the _____ area of Park Savannah.

a. northeast

b. southeast

c. southwest

d. northwest

70. The streets that provide direct routes from Lapeyrouse Cemetery to Park Savannah are

a. Cipriani Boulevard, Stanmore Avenue, and Victoria Avenue.

b. Cipriani Boulevard and Victoria Avenue.

c. Stanmore Avenue and Dundonald Street.

d. Stanmore Avenue, Victoria Avenue, and Borde Street.

Directions: You will have ten minutes to read and study the following passage. Then, answer questions 71 through 80 without referring back to the passage.

On Wednesday, January 11, 2006, three defendants were assaulted at the Camden Courthouse. At approximately 1:30 P.M., a blond suspect attacked defendants John Dendler, Erin Finkle, and Fred Gussoni with a knife. Officer Martin Thomas recognized that defendant Dendler appeared to have been stabbed in the thigh. He immediately called 911, and EMT personnel transported Dendler to the St. Joseph's Medical Center, where he was discharged the next day. The two other defendants sustained minor injuries and were treated at the scene of the incident.

At approximately 3:00 P.M., the suspect in the assault was removed from the courthouse by Officer Ryan Morton and Officer Ed Buckworth. During the removal, the suspect, William Dawkins, became unruly and attempted to strike Officer Buckworth in the head with his own head. Dawkins was restrained by Morton.

At 6:30 P.M., Officer Delongo questioned Defendant Dendler at St. Joseph's Medical Center regarding the assault. Dendler denied that the incident was drug related and claimed that prior to that afternoon, he had only spoken to Dawkins once before, in passing.

At 9:30 A.M. on Thursday, January 12, 2006, Officer Delongo questioned defendants Finkle and Gussoni at their respective residences. All statements made by defendants Finkle and Gussoni closely corroborated with inmate Dendler's statements regarding the assault.

71. What day of the week did the assault occur?
   a. Wednesday
   b. Saturday
   c. Monday
   d. Thursday

72. Which defendant was stabbed in the thigh?
   a. Finkle
   b. Gussoni
   c. Dendler
   d. Dawkins

73. In which courthouse were the three defendants assaulted?
   a. Camden Courthouse
   b. Central Courthouse
   c. Central Community Courthouse
   d. Camdall Courthouse

74. Who transported the defendant who had been stabbed in the thigh to the medical center?
   a. Thomas
   b. Buckworth
   c. EMT personnel
   d. Delongo

75. Which officer did William Dawkins attempt to strike?
   a. Thomas
   b. Morton
   c. Buckworth
   d. Bush

76. At approximately what time was the suspect in the assault removed from the courthouse?
   a. 1:30 P.M.
   b. 3:00 P.M.
   c. 6:30 P.M.
   d. 9:30 A.M.

77. Where were the two other stabbed defendants treated?
   a. at their residences
   b. at the courthouse
   c. at the medical center
   d. in the ambulance

78. What color hair did the attacker have?
   a. brown
   b. black
   c. blond
   d. gray

79. Defendant Dendler had spoken to the suspect
   a. never.
   b. once before in passing.
   c. three times in the courtroom.
   d. numerous times.

80. Who was treated at the scene of the incident?
   a. Gussoni and Dawkins
   b. Gussoni and Dendler
   c. Finkle and Dendler
   d. Gussoni and Finkle

Directions: Read the following passage, then answer questions 81 through 87.

Henry Allen, a fiscally conservative candidate for city council, contacted the Internal Security Division of the Internal Revenue Service and alleged that an IRS employee was giving Allen's tax information to an opponent, Susan Vickers. Vickers was threatening to release information that Allen's business had been operating at a loss the last five years. Molly Hepplewhite, an internal security inspector for the IRS, commenced an investigation.

During the course of the investigation, the following statements were made:

1. Milton Banks, Susan Vickers's neighbor, said that he once caught Vickers going through his trash.

2. Bill Pushman, Henry Allen's campaign manager, said he dated Alice West in college. Alice now works at the IRS.

3. Shelby Gray, Susan Vickers's sister, said Susan would always do whatever she needed to do to get what she wanted.

4. Calvin Morris, Susan Vickers's campaign manager, said that his sister-in-law, Mary Yate, works at the IRS, but they haven't spoken in months.

5. IRS employee Doug Edwards said that Mary Yate and Alice West have lunch together almost every day.

6. Frank Luther, Henry Allen's neighbor, said that Allen has no business running for city council when he can't even keep his dog in his own yard.

7. Felicia Dial said that she plans to vote for Henry Allen because he promises to run the city as efficiently as he runs his business.

8. IRS employee Mary Yate said that Frank Luther and Doug Edwards have been friends since grade school.

9. IRS employee Avery Page said that Alice West makes a lot of personal phone calls and once he heard her say, "He can't treat you like that!"

10. Henry Allen said that current council member Mavis Wright said that Susan Vickers said she'd do anything to win this election.

81. Which statement is most damaging to the Susan Vickers campaign?
   a. Statement 1
   b. Statement 3
   c. Statement 4
   d. Statement 10

82. Which statement is least helpful to the investigation?
   a. Statement 1
   b. Statement 8
   c. Statement 2
   d. Statement 6

83. Which two statements are hearsay?
   a. Statements 1 and 2
   b. Statements 9 and 10
   c. Statements 5 and 6
   d. Statements 3 and 4

84. Which statement represents circumstantial evidence?
   a. Statement 5
   b. Statement 2
   c. Statement 4
   d. Statement 7

85. Which statement indicates that an IRS employee is providing information to the Vickers campaign?
   a. Statement 1
   b. Statement 3
   c. Statement 10
   d. Statement 4

86. Which two statements imply the possibility that the Allen campaign is attempting to make the Vickers campaign appear guilty?
   a. Statements 4 and 8
   b. Statements 1 and 3
   c. Statements 2 and 5
   d. Statements 8 and 10

87. Which two statements tend to implicate Frank Luther?
   a. Statements 6 and 8
   b. Statements 1 and 5
   c. Statements 2 and 9
   d. Statements 4 and 5

Directions: Read the following passage, then answer questions 88 through 94.

Bert Hines was imprisoned in a federal facility for forgery. Hines, along with three other prisoners and two guards, was taken from lock-up to a local optometrist's office on January 17. The four prisoners were secured by handcuffs to an eight-foot length of chain during transport. While sitting in the optometrist's waiting room, Hines was released from the chain and taken to the examination room, where a preliminary eye exam was conducted. He was then escorted back to the waiting room. While another prisoner was being released, Hines, who had not been reshackled, seized a gun from one of the guards and managed to escape. He took Michelle Rogers, the optometrist's receptionist, hostage and fled with her. He released her within 30 minutes, when he stole a car. During the course of the investigation, the following statements were made:

1. Jeff Reynolds, one of the four prisoners, said that Hines's cellmate told him Hines had a girlfriend in town.
2. The optometrist said that Hines acted "weird" during the exam.
3. Jessie Seymour, one of the guards, said that Hines was not reshackled because his exam was not complete.
4. Mary Hobbes, the guard whose gun was stolen, said that the gun was not regulation.
5. Maurice Chang, one of the four prisoners, said Hines made eye contact with a female passerby as the prisoners were led into the office.
6. Martin Steffins, Michelle Rogers's fiancé, said Michelle was always afraid on the days prisoners came to the office.
7. Michelle Rogers said that Hines retrieved a package from the planter in front of the office and later showed her a passport and an envelope containing several thousand dollars.

8. Rachel Firth, the owner of the stolen car, said that one of her husband's suits, which she had picked up at the dry cleaner, was hanging in the car.
9. Michael Jones, Rachel's husband, said the car tended to cut out at speeds over 60 miles per hour.
10. Raymond Diaz, Hines's cellmate, said that Hines spoke French fluently.

88. Which statement is hearsay?
   a. Statement 1
   b. Statement 2
   c. Statement 4
   d. Statement 7

89. Which two statements indicate that Hines may have been planning to leave the country?
   a. Statements 7 and 8
   b. Statements 2 and 10
   c. Statements 8 and 10
   d. Statements 7 and 10

90. Which two statements, along with Statement 2, are least likely to be of use in this investigation?
   a. Statements 3 and 5
   b. Statements 4 and 6
   c. Statements 1 and 7
   d. Statements 8 and 10

91. Which two statements indicate the escape was planned, rather than spontaneous?
   a. Statements 2 and 5
   b. Statements 3 and 7
   c. Statements 2 and 3
   d. Statements 5 and 7

92. Which statement indicates an avoidable mistake on the part of prison guards?
   a. Statement 2
   b. Statement 3
   c. Statement 1
   d. Statement 5

93. Assuming law enforcement officers spot Hines driving Firth's car, which statement would lead officers to consider commencing a high-speed chase?
   a. Statement 7
   b. Statement 8
   c. Statement 6
   d. Statement 9

94. Which statement indicates officers should contact security at the local airport?
   a. Statement 7
   b. Statement 8
   c. Statement 9
   d. Statement 10

95. In the K-9 Corps, Officer Thomas is partnered with Ranger, Officer Cain is partnered with Scout, Officer Stern is partnered with Laddie, and Officer Walker is partnered with Astro. If Officer Thomas switches partners with Officer Stern and Officer Stern then switches with Officer Cain, who is Officer Stern's new partner?
   a. Ranger
   b. Scout
   c. Laddie
   d. Astro

96. Officers aren't always required to make a custody arrest that very moment even though the law has been broken. A warrant can always be issued at a later date for the suspect if the person can be identified. Which of the following situations best illustrates this point?
   a. Jeremy is well known in his community for his appearance at political demonstrations. Police are called to the scene of a massive riot where Jeremy has incited over 100 college students to throw rocks and attack the outnumbered police force.
   b. Melody is walking along the street when a man jumps out from the shadows, grabs her purse, and takes off running. Officer Bentley catches him one block later.
   c. Antonio tells Officer DiAngelo that his cousin has been threatening to come burn his house down. While Antonio is telling this story, a gasoline can comes crashing through the living room window.
   d. Rachel walks up to Officer Xavier dragging a teenager by the jacket. She tells the officer that she caught the young man putting his hand into her coat pocket when she was waiting at the bus stop.

Directions: Read the following passage, then answer questions 97 and 98.

Police officers are required to give out physical descriptions of suspects over police radios for other officers to assist in locating the person. A description should be given out in the following order:

1. race and sex
2. weapons the suspect may be carrying
3. approximate height and weight
4. color and length of hair
5. baseball cap or other headgear
6. coat, jacket, or shirt
7. long or short pants
8. footwear

97. Officer Lundy was on patrol when he saw a man on a sidewalk waving wildly at him. The man told him he'd been robbed about one block away by a white male carrying a lock-blade knife. The suspect has on white tennis shoes, olive drab fatigue pants, a black turtleneck, and a black baseball cap. He's about 6 feet tall and weighs about 180 pounds. What is the first thing Officer Lundy should put out over the radio when he begins describing the suspect?
   a. a description of the suspect's knife
   b. a description of the suspect's race and sex
   c. a description of the suspect's pants
   d. a description of the suspect's speaking voice

98. Officer Scott is taking a report of a purse-snatching at the mall. The victim says the thief was 5′10″ tall, weighed about 160 pounds, had short red hair, and was wearing a New York Yankees baseball cap with gray warm-up pants and a gray sweatshirt. He was wearing black jogging shoes, was a white male, and appeared to be without weapons. Officer Scott begins his description with the race and sex of the suspect, but is interrupted by the victim. When he resumes his description, Officer Scott should begin with the
   a. suspect's footwear.
   b. suspect's headgear.
   c. suspect's height and weight.
   d. suspect's weapon.

99. Officer Mattox is listening to Claude, an angry citizen. Claude is furious with Officer Mattox because he feels that he doesn't deserve a ticket for running a stop sign. At what point should the officer consider physically arresting Claude?
   a. Claude is seated in his automobile shouting, "Why aren't you out catching real crooks?" while the officer opens his ticket book.
   b. Claude is standing beside his car on the sidewalk holding his arms out, with palms up, at passing cars while the officer writes the ticket.
   c. Claude points his pen at Officer Mattox and says, "I want your name and badge number because I'm calling your supervisor."
   d. Claude pokes his forefinger in Officer Mattox's chest and tells him he doesn't know what he's talking about.

100. During the graduation ceremony at the police academy, Cadet Jurgens is standing immediately to Cadet Shirley's left. Cadet Shirley is immediately to the left of Cadet Davis. Cadet Riley is to the right of Cadet Shirley. There are no other cadets in this row. In what order are the cadets standing?
  a. Jurgens, Shirley, Davis, Riley
  b. Riley, Jurgens, Shirley, Davis
  c. Shirley, Davis, Riley, Jurgens
  d. Davis, Riley, Jurgens, Shirley

▶ Answers

1. d. The yelling the officers hear coming from inside Mr. Hayes's house is most likely Mr. Hayes, given all the circumstances described in the passage. The other choices are less certain as they are statements made by Mr. Weber when he was upset, and no witnesses are present to confirm them.

2. c. Alan Weber most likely made the call from his home at 1807 Clarkson.

3. a. According to the second sentence of the passage, Alan Weber told police he was kept awake by the noise coming from Mr. Hayes's home.

4. b. According to the passage, Mr. Hayes's first words to the police were, "It's about time you got here."

5. a. According to the next-to-last sentence of the passage, Mr. Hayes told police he had been protecting himself.

6. d. The last sentence of the passage says that no arrests were made.

7. d. The passage presents two reasons for punishment. The second sentence notes a view that *some people* hold. The first line of the second paragraph indicates *another view*.

8. b. This is the main idea of the first paragraph.

9. a. The deterrence theory promotes punishment to discourage future crimes.

10. c. The first sentence indicates that the passage is about punishment. The first paragraph is about retribution; the second is about deterrence.

11. d. The second paragraph notes that one reason behind the deterrence theory is the effect of deterring not only criminals, but also the public.

12. d. See the first sentence of the passage. The officers were initially in the uptown-bound train. The subway platform is where the questioning occurred.

13. c. Although Ms. Simpson allegedly assaulted the complainant and created a disturbance, she was arrested for the concealed weapon.

14. a. Alan Sterns is identified as the complainant in the second sentence of the passage.

15. d. See the next-to-last sentence in the passage.

16. a. According to Mr. Sterns, Ms. Simpson struck him when he attempted to move her bags.

17. d. This idea is stated in the second sentence and discussed throughout the passage.

18. b. Proof of guilt is the whole point of gathering evidence, but this is never referred to in the passage.

19. c. This is stated in the third sentence. Choice **a** is incorrect because, though rules of evidence protect the accused, that is not the reason the passage gives that an officer must know them.

20. a. The pragmatic, or practical, intent the author refers to in the second sentence is the purpose of shaping police procedure before arrest.

21. b. The sentence does not require any punctuation other than the period at the end. Also, *who*, not *that* should be used with *people*.

22. c. This is a declarative sentence; it asks an indirect question, so a question mark should not be used. Also, the comma is unnecessary.

23. a. The sentence requires a comma before the phrase *isn't it*.

24. a. The phrase *a virus* is a nonessential element in the sentence and needs to be set off with commas.

25. d. Commas separate dates and addresses.

26. a. In this choice, the order is chronological. In sentence 4, they take Grandma to the Greyhound station. In sentence 2, the bus has not yet moved away from the station. In sentence 1, the bus jolts away but is still in town. In sentence 3, the bus (at least in the narrator's mind) is out on the open highway.

27. a. Sentence 1 is the topic sentence. Sentence 4 defines the term *double jeopardy* used in sentence 1; sentence 2 gives another definition, signaled by *also*; sentence 3 begins with the word *Finally* and gives the last definition.

28. c. Sentence 3 is the general topic sentence. Sentence 2 repeats the word *images* to make a link to the topic sentence. Sentence 3 gives the details of the example; sentence 1 offers an explanation for the idea presented in the topic sentence.

29. a. Sentence 2 sets the stage—this is a memory. After that, the order is chronological: In sentence 1, the man tries to teach his son how to pitch. In sentence 4, he wasn't interested, so the man gave up. Sentence 3 logically follows—the memory of giving up makes him feel sad and guilty.

30. c. This choice makes use of parallel structure because the list of the drivers' obligations are all expressed in the same subject/verb grammatical form: Bus drivers *will wait, will allow, will not allow*. In choices **a**, **b**, and **d**, the parallelism of the list is thrown off by the last item in the list, which changes the subject of its verb from *operators* to *passengers*.

31. c. This choice adds the subject *he* in the second sentence, eliminating the dangling modifier *walking down the street*. Otherwise, the sentence reads as if the leaves are walking down the street. All other choices ignore the problem of the dangling modifier and add grammatical mistakes to the sentences.

32. c. The other choices contain unnecessary shifts in person, from *people* to *their* and *we* in choice **a**, to *your* and *one* in choice **b**, and to *our* and *they* in choice **d**.

33. b. The correct preposition is *by*; choices **a**, **c**, and **d** contain the incorrect prepositions *of*, *off of*, and *from*.

34. b. There is no subject-verb agreement. The verb should be plural (*do not make*) because the subject is *words*, which is plural.

35. a. *Either* is incorrect. Use *either* with *or* and *neither* with *nor*.

36. c. The correct pronoun is *I*, not *me*. *I* is the choice because along with *Gabriel*, it is the compound subject of the sentence (subjective or nominative case).

37. a. The adjective *sad* should be replaced with the adverb *sadly*, which modifies the verb *wandered*.

38. b. This is a sentence fragment; the other answer choices are complete sentences.

39. d. The verb needs to be plural because the subject (*causes*) is plural. Replacing *is* with *are* would correct this sentence.

40. d. *Most awfulest* is a double superlative and is, therefore, redundant.

41. b. The first plane is actually the triangle's right vertex. The distance between Dorothy and the second plane is the hypotenuse. Plug the known measurements into the Pythagorean theorem: $300^2 + b^2 = 500^2$. $90,000 + b^2 = 250,000$. $b^2 = 160,000$. $b = 400$. Notice that if you divide each side by 100, this is another 3-4-5 triangle.

42. a. Divide the total amount of marijuana (6,000 kg) by the amount in each bag (5 kg), to get the number of bags (1,200).

43. c. Add the hours first, then the minutes: 1 hour + 3 hours = 4 hours and 20 minutes + 30 minutes = 50 minutes. Combine the two: 4 hours 50 minutes.

44. c. Because the distance from the wall is known, the formula would be $(x \div 5) + 2 = 10$. To find x, start by subtracting 2 from both sides, so you have $x \div 5 = 8$. Then, multiply both sides by 5, and you end up with $x = 40$.

45. b. Rearrange $D = RT$ to $R = D \div T = 220 \div 4 = 55$ mph.

46. c. $100^2 = (100)(100)$, or 10,000. $(10,000)(2.75) = 27,500$.

47. a. The expression $5n$ means 5 times n. The addition sign before the 7 indicates the phrase *more than*.

48. a. This is a basic addition problem: 108 pounds + 27 pounds = 135 pounds.

49. d. Substitute 3 for x in the expression $5 + 4x$ to determine that y equals 17.

50. c. This is an alternating repetition series, with a random number, 22, introduced as every third number into an otherwise simple addition series. In the addition series, 4 is added to each number to arrive at the next number. Thus, the next two numbers will be 22 (the random number), followed by 24 + 4, or 28.

51. b. You are adding numbers that have different signs; therefore, subtract the smaller number from the larger number. In this case, the larger number is a negative number, so the answer is –4.

52. d. This is a multiplication problem. The simplest way to solve this problem is to temporarily take away the five zeros, then multiply: $365 \times 12 = 4,380$. Now add back the five zeros for a total of 438,000,000. If you selected choice **a**, you divided when you should have multiplied.

53. d. You need to multiply 37 and 60, then multiply that amount by 3.

54. b. This is a subtraction problem. Be sure to align the decimal points: $99.0 - 97.2 = 1.8$.

55. d. Use the place value of each of the non-zero numbers. The 4 is in the ten-thousands place, so it is equal to 40,000. The 5 is in the hundreds place, so it is equal to 500. The 3 is in the ones place, so it is equal to 3.

56. b. When she made the left turn, State Trooper Fitzgerald was heading south.

57. a. The Honda was heading east, with its right side facing south. The car that hit it was, therefore, heading north.

58. d. If the ambulance is traveling southwest, the merge on the left is a merge from the east and is heading to the west.

59. c. State Trooper Ahmed is heading west after making the right turn, so the Ford is heading east.

60. c. On a southbound highway, east is on the left side, so State Trooper Troncellito should turn into the next exit to the east.

61. d. If Trooper Smith is traveling west on Elm Street and makes a left, he is now heading south on Beaver Street. His right turn will take him west on Providence Avenue, and the next right turn will take him north on Michigan Avenue. The final left turn will put Trooper Smith back on Elm Street heading west.

62. b. The SUV was traveling west, so the police car to the right is traveling south.

63. b. The vehicle would need to go up around the circle (north), then continue west.

64. c. Your unit would need to go down around the circle (south), then continue east.

65. b. State Trooper Gates is entering from the right and must drive north because of the direction of the arrows in the traffic circle.

66. c. Rhode Island Avenue does not run directly north and south, so choices **a** and **b** can be eliminated. Rhode Island Avenue runs south on the bottom of the map, but it runs northeast on the top of the map. Therefore, Rhode Island Avenue runs south *and* northeast, not south *to* northeast.

67. a. It is the most direct route from the northwest corner of Woodford Square to the southeast corner of Victoria Square.

68. d. Using the directional coordinates given to you in the description, the cemetery is northwest of Victoria Square.

69. c. Using the directional coordinates given to you in the description, Newtown is nestled against the southwestern corner of Park Savannah.

70. a. These are the only three streets that provide direct access from the cemetery to the park.

71. a. The assault occurred on a Wednesday. Choice **d**, Thursday, was the day that Officer Delongo questioned defendants Finkle and Gussoni at their respective residences.

72. c. The passage does not state that Finkle or Gussoni, choices **a** and **b**, was stabbed in the thigh. Choice **d**, Dawkins, was the person who assaulted the defendants with the knife.

73. a. The courthouses mentioned in choices **b**, **c**, and **d** are not mentioned in the passage.

74. c. Choice **a** is tricky—Senior Court Officer Thomas called 911, but he did not escort the defendant to the medical center.

75. c. Choices **a** and **b** were not involved in the attempted assault, and choice **d** is not mentioned in the passage.

76. b. The times in the other choices are all mentioned in the passage, but they describe other events.

77. b. The passage states that the defendants were treated *at the scene*: in this case, the Camden Courthouse.

78. c. The second sentence of the passage states that *a blond suspect attacked* the defendants.

79. b. The passage states that Dendler had spoken to Dawkins only once before, in passing.

80. d. Choice **a** is incorrect, because Dawkins was the stabbing suspect, not one of the defendants who was stabbed. Dendler was not treated at the scene, so choices **b** and **c** can be ruled out.

81. c. Statement 4 provides information on the opportunity the Vickers campaign had to receive information from the IRS.

82. d. Statement 6 is not related to the investigation at all.

83. b. Statements 9 and 10 are statements made without personal knowledge, simply repeating what others said.

84. a. Circumstantial evidence is evidence from which the presence of a principal fact of the case can be inferred. The fact that Mary Yate and Alice West frequently have lunch together proves nothing by itself; however, one may infer it means they have a closer relationship than coworkers normally have.

85. d. Statement 4 provides the opportunity for the campaign to receive information from the IRS.

86. c. Statements 2 and 5 indicate a connection from the Allen campaign to the IRS and then to the Vickers campaign.

87. a. Statements 6 and 8 show that Luther holds a grudge against Allen and has access to the IRS through Doug Edwards.

88. a. Statement 1 is a statement made without personal knowledge, simply repeating what others said.

89. d. Statement 7 demonstrates that Hines has the means—a passport and money—to leave the country, and Statement 10 contains the information that Hines speaks a foreign language, facilitating Hines going to another country.

90. b. Statements 4 and 6. The fact that the guard was carrying a nonregulation firearm has no bearing on the investigation into Hines' disappearance; neither does the fact that Michelle Rogers was not comfortable with the prisoners.

91. d. Statements 5 and 7 indicate that someone left the package outside the office for Hines, requiring prior planning.

92. b. Statement 3 was an entirely avoidable mistake; Hines should have been reshackled when he returned to the waiting room.

93. d. Statement 9 indicates that the car may experience mechanical difficulties at speeds over 60 miles an hour; if the officers can force Hines to drive faster than that, the car might be disabled.

94. a. Statement 7 provides information that Hines is planning to go where he will need a passport. Chances are that this will require him to travel by air.

95. b. After all the switches were made, Officer Stern's partner was Scout. Officer Thomas's partner was Laddie, Officer Cain's was Ranger, and Officer Walker's was Astro.

96. a. Outnumbered officers attempting to control a hostile crowd may not be able to arrest the instigator safely; however, according to the situation, they will likely be able to find him later, because they are aware of his identity. In the other situations, custody arrests are appropriate and more easily accomplished. Although in choice **c** it seems apparent that Antonio knows his cousin's identity, and that a warrant could therefore be issued at a later date, the violence of the situation makes immediate action necessary.

97. b. The first step is to give the race and sex of the suspect. In this case, the victim has provided that information.

98. c. The next information the officer can give out is a height and weight description. Because no weapon was seen, choice **d** is not possible.

99. d. Claude has just assaulted Officer Mattox by poking him in the chest. This is a safety issue for the officer, and he should not allow contact of this nature. Allowing an angry citizen to vent and release a certain amount of frustration, as in the other options, is appropriate in many situations.

100. a. The order of the cadets is Jurgens, Shirley, Davis, Riley. Jurgens is on Shirley's immediate left, and Davis is on Shirley's immediate right. Riley is therefore on Davis's immediate right.

14 ▶ State Trooper Practice Test 4

CHAPTER SUMMARY

This is the fourth practice test in the book based on the most commonly tested areas on the state trooper exam.

The practice test consists of 100 multiple-choice questions in the following areas: reading comprehension, writing and information ordering, mathematics, spatial and directional orientation, memory and observation, and problem solving. As with the previous practice tests, you should give yourself two hours to take this practice test.

State Trooper Practice Test 4

1.	ⓐ	ⓑ	ⓒ	ⓓ	36.	ⓐ	ⓑ	ⓒ	ⓓ	71.	ⓐ	ⓑ	ⓒ	ⓓ
2.	ⓐ	ⓑ	ⓒ	ⓓ	37.	ⓐ	ⓑ	ⓒ	ⓓ	72.	ⓐ	ⓑ	ⓒ	ⓓ
3.	ⓐ	ⓑ	ⓒ	ⓓ	38.	ⓐ	ⓑ	ⓒ	ⓓ	73.	ⓐ	ⓑ	ⓒ	ⓓ
4.	ⓐ	ⓑ	ⓒ	ⓓ	39.	ⓐ	ⓑ	ⓒ	ⓓ	74.	ⓐ	ⓑ	ⓒ	ⓓ
5.	ⓐ	ⓑ	ⓒ	ⓓ	40.	ⓐ	ⓑ	ⓒ	ⓓ	75.	ⓐ	ⓑ	ⓒ	ⓓ
6.	ⓐ	ⓑ	ⓒ	ⓓ	41.	ⓐ	ⓑ	ⓒ	ⓓ	76.	ⓐ	ⓑ	ⓒ	ⓓ
7.	ⓐ	ⓑ	ⓒ	ⓓ	42.	ⓐ	ⓑ	ⓒ	ⓓ	77.	ⓐ	ⓑ	ⓒ	ⓓ
8.	ⓐ	ⓑ	ⓒ	ⓓ	43.	ⓐ	ⓑ	ⓒ	ⓓ	78.	ⓐ	ⓑ	ⓒ	ⓓ
9.	ⓐ	ⓑ	ⓒ	ⓓ	44.	ⓐ	ⓑ	ⓒ	ⓓ	79.	ⓐ	ⓑ	ⓒ	ⓓ
10.	ⓐ	ⓑ	ⓒ	ⓓ	45.	ⓐ	ⓑ	ⓒ	ⓓ	80.	ⓐ	ⓑ	ⓒ	ⓓ
11.	ⓐ	ⓑ	ⓒ	ⓓ	46.	ⓐ	ⓑ	ⓒ	ⓓ	81.	ⓐ	ⓑ	ⓒ	ⓓ
12.	ⓐ	ⓑ	ⓒ	ⓓ	47.	ⓐ	ⓑ	ⓒ	ⓓ	82.	ⓐ	ⓑ	ⓒ	ⓓ
13.	ⓐ	ⓑ	ⓒ	ⓓ	48.	ⓐ	ⓑ	ⓒ	ⓓ	83.	ⓐ	ⓑ	ⓒ	ⓓ
14.	ⓐ	ⓑ	ⓒ	ⓓ	49.	ⓐ	ⓑ	ⓒ	ⓓ	84.	ⓐ	ⓑ	ⓒ	ⓓ
15.	ⓐ	ⓑ	ⓒ	ⓓ	50.	ⓐ	ⓑ	ⓒ	ⓓ	85.	ⓐ	ⓑ	ⓒ	ⓓ
16.	ⓐ	ⓑ	ⓒ	ⓓ	51.	ⓐ	ⓑ	ⓒ	ⓓ	86.	ⓐ	ⓑ	ⓒ	ⓓ
17.	ⓐ	ⓑ	ⓒ	ⓓ	52.	ⓐ	ⓑ	ⓒ	ⓓ	87.	ⓐ	ⓑ	ⓒ	ⓓ
18.	ⓐ	ⓑ	ⓒ	ⓓ	53.	ⓐ	ⓑ	ⓒ	ⓓ	88.	ⓐ	ⓑ	ⓒ	ⓓ
19.	ⓐ	ⓑ	ⓒ	ⓓ	54.	ⓐ	ⓑ	ⓒ	ⓓ	89.	ⓐ	ⓑ	ⓒ	ⓓ
20.	ⓐ	ⓑ	ⓒ	ⓓ	55.	ⓐ	ⓑ	ⓒ	ⓓ	90.	ⓐ	ⓑ	ⓒ	ⓓ
21.	ⓐ	ⓑ	ⓒ	ⓓ	56.	ⓐ	ⓑ	ⓒ	ⓓ	91.	ⓐ	ⓑ	ⓒ	ⓓ
22.	ⓐ	ⓑ	ⓒ	ⓓ	57.	ⓐ	ⓑ	ⓒ	ⓓ	92.	ⓐ	ⓑ	ⓒ	ⓓ
23.	ⓐ	ⓑ	ⓒ	ⓓ	58.	ⓐ	ⓑ	ⓒ	ⓓ	93.	ⓐ	ⓑ	ⓒ	ⓓ
24.	ⓐ	ⓑ	ⓒ	ⓓ	59.	ⓐ	ⓑ	ⓒ	ⓓ	94.	ⓐ	ⓑ	ⓒ	ⓓ
25.	ⓐ	ⓑ	ⓒ	ⓓ	60.	ⓐ	ⓑ	ⓒ	ⓓ	95.	ⓐ	ⓑ	ⓒ	ⓓ
26.	ⓐ	ⓑ	ⓒ	ⓓ	61.	ⓐ	ⓑ	ⓒ	ⓓ	96.	ⓐ	ⓑ	ⓒ	ⓓ
27.	ⓐ	ⓑ	ⓒ	ⓓ	62.	ⓐ	ⓑ	ⓒ	ⓓ	97.	ⓐ	ⓑ	ⓒ	ⓓ
28.	ⓐ	ⓑ	ⓒ	ⓓ	63.	ⓐ	ⓑ	ⓒ	ⓓ	98.	ⓐ	ⓑ	ⓒ	ⓓ
29.	ⓐ	ⓑ	ⓒ	ⓓ	64.	ⓐ	ⓑ	ⓒ	ⓓ	99.	ⓐ	ⓑ	ⓒ	ⓓ
30.	ⓐ	ⓑ	ⓒ	ⓓ	65.	ⓐ	ⓑ	ⓒ	ⓓ	100.	ⓐ	ⓑ	ⓒ	ⓓ
31.	ⓐ	ⓑ	ⓒ	ⓓ	66.	ⓐ	ⓑ	ⓒ	ⓓ					
32.	ⓐ	ⓑ	ⓒ	ⓓ	67.	ⓐ	ⓑ	ⓒ	ⓓ					
33.	ⓐ	ⓑ	ⓒ	ⓓ	68.	ⓐ	ⓑ	ⓒ	ⓓ					
34.	ⓐ	ⓑ	ⓒ	ⓓ	69.	ⓐ	ⓑ	ⓒ	ⓓ					
35.	ⓐ	ⓑ	ⓒ	ⓓ	70.	ⓐ	ⓑ	ⓒ	ⓓ					

▶ State Trooper Practice Test 4

Directions: Read the following passage, then answer questions 1 through 10.

The Advisory Committee of the State Police has issued the following guidelines for establishing a roadblock in order to identify and apprehend drunk drivers:

Selecting the location. The roadblock must be established in a location that affords motorists a clear view of the stop. It cannot be established, for example, just over a hill or around a curve. Motorists must be able to see that a roadblock is ahead and that cars are being stopped.

Staffing the location. A roadblock must display visible signs of police authority. Therefore, uniformed officers in marked patrol cars should primarily staff the roadblock. Plainclothes officers may supplement the staff at the roadblock, but the initial stop and questioning of motorists should be conducted by uniformed officers. In addition to the officers conducting the motorist stops, officers should be present to conduct field sobriety tests on suspect drivers. A command observation officer must also be present to coordinate the roadblock.

Operation of the roadblock. All cars passing through the roadblock must be stopped. It should not appear to an approaching motorist that cars are being singled out for some reason while others are not stopped, as this will generate unnecessary fear on the part of the motorist. The observation vehicle that is present at the roadblock will be able to pursue any motorists who refuse to stop.

Questioning the drivers. Each motorist stopped by the roadblock should be questioned only briefly. In most cases, an officer should ask directly if the driver has been drinking. In suspicious cases, an officer may engage in some further questioning to evaluate the driver's sobriety. A driver who appears to have been drinking should be directed to the side of the road, out of the line of traffic, where other officers may conduct a field sobriety test. Each non-suspicious driver should be stopped only briefly, for approximately a minute or less.

Duration of operation. No drunk-driving roadblock should be in operation for more than two hours. Roadblocks in place for longer periods lose their effectiveness as word spreads as to location of the roadblock, and motorists who have been drinking will avoid the area. In addition, on average only about 1% of all the drivers who pass through a roadblock will be arrested for drunk driving, and, after a short period of time, officers can be used more efficiently elsewhere.

Charges other than drunk driving. A roadblock may only be established for a single purpose—in this case, detecting drunk drivers—and should not be seen as an opportunity to check for a variety of motorist offenses. However, officers are not required to ignore what is plainly obvious. For example, motorists and passengers who are not wearing seat belts should be verbally warned that failure to do so is against the law. Detaining and ticketing such drivers is not the purpose of the roadblock and would unduly slow down the stops of other cars. An officer who spots a situation that presents a clear and present danger should follow through by directing the motorist to the side of the road where the officers are conducting field sobriety tests. These officers can then follow through on investigating the driver for crimes other than drunk driving.

1. According to the roadblock guidelines, officers must be sure they set up a drunk-driving roadblock that
   a. can be seen by motorists from a distance.
   b. provides a well hidden place for officers to park their cars.
   c. is near a bar or tavern.
   d. is near a busy street or highway.

2. While questioning motorists at a drunk-driving roadblock, Officer Firth notices that, although the driver of a particular car seems sober, the passenger in that car seems extremely nervous and has bruises on his face. She asks the passenger if he is all right, and after glancing at the driver, the passenger nods "yes." According to the guidelines, Officer Firth should
   a. let the car pass because the driver is not drunk.
   b. question the passenger and the driver further about the passenger's condition.
   c. arrest the driver on suspicion of assault.
   d. direct the driver to pull to the side of the road where other officers can investigate further.

3. Officers have been conducting a drunk-driving roadblock since 7:00 P.M. and have made 35 drunk-driving arrests, which is one-quarter of all cars stopped. It is now 9:00 P.M. According to the guidelines, the officers should
   a. continue the roadblock because they are making a high percentage of arrests.
   b. reestablish the roadblock one-quarter mile down the road.
   c. ask the Advisory Committee for permission to operate the roadblock longer.
   d. dismantle the roadblock, because it has been in operation for two hours.

4. Officers have been directed to operate a drunk-driving roadblock from 6:00 P.M. to 8:00 P.M. at the corner of Greene and First. At 6:45, the unusually heavy traffic begins to back up. According to the guidelines, the officers should NOT
   a. dismantle the roadblock early.
   b. begin stopping only every third car.
   c. move the roadblock to a quieter intersection.
   d. ask for extra officers to help staff the roadblock.

5. According to the guidelines, the officers stopping and questioning motorists at a drunk-driving roadblock should be in uniform so that motorists
   a. will take the roadblock more seriously.
   b. will answer their questions more truthfully.
   c. can identify which agency they are from.
   d. can tell from a distance that this is an official activity.

6. Officer Robb is stopping and questioning eastbound cars at the drunk-driving roadblock on Highway 7. He asks one driver if she has been drinking. The driver says, "No, Officer, I haven't," but she slurs her words. According to the guidelines, Officer Robb should
   a. ask the driver a few more questions.
   b. arrest the driver for drunk driving.
   c. ask the driver to take a field sobriety test.
   d. pass the driver through with a warning.

7. A car approaching a drunk-driving roadblock slows downs, then at the last minute speeds up and passes through the roadblock without stopping. According to the guidelines,
   a. officers should note the car's license number and radio headquarters.
   b. the officers should request backup to pursue the car.
   c. the officer in the command observation vehicle should pursue the motorist.
   d. the officers conducting field sobriety tests should pursue the vehicle.

8. Based on the guidelines, which of the following statements is true?
   a. Guidelines for drunk-driving roadblocks are determined by the State Police.
   b. Guidelines for drunk-driving roadblocks are determined by local police departments.
   c. Guidelines for drunk-driving roadblocks are determined by the state legislature.
   d. Guidelines for drunk-driving roadblocks are determined by the county sheriff.

9. According to the guidelines, officers operating a drunk-driving roadblock can expect
   a. cooperation from most drivers.
   b. to arrest only about 1% of the drivers stopped.
   c. to issue several tickets for failure to wear a seat belt.
   d. that many cars will refuse to stop.

10. According to the guidelines, the main role of the command observation officer at a drunk-driving roadblock is to
    a. conduct field sobriety tests.
    b. establish the official police presence.
    c. determine when to dismantle the roadblock.
    d. coordinate the roadblock.

Directions: Read the following passage, then answer questions 11 through 15.

At 9:20 A.M., Officers Torres and Verona investigated a burglary at 212 Hawkins Drive, Apartment 2107. Robert Larkin reported that he left for work at 10 P.M. and returned at 8:15 A.M. to find his television, VCR, CD player, and several CDs missing. After calling the police, he reported hearing music coming through the ceiling and stated that he suspected his upstairs neighbor, Lawrence Cole, who lives in Apartment 3107. Mr. Larkin stated that Mr. Cole had a key to Mr. Larkin's apartment and that there was no sign of forced entry.

Further, he said that Mr. Cole had not previously owned a CD player. Mr. Larkin reported that the two had recently had a falling out. The officers questioned Mr. Cole, who claimed that he had been at the apartment of his girlfriend, Teresa Romero, 210 Hawkins Drive, Apartment 3112, from 9:30 P.M. until 8:30 A.M. Ms. Romero confirmed this. Mr. Larkin could not produce receipts for the merchandise in question, save for the CD player. The receipt supported Mr. Larkin's claim that he purchased the CD player from his neighbor, Irene Franklin, in Apartment 3218. The serial numbers on the CD player were filed off. Ms. Franklin could not be located, and the officers decided to investigate further.

11. Who reported the crime?
    a. Robert Larkin
    b. Lawrence Cole
    c. Irene Franklin
    d. Teresa Romero

12. Where does the suspect's girlfriend live?
    a. 212 Hawkins Drive, Apartment 3107
    b. 212 Hawkins Drive, Apartment 3218
    c. 210 Hawkins Drive, Apartment 3218
    d. 210 Hawkins Drive, Apartment 3112

13. Who failed to produce a receipt for the VCR?
    a. Mr. Larkin
    b. Ms. Franklin
    c. Ms. Romero
    d. Mr. Cole

14. Who may have been in possession of stolen merchandise?
    a. only the victim
    b. only the suspect and the neighbor
    c. only the neighbor
    d. the suspect, the victim, and the neighbor

15. When did the burglary take place?
   a. approximately 9:20 A.M.
   b. between 8:15 P.M. and 9:20 A.M.
   c. approximately 9:30 P.M.
   d. between 10:00 P.M. and 8:15 A.M.

Directions: Read the following passage, then answer questions 16 through 20.

According to the National Highway and Traffic Safety Administration, more than 40,000 members of the general population of the United States lost their lives in traffic-related fatalities in 2004. The investigation of traffic collisions is an important part of a state trooper's job. Any information obtained during these investigations helps law enforcement, traffic engineering, and driver education personnel in making roadways safer places to travel.

A state trooper should arrive at the collision scene promptly to identify and aid any injured parties and prevent traffic congestion or secondary collisions. In addition, getting to the scene quickly will enable a state trooper to identify witnesses.

Use of emergency signaling equipment while responding is authorized if injuries are known to exist and the extents of the injuries are not known, or if it is unknown if injuries exist (a "no detail" collision).

The collision investigation begins as a state trooper approaches the collision scene. He or she should note any conditions that may have contributed to the collision, such as:

- reduced visibility
- obstructed views
- hazards in the roadway
- malfunctioning traffic control devices
- roadway construction
- weather conditions
- unusually narrow lane widths
- unusual roadway surface conditions

If a hit-and-run collision has occurred, responding state troopers should be alert for suspicious or damaged vehicles leaving the area. If such a vehicle is observed, the state trooper assigned to respond to the scene should continue the response and notify other responding units of the vehicle's description, direction of travel, number of occupants, rate of speed, and any other information that could aid these other officers in stopping that vehicle for questioning.

When en route to any collision scene, a state trooper should obtain the following information from the dispatcher:

- exact location of the collision
- whether medical help has been dispatched
- existence and extent of any injuries

This information is vital to making intelligent decisions governing the response to the scene.

Upon arriving at a collision scene, the state trooper should do the following:

1. Have all drivers move all vehicles not in need of a tow truck out of the roadway.
2. Position the patrol car behind disabled vehicles to keep other traffic from becoming involved.
3. Turn on emergency lights so other traffic is warned of the problem.
4. Call tow trucks if needed.
5. Put on reflective traffic vest if traffic direction becomes necessary.
6. Have the drivers, passengers, and witnesses step out of the roadway.
7. Collect information from drivers, passengers, and witnesses.

16. According to the passage, which is NOT a reason that a state trooper should arrive at the collision scene in a prompt manner?
   a. to aid any injured people
   b. to prevent involved parties from leaving the scene
   c. to help prevent additional car accidents
   d. to locate witnesses

17. What is a "no detail" collision?
   a. a collision in which it is unknown if injuries exist
   b. a collision in which it is unknown how many parties are involved
   c. a collision in which it is unknown how many vehicles are involved
   d. a collision in which it is unknown where the collision occurred

18. When heading to a collision scene, what information is NOT necessary for a state trooper to obtain from the dispatcher?
   a. that the vehicle driver has a concussion
   b. the cross streets of the accident
   c. that the vehicle driver has a suspended license
   d. that the EMT has been dispatched to the scene

19. According to the passage, as a state trooper approaches a collision scene, he or she should note
   a. local businesses.
   b. functioning traffic control devices.
   c. construction zones.
   d. parked cars.

20. Officer Gallagher has been dispatched to a four-car collision at Maple and Walnut. When he arrives, he notices that all four cars are in the same lane of traffic and have apparently run into each other. What is the first thing he should do?
   a. Call for four tow trucks to be sent to his location.
   b. Have the drivers move all drivable cars into a nearby parking lot.
   c. Put on his reflective vest.
   d. Collect information from all drivers, passengers, and witnesses.

Directions: For questions 21 through 25, choose the answer choice that best rephrases the underlined portion of the given sentence.

21. Cats make wonderful <u>pets even though they</u> seem closer to being wild than dogs are.
   a. pets, even though, they
   b. pets, even though they
   c. pets. Even though they
   d. pets; even though they

22. Many people believe in <u>UFO's however I've</u> never seen one.
   a. UFO's however: I've
   b. UFO's, however, I've
   c. UFO's however, I've
   d. UFO's; however, I've

23. "Am I <u>crazy," asked Samantha, "Am I</u> the only one who thinks volleyball is a waste of time?"
   a. crazy?" asked Samantha. "Am
   b. crazy?" asked Samantha, "Am
   c. crazy," asked Samantha? "Am
   d. crazy?" asked Samantha, "Am

24. Some scientists <u>maintain: that we</u> are born with a fear of snakes.
a. maintain, that we
b. maintain that, we
c. maintain that we
d. maintain—that we

25. After the dog frightened the mail <u>carrier, the dogs</u> owner apologized over and over.
a. carrier the dogs
b. carrier, the dog's
c. carrier, the dogs'
d. carrier the dogs'

26. Look at the four numbered sentences below. Choose the sentence order that would result in the best paragraph.
(1) If there are expenses incurred, complete report form 103; if there was damage to equipment, complete form 107.
(2) If form 107 and form 103 are required, complete form 122 also.
(3) Log on to the computer and go to the directory that contains the report forms.
(4) As an employee, you must complete all paperwork.
a. 3, 2, 1, 4
b. 1, 3, 4, 2
c. 2, 1, 4, 3
d. 4, 3, 1, 2

27. Look at the three numbered sentences below. Choose the sentence order that would result in the best paragraph.
(1) In some areas, the salt is combined with calcium chloride, which is more effective in below-zero temperatures and which melts ice better.
(2) After a snow- or icefall, city streets are treated with ordinary rock salt.
(3) This combination of salt and calcium chloride is also less damaging to foliage along the roadways.
a. 2, 1, 3
b. 1, 3, 2
c. 3, 2, 1
d. 2, 3, 1

28. Look at the four numbered sentences below. Choose the sentence order that would result in the best paragraph.
(1) Yet the human brain is the most mysterious and complex object on earth.
(2) It has created poetry and music, planned and executed horrific wars, devised intricate scientific theories.
(3) It thinks and dreams, plots and schemes, and easily holds more information than all the libraries on earth.
(4) It weighs less than three pounds and is hardly more interesting to look at than an overly ripe cauliflower.
a. 1, 3, 4, 2
b. 2, 1, 4, 3
c. 3, 1, 2, 4
d. 4, 1, 2, 3

29. Look at the four numbered sentences below. Choose the sentence order that would result in the best paragraph.

(1) Before you begin to compose a business letter, sit down and think about your purpose in writing the letter.

(2) Do you want to request information, order a product, register a complaint, or apply for something?

(3) Always keep your objective in mind.

(4) Do some brainstorming and gather information before you begin writing.

    a. 4, 3, 2, 1

    b. 2, 4, 3, 1

    c. 1, 2, 4, 3

    d. 3, 2, 1, 4

30. Choose the sentence that expresses the idea most clearly and correctly.

    a. Dr. Richard K Brown, CEO of the company, will speak to the scientists at Brookhaven National Laboratory on Wed at 9:00 A.M.

    b. Dr Richard K Brown, CEO of the company, will speak to the scientists at the Brookhaven National Laboratory on Wed. at 9:00 A.M.

    c. Dr. Richard K. Brown, CEO of the company, will speak to the scientists at the Brookhaven National Laboratory on Wed. at 9:00 A.M.

    d. Dr. Richard K. Brown, CEO of the company, will speak to the scientists at the Brookhaven National Laboratory on Wed at 9:00 A.M.

31. Choose the sentence that expresses the idea most clearly and correctly.

    a. As soon she realized that the hurricane was going to strike, the mayor told the residents to evacuate the city.

    b. As soon she realized that the hurricane was going to strike, the city residents were told to evacuate by the mayor.

    c. As soon she realized that the hurricane was going to strike, the mayor tells the city residents of her decision to evacuate.

    d. As soon she realized that the hurricane was going to strike, the residents of the city were told to evacuate by the mayor.

32. Choose the sentence that expresses the idea most clearly and correctly.

    a. A sharpshooter for many years, a pea could be shot off a person's shoulder from 70 yards away by Miles Johnson.

    b. A sharpshooter for many years, Miles Johnson could shoot a pea off a person's shoulder from 70 yards away.

    c. A sharpshooter for many years, from 70 yards away off a person's shoulder Miles Johnson could have shot a pea.

    d. A sharpshooter for many years, Miles Johnson could shoot from 70 yards away off a person's shoulder a pea.

33. Choose the sentence that expresses the idea most clearly and correctly.
   a. By the time they are in the third or fourth grade, the eyes of most children in the United States are tested.
   b. Most children by the time they are in the United States have their eyes tested in the third or fourth grade.
   c. Most children in the United States have their eyes tested by the time they are in the third or fourth grade.
   d. In the United States by the time of third or fourth grade, there is testing of the eyes of most children.

34. Choose the sentence that expresses the idea most clearly and correctly.
   a. Recession, as well as budget cuts, is hard on the cop on the beat.
   b. Recession and budget cuts is hard on the cop on the beat.
   c. Recession, as well as budget cuts, are hard on the cop on the beat.
   d. Budget cuts, as well as the recession, is hard on the cop on the beat.

Directions: For questions 35 through 37, choose the sentence that best combines the two sentences.

35. Recently there have been government cutbacks in funds. Experts foresee steady hiring in the government's future.
   a. Despite recent government cutbacks in funds, experts foresee steady hiring in the government's future.
   b. Whereupon recent government cutbacks in funds, experts foresee steady hiring in the government's future.
   c. So that there have been recent government cutbacks in funds, experts foresee steady hiring in the government's future.
   d. Nonetheless there have been recent government cutbacks in funds, experts foresee steady hiring in the government's future.

36. The federal government has diversity of jobs and geographic locations. The federal government offers flexibility in job opportunities that is unmatched in the private sector.
   a. In spite of its diversity of jobs and geographic locations, the federal government offers flexibility in job opportunities that is unmatched in the private sector.
   b. No matter its diversity of jobs and geographic locations, the federal government offers flexibility in job opportunities that is unmatched in the private sector.
   c. Because of its diversity of jobs and geographic locations, the federal government offers flexibility in job opportunities that is unmatched in the private sector.
   d. The federal government has diversity of jobs and geographic locations, so it offers flexibility in job opportunities that is unmatched in the private sector.

37. There have been great strides in the practical application of quantum physics in the last decade. We are no closer to actually understanding it than were the physicists of the 1920s.

   a. Unless there have been great strides in the practical application of quantum physics in the last few decades, we are no closer to actually understanding it than were the physicists of the 1920s.

   b. In the last few decades, we are no closer to actually understanding it than were the physicists of the 1920s, until there have been great strides in the practical application of quantum physics.

   c. Although there have been great strides in the practical application of quantum physics in the last few decades, we are no closer to actually understanding it than were the physicists of the 1920s.

   d. In the last few decades, if there have been great strides in the practical application of quantum physics we are no closer to actually understanding it than were the physicists of the 1920s.

Directions: For questions 38 through 40, fill in the blank with the word that creates the most logical sentence.

38. _____ strip mining is the cheapest method of mining, it is often harmful to the environment.

   a. Besides

   b. Unless

   c. Nevertheless

   d. Although

39. Joelle's favorite beverages are herb tea and mineral water. Chelsea, _____, drinks only milk or juice.

   a. however

   b. therefore

   c. then

   d. too

40. Sandra Day O'Connor, the first woman to serve on the United States Supreme Court, _____ appointed by President Ronald Reagan in 1981.

   a. she

   b. and

   c. but

   d. was

41. During a race, markers will be placed along a roadway at regular 0.2-mile intervals. If the entire roadway is 10,560 feet long, how many such markers will be used?

   a. 10

   b. 100

   c. 20

   d. 200

42. If the ratio of union workers to nonunion workers is 2:3 and there are 360 nonunion workers, how many workers are there in all?

   a. 240

   b. 360

   c. 600

   d. 720

43. An elevator sign reads "Maximum weight 600 pounds." Which of the following may ride the elevator?
   a. three people: one weighing 198 pounds, one weighing 185 pounds, one weighing 200 pounds
   b. one person weighing 142 pounds with a load weighing 500 pounds
   c. one person weighing 165 pounds with a load weighing 503 pounds
   d. three people: one weighing 210 pounds, one weighing 101 pounds, one weighing 298 pounds

44. Kira's register contains 10 twenty-dollar bills, 3 five-dollar bills, 98 one-dollar bills, 88 quarters, 52 dimes, 200 nickels, and 125 pennies. How much money is in the register?
   a. $351.45
   b. $351.20
   c. $350
   d. $345.51

45. A work crew paves a 120-yard section of road in four hours. If each crew member works at the rate of 10 yards per hour, how many people are working?
   a. 3
   b. 4
   c. 12
   d. 36

46. Two times a number is the result when 7 times a number is taken away from 99. What is the number?
   a. 85
   b. 11
   c. 46
   d. 9

47. When Anthony and Dave work together, they can complete a task in 3 hours. When Anthony works alone, he can complete the same task in 8 hours. How long would it take for Dave to complete the task alone?
   a. $6\frac{1}{2}$ hours
   b. 6 hours
   c. $4\frac{4}{5}$ hours
   d. 4 hours

48. Denise had $120. She gave $\frac{1}{8}$ of this amount to Suzanne. She then gave $\frac{1}{4}$ of the remainder to Darlene. How much money does Denise have left?
   a. $26.25
   b. $30
   c. $78.75
   d. $80

49. Officer Jozwiak has made a vow to jog five days a week for an average of one hour daily. He cut his workout short on Wednesday by 40 minutes but was able to make up 20 minutes on Thursday and 13 minutes on Friday. How many minutes of jogging did Officer Jozwiak lose for the week?
   a. 3 minutes
   b. 7 minutes
   c. 13 minutes
   d. 20 minutes

50. If Martin exchanges 120 quarters, 300 dimes, 600 nickels, and 500 pennies for bills, he may get
   a. 4 twenty-dollar bills, 2 ten-dollar bills, and 1 five-dollar bill.
   b. 3 twenty-dollar bills, 1 ten-dollar bill, and 1 five-dollar bill.
   c. 2 fifty-dollar bills and 1 twenty-dollar bill.
   d. 1 fifty-dollar bills, 2 twenty-dollar bills, and 1 five-dollar bill.

51. Pete made $4,000 in January, $3,500 in February, and $4,500 in March. If he put 30% of his total earnings into his savings account and the rest into his checking account, how much money does he have in his savings account?
   a. $3,600
   b. $4,200
   c. $6,300
   d. $8,400

52. A police precinct is purchasing 5 computer monitors at $175 each, 3 printers at $120 each, and 8 surge suppressors at $18 each. If the precinct receives a 12% discount, what is the final cost (excluding tax)?
   a. $1,379
   b. $1,313.52
   c. $1,213.52
   d. $1,200

53. A map drawn to scale shows that the distance between two towns is 31 inches. If the scale is such that 1 inch equals 1.5 km, how far away are the two towns in kilometers?
   a. 15.5 km
   b. 31 km
   c. 46.5 km
   d. 47 km

54. If Michael runs at a constant rate of 2.5 meters per second, how long will it take him to run 1 kilometer?
   a. 4 minutes
   b. 40 minutes
   c. 400 seconds
   d. 4,000 seconds

55. Amy can run 8 miles at a constant rate in 40 minutes. Sharon can run 12 miles at a constant rate in an hour. Who has a faster rate?
   a. Amy
   b. Sharon
   c. They both run at the same rate.
   d. It cannot be determined by the information given.

56. Your unit is driving west on the interstate and makes a right to turn onto Lake Street. A fallen tree branch on Lake Street forces your unit to make a left onto Littlefield Road. What direction is your unit now traveling?
   a. north
   b. south
   c. east
   d. west

57. State Trooper Rudy Levin is driving north on Main Street when he makes a left turn. If he makes a second left turn, what direction will he be heading?
   a. north
   b. south
   c. east
   d. west

58. Your unit is driving east, makes a left turn, then makes a right turn. What direction is your unit heading now?
   a. north
   b. south
   c. east
   d. west

Directions: Answer the following questions based on the map below. The arrows indicate traffic flow. One arrow indicates a one-way street going in the direction of the arrow; two arrows represent a two-way street. You are not allowed to go the wrong way on a one-way street.

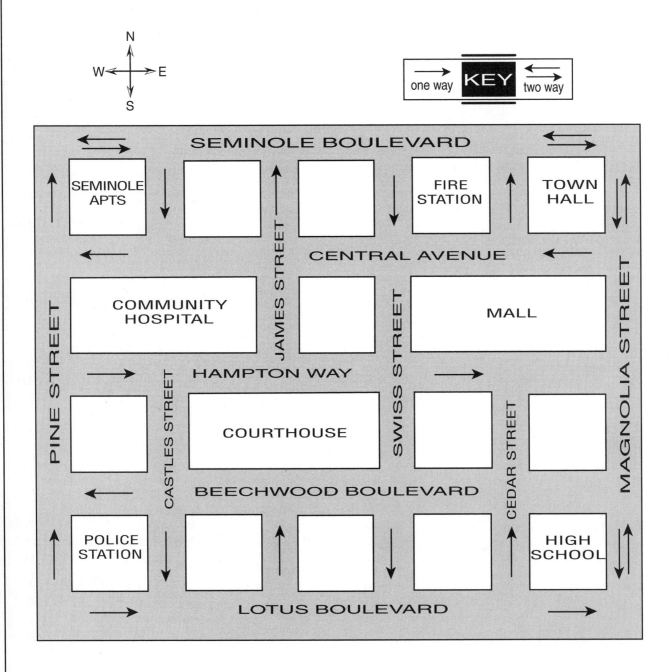

59. You are driving north on Pine Street at Central Avenue and need to pick up a friend at the south entrance of the mall. How many turns will you make, taking the most direct legal route?

   a. 3

   b. 4

   c. 5

   d. 6

60. State Trooper DeSiervo has just come off duty and is driving west on Central Avenue. He makes a right onto James Avenue, then a left onto Seminole Boulevard, then a left onto Castles Street. What direction is he facing?

   a. east

   b. south

   c. west

   d. north

61. Your unit is southbound on Magnolia Street and has just crossed Hampton Way, when a call comes in about a domestic disturbance at the Seminole Apartments. What is the quickest route for your unit to take to the incident?

   a. Keep driving south, turn west onto Lotus Boulevard, turn north onto Pine Street, and turn east onto Seminole Boulevard.

   b. Keep driving south, turn west onto Beechwood Boulevard, turn north onto Pine Street, and turn east onto Seminole Boulevard.

   c. Keep driving south. Turn west onto Beechwood Boulevard, turn north onto Cedar Street, and west onto Hampton Way.

   d. Keep driving south, turn west onto Beechwood Boulevard, turn north onto Swiss Street, and turn west onto Seminole Boulevard.

Directions: Answer the following questions based on the map below.

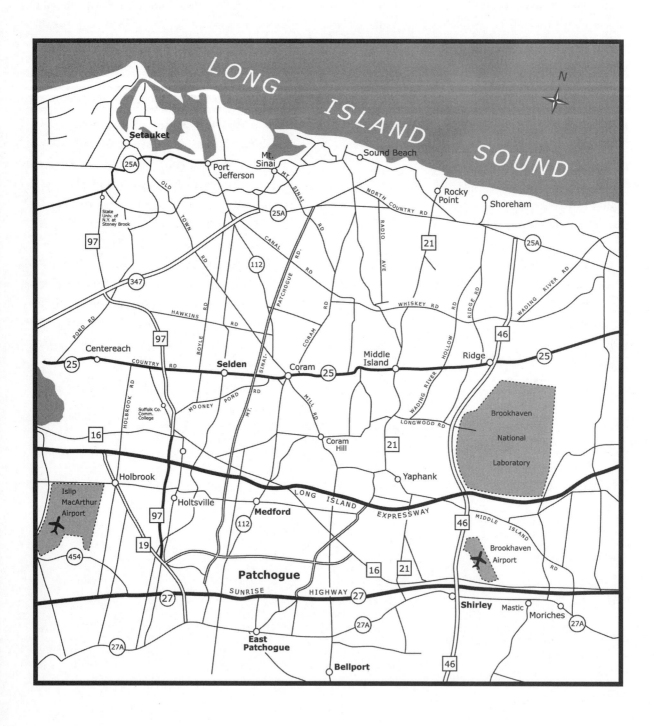

62. The town of Port Jefferson is _____ of the town of Medford.
a. northwest
b. northeast
c. southwest
d. southeast

63. Three towns that are located along a major east/west highway are
a. Holtsville, Medford, and Selden.
b. Selden, Coram, and Middle Island.
c. Coram, Yaphank, and Shirley.
d. Bellport, Shirley, and Coram.

64. You received instructions to drive from East Patchogue to Shirley. The roadway that seems to provide the most direct route is
a. Route 27.
b. Route 27A.
c. the Sunrise Highway.
d. Route 46.

65. What is the one local roadway that leads into the Brookhaven National Laboratory?
a. Ridge Road
b. Route 25
c. Route 46
d. Longwood Road

66. The direction of the drive from Islip MacArthur Airport to Brookhaven National Laboratory is _____ .
a. northwest
b. northeast
c. southwest
d. southeast

67. The most direct route to travel from the State University of New York at Stony Brook to Suffolk County Community College is via
a. Pond Road.
b. Mooney Pond Road.
c. Route 97.
d. Stony Brook Road.

Directions: Answer the following questions based on the map below. The arrows indicate traffic flow. One arrow indicates a one-way street going in the direction of the arrow; two arrows represent a two-way street. You are not allowed to go the wrong way on a one-way street.

68. Officer Harolds is sitting at a red light at the intersection of Fourth Street and Washington Road facing southbound. The dispatcher sends him on a one-vehicle collision call. A motorist has run into the northwest corner of the City Hall building. What is the quickest route for Officer Harolds to take to City Hall?

a. Turn west onto Washington Road, then south on Third Street, and then west on Main Street to Parker Road.

b. Turn west onto Washington Road, then south onto Parker Road.

c. Turn west onto Washington Road, south onto Second Street, and then east onto Main Street to Parker Road.

d. Turn west onto Washington Road, then south onto Parker Road, and then east onto Main Street.

69. Officer Watson is driving eastbound on Main Street at Fourth Street. If he makes a U-turn on Main Street, turns onto Third Street, and then makes another U-turn, what direction will he be facing?

a. east

b. west

c. north

d. south

70. On a rainy night, Officers Epps and Burton are dispatched to a burglar alarm at a business on Ash Road and Church Street. They are driving north on First Street and have just passed Washington Road. What is the quickest route they can take?

a. North on First Street, then west on River Road, then south on Parker Road, then east on McArthur Boulevard, then north on Church Street to Ash Road.

b. North on First Street, then east on River Road, then south on Third Street, then east on Main Street, then north on Church Street to Ash Road.

c. North on First Street, then east on River Road, then south on Church Street to Ash Road.

d. North on First Street, then west on River Road, then south on Parker Road, then east on Lincoln Avenue, then south on Second Street, then east on McArthur Boulevard, then north on Church Street to Ash Road.

Directions: You will have ten minutes to read and study the following passage. Then, answer questions 71 through 80 without referring back to the passage.

On Friday, May 12, Corrections Officer Todd Rodriguez reported to his new assignment in the visitors' room in the main building of Rockland Prison. Senior Corrections Officer Emma Ling was training him on the day shift. Officer Rodriguez had graduated from the academy just two months earlier. Besides Officer Ling, Officer Rodriguez would also be working with Officer Keisha White and Officer Jim Tuttle. They were veterans with three and four years of day shift experience, respectively.

At 8 A.M. sharp, Officer Rodriguez reported to duty. Officer Ling took Officer Rodriguez into the visitors' room and told him to familiarize himself with the layout of the room. He was introduced to Officers White and Tuttle. Ling told the officer that the room holds a maximum of 16 inmates at a time. One inmate and one visitor are to sit at one of the 16 metal tables. Each table has two metal chairs, one on each side of each table. All furnishings are bolted to the floor in the room. The concrete floor is painted white, except for a red line leading from the inner hallway that the inmates use to get to the visitors' room. The red line is painted 14 inches from the right-hand side of the wall and goes completely around the room to end up back

at the doorway. Officer Ling instructed Officer Rodriguez that all inmates are expected to walk along the red line to enter and exit the room. If they refuse to walk the line, their visiting privileges are immediately revoked. The walls are white and the ceiling is gray. There are no windows.

Officer Ling told Officer Rodriguez that he is responsible for doing a pat-down search of each inmate before allowing the inmate into the room. The visitors are all thoroughly searched before they are allowed to enter the room. After Officer Rodriguez pats the inmates down, he is to allow the visitors into the room. Each visitor is allowed a maximum of 30 minutes with the inmate. If the inmate has two visitors, one visitor must remain in the waiting room next door until it is his or her turn. No matter how many visitors come for an inmate, the inmate is allowed only one session of 30 minutes. At the end of this time period, the officer is to make sure the visitors stay seated while the inmates are escorted to the doorway leading back into the corridor. Officer Rodriguez is to do another pat-down search of each inmate before the inmate passes through the doorway and into the hall. After each inmate is searched and turned over to the escorting officer, Officer Rodriguez is to let the visitors know that they may exit the room.

71. What color is the line painted on the floor of the visitors' room?
a. beige
b. yellow
c. red
d. green

72. What is Officer Rodriguez's training officer's last name?
a. Lang
b. White
c. Tuttle
d. Ling

73. What is the maximum number of inmates allowed into the visitors' room at one time?
a. 15
b. 16
c. 14
d. 12

74. What time did Officer Rodriguez report for duty on his first day at his new assignment?
a. 8:00 A.M.
b. 7:30 A.M.
c. 7:00 A.M.
d. 6:45 A.M.

75. What should Officer Rodriguez instruct visitors to do while inmates are exiting the visitors' room?
a. exit by another door
b. remain seated until the inmates have left
c. stand by their chairs and wait to be searched
d. stand on the line on the floor until the inmates have left

76. How far from the wall is the painted line that the inmates are required to walk along?
a. 10 inches
b. 12 inches
c. 14 inches
d. 16 inches

77. What day of the week did Officer Rodriguez report to his new duty assignment?
a. Monday
b. Friday
c. Thursday
d. Wednesday

78. What kind of search is Officer Rodriguez required to conduct on each inmate?
a. strip
b. spread
c. pat-down
d. full-body

79. How long is a visitor permitted to see an inmate?
a. 15 minutes
b. 20 minutes
c. 25 minutes
d. 30 minutes

80. What color is the ceiling in the visitors' room?
a. gray
b. red
c. white
d. blue

Directions: Read the following passage, then answer questions 81 through 89.

Customs Inspector Ellen Mitchell noticed several boxes marked "Assorted hand-carved wooden figures from Cameroon," which were being unloaded from a United Express cargo plane. The boxes were sent from Mandara Exports, Ltd. to Freddy Jones Imports. Inspector Mitchell was suspicious of the shipment for several reasons. It was a large shipment, and she had never heard of Freddy Jones Import before; the boxes were triple-sealed; and Jones himself was there waiting to claim the boxes. Mitchell opened one of the crates and found figures carved of ivory. During the course of the investigation, the following statements were made.

1. Freddy Jones stated that he had ordered wooden figures and he had the invoice to prove it.
2. Margaret Woo, United Express employee, said she picked up this shipment from another plane in Madrid and looked only at the bill of lading, which indicated the crates contained hand-carved wooden figures from Cameroon. Her supervisor happened to be present at the pickup.
3. In Cameroon, Michelle Eseka, president of Mandara Exports, Ltd., stated she obtains the carved wooden figurines from several suppliers and cooperatives.
4. William Calabar, head of purchasing for Mandara Exports, said he has recently been dealing mostly with Francis Onitsha, a supplier from eastern Cameroon, for the wooden carvings.
5. Rosemary Ndele, Michelle Eseka's administrative assistant, said that William Calabar was a compulsive gambler.
6. Michelle Eseka said she had told Calabar not to deal with Onitsha, because Onitsha once asked her to send some contraband along with one of her regular shipments.

7. Kenneth Yokadouma, Michelle Eseka's banker, said that Mandara Exports had been losing money lately and that Eseka was in danger of losing the business.
8. A member of Women's Hands, a cooperative that carves figures and makes jewelry, said that Francis Onitsha asked them to do some ivory carvings.
9. Francis Onitsha said that Rosemary Ndele put Freddy Jones in touch with Mandara Exports.
10. Customs officials in Douala, Cameroon, said they had no record of this shipment.

81. Which statement is most damaging to Francis Onitsha?
a. Statement 6
b. Statement 8
c. Statement 2
d. Statement 4

82. Which statement appears to be an attempt by the speaker to establish innocence?
a. Statement 7
b. Statement 9
c. Statement 10
d. Statement 6

83. Which statement indicates that United Express employees knew nothing about the illegal shipment?
a. Statement 4
b. Statement 6
c. Statement 2
d. Statement 10

84. Which statement causes one to be suspicious of the information provided by Rosemary Ndele?
a. Statement 9
b. Statement 8
c. Statement 4
d. Statement 5

85. Which statement provides a motive for Michelle Eseka to make the illegal shipment?
- **a.** Statement 6
- **b.** Statement 8
- **c.** Statement 9
- **d.** Statement 7

86. Which two statements cast the greatest suspicion on William Calabar?
- **a.** Statements 3 and 4
- **b.** Statements 7 and 10
- **c.** Statements 5 and 6
- **d.** Statements 1 and 2

87. Which statement illustrates cooperation between U.S. and Cameroon law enforcement agencies?
- **a.** Statement 8
- **b.** Statement 3
- **c.** Statement 10
- **d.** Statement 7

88. Which statement implies Freddy Jones had knowledge of the illegal shipment?
- **a.** Statement 1
- **b.** Statement 9
- **c.** Statement 2
- **d.** Statement 10

89. Which two statements indicate the bill of lading may have been tampered with?
- **a.** Statements 2 and 10
- **b.** Statements 1 and 6
- **c.** Statements 3 and 9
- **d.** Statements 2 and 6

Directions: Read the following passage, then answer questions 90 through 96.

The president was scheduled to speak at the Civic Arena. There was no charge to attend the event, but audience members had to obtain a ticket beforehand in order to be admitted to the arena the day of the speech. One week before the event, the Secret Service arrived to finalize security plans. The next day, the box office at the arena received a letter containing a threat on the president's life. During the course of the investigation, the following statements were made.

1. Edna Thurber, box office manager, said that mail was always delivered into a locked box and only she and Bob White, the arena manager, had keys.
2. Randy Shoemaker, a box office employee, said the tickets were all distributed two weeks before the speech.
3. After examining the envelope in which the threat arrived, Police Officer Connie Hall noted that the stamp was not canceled.
4. Rita Lawe, a box office employee, said that several people had tried to obtain tickets in the last week; a short, thin, scruffy man had come to the box office several times.
5. Bob White said he knew for a fact that Edna Thurber had volunteered for a "get out the vote drive" in the last election.
6. Randy Shoemaker said that Rita Lawe was mad at the president because she was being harassed to repay her student loans.
7. Special Agent Maury Thurston said that several members of the public had spoken to him while he was examining the exterior of the arena. He remembered a thin man in a shabby raincoat who asked if there would be bomb-sniffing dogs.

8. Edna Thurber said that Alan Pip, Bob White's assistant, was always talking about how members of the government were also members of a satanic cult.

9. Bob White said that prior to getting the job managing the arena, he was in the military.

10. Alan Pip said that, last week when he went out on the loading dock to have a cigarette, he saw a man looking around the area. He said the man was thin and wearing a dirty sweatshirt.

90. Which statements, along with statement 4, indicate the threat was made by someone who does not work at the arena?
  a. Statements 3 and 6
  b. Statements 7 and 10
  c. Statements 1 and 5
  d. Statements 6 and 8

91. Which statement leads one to question the reliability of Alan Pip?
  a. Statement 1
  b. Statement 10
  c. Statement 3
  d. Statement 8

92. Which two statements are most damaging to Bob White?
  a. Statements 1 and 3
  b. Statements 5 and 9
  c. Statements 4 and 8
  d. Statements 2 and 10

93. Which statement is least damaging to Edna Thurber?
  a. Statement 8
  b. Statement 1
  c. Statement 5
  d. Statement 3

94. Which statement represents an idle threat?
  a. Statement 4
  b. Statement 6
  c. Statement 7
  d. Statement 9

95. Which two statements indicate cooperation between the Secret Service and local police?
  a. Statements 5 and 9
  b. Statements 1 and 3
  c. Statements 5 and 7
  d. Statements 3 and 7

96. Which statement is the least helpful in solving the case?
  a. Statement 8
  b. Statement 6
  c. Statement 5
  d. Statement 2

97. When an officer goes to a business to pick up a shoplifter who is already in the custody of private security guards, the officer should take the following steps in the order listed:

1. Check with store security personnel to verify that the circumstances fit the criteria for shoplifting.
2. Have store personnel fill out witness statements and a complaint form for shoplifting.
3. Take a photograph of the evidence, and return the evidence to the store.
4. Search the suspect for weapons or contraband.
5. Place the suspect in the patrol car and secure his or her seat belt.
6. Transport the suspect directly to jail.

Officer O'Brien is dispatched to the Blue Moon Art Gallery to pick up a shoplifter. When she arrives, she talks to Jeffrey, the store security guard, who tells her that he watched a man pick up a five-inch-long statue, stuff it in his coat pocket, and walk out the front door of the shop. He chased the man down and brought him back to the store. Jeffrey takes Officer O'Brien into the back room, where he gives her a photograph of the statue for her to turn in as evidence. Officer O'Brien searches the prisoner for weapons and then places him in the patrol car, seat belting him in securely. They drive straight to the jail where O'Brien books the suspect for shoplifting. Officer O'Brien's actions were

a. proper, because the incident was obviously a shoplifting.
b. improper, because she did not take the statue itself in as evidence.
c. proper, because the security guard watched the man carefully before accusing him of anything.
d. improper, because she did not have the guard fill out a witness statement or complaint form.

98. The police department is staking out a warehouse. Officer Walters is stationed north of Officer Smits. Officer Foster is stationed north of Officer Walters. Officer Balboa is stationed south of Officer Foster. Given these facts, which of the following statements is definitely true?

a. Officer Walters is the farthest north of all the officers.
b. Officer Balboa is the farthest south of all the officers.
c. Officer Smits is stationed south of Officer Foster.
d. Officer Balboa is stationed south of Officer Walters.

99. In many smaller police departments, the first officer to arrive at the scene of a homicide is often the same officer who will be responsible for taking photographs to preserve the scene. That officer should take the following steps in the order listed:

1. Make sure the crime scene is secure and assign another officer to be responsible for who comes in and out of the area.
2. Leave the crime scene as it is, not moving any objects or specific items of evidence until photos can be taken of the scene as it first appears to the officer.
3. Take a picture of the overall crime scene area, then take a more specific photo of the area where the body is, and then take photos of specific pieces of evidence.
4. After the first set of photographs is taken, shoot another set and put in an object such as a ruler that will give whoever looks at the pictures a sense of perspective.
5. Place the film in a container and write on the container the case number, the photographer's name and employee number, the date, and the location where the photographs were taken.
6. Take the film to the department photo lab to be developed.

Officer Scales received a call at 8:00 A.M. of a headless body found in a trash bin in an alley behind 4501 W. Thompson St. He arrives on scene and secures the area by having everyone step away from the trash bin and by assigning backup Officer Angel to keep onlookers away from the scene. He reaches inside the trash bin and moves a cardboard box so that he can see the body better. He steps back, takes an overall shot of the scene, then moves in closer and takes specific shots of the body and then of all items that appear to be potential evidence. He takes a second set of photographs of the scene using a ruler for a marker. He then places the film in an evidence container and writes the case number, his name and employee number, the date, and the location of where the photos were taken. He takes the film to the department photo lab. Based on the information in the passage, Officer Scales's actions were

a. improper, because he needed a flash unit given that the inside of the trash bin is dark.

b. improper, because he didn't witness the development of the film himself to protect the chain of evidence.

c. improper, because he moved the cardboard box before taking photographs of the scene as it first appeared.

d. proper, because he fulfilled all the duties as outlined in the procedures.

100. The police department files information on crimes by date committed. Baker robbed a bank before Mitchell assaulted a police officer, but after Nelson stole a car. Edgar burgled a warehouse before Nelson committed his crime. In what order do these files appear at the police department?
a. Nelson, Baker, Mitchell, Edgar
b. Edgar, Nelson, Baker, Mitchell
c. Baker, Mitchell, Edgar, Nelson
d. Edgar, Mitchell, Nelson, Baker

▶ Answers

1. a. The passage states, *Motorists must be able to see that a roadblock is ahead and that cars are being stopped.*

2. d. The passage states that *an officer who spots a situation that presents a clear and present danger should follow through by directing the motorist to the side of the road where the officers are conducting field sobriety tests. These officers can then follow through on investigating the driver for crimes other than drunk driving.*

3. d. According to the passage, *no drunk driving roadblock should be in operation for more than two hours.*

4. b. The passage notes that every car passing through a roadblock must be stopped; at no time should motorists feel that certain cars are being singled out.

5. c. The passage states that a roadblock should display visible signs of police authority, such as uniforms and marked patrol cars.

6. a. The passage says that *in suspicious cases, an officer may engage in some further questioning to allow him or her to evaluate the driver's sobriety.*

7. c. The passage states that the observation vehicle *will be able to pursue any motorists that refuse to stop.*

8. a. According to the selection, the guidelines are issued by the Advisory Committee of the State Police.

9. b. The passage notes that *on average only about 1% of all the drivers who pass through a roadblock will be arrested for drunk driving.*

10. d. The passage states that a command observation officer *must . . . be present to coordinate the roadblock.*

11. a. Robert Larkin called the police to report that his television, VCR, CD player, and several CDs were missing.

12. d. Ms. Romero lives at 210 Hawkins Drive, Apartment 3112.

13. a. Mr. Larkin, the victim, is the one who could not produce receipts for the stolen merchandise.

14. d. Clearly Mr. Cole, the suspect, may have stolen merchandise. However, because the serial numbers have been filed off the CD player and there is no way of knowing when this occurred, it is possible that it was stolen property when both Ms. Franklin, the neighbor, and Mr. Larkin, the victim, were in possession of it. The officers cannot know whether Ms. Franklin did indeed have possession of the merchandise and where it came from without further investigation.

15. d. The burglary took place while Mr. Larkin was at work from 10:00 P.M. to 8:15 A.M.

16. b. The passage never states that an officer should arrive at a collision scene quickly to prevent individuals from fleeing the scene.

17. a. According to the passage, a "no detail" collision is one in which it is unknown if injuries exist.

18. c. A dispatcher does not need to tell a state trooper that the vehicle driver has a suspended license. All the other answer choices contain vital information.

19. c. The state trooper should note any conditions that may have contributed to the collision, including roadway construction. Choice **b** would be correct if it was *malfunctioning* traffic control devices.

20. b. The first step in the procedure is to move all drivable vehicles, and that should be Officer Gallagher's first move.

21. b. The comma separates the main clause from the long, descriptive subordinate clause.

22. d. The semicolon can be used to separate two main clauses, which could each stand alone as complete sentences.

23. a. The quotation is a question, and the tag *asked Samantha* ends the sentence.

24. c. No puncuation is needed before or after the word *that* in this sentence.

25. b. The word *dog's* is possessive and needs an apostrophe; the comma is optional.

26. d. Sentence 4 sets the reader up to expect a discussion of a procedure, the writing of reports of a fire. Sentence 3 tells how you can find the right report forms. Sentence 1 leads logically into sentence 2.

27. a. Sentence 2 is the topic sentence. Sentence 1 provides reasons for the procedure described in the topic sentence. Sentence 3 gives further definition as a conclusion.

28. d. The word *Yet* at the beginning of sentence 1 is a clue that this is not the beginning sentence. Sentences 4 and 1 are the only ones that logically follow each other, so the other choices can be ruled out.

29. c. Sentence 1 is the topic sentence and states the general situation. Sentence 2 poses a question about the situation in the topic sentence. Sentence 4 offers the response. Sentence 3 concludes the paragraph as it gives a reminder about the original goal.

30. c. Periods are correctly placed after all abbreviations in this sentence.

31. a. This choice is clear, has no misplaced modifiers, and has no shifts in verb tense. Choices **b** and **d** have misplaced modifiers and result in unclear sentences; choice **c** has an unnecessary shift from past to present tense.

32. b. This is the only choice that does not have a misplaced modifier. Because Miles Johnson is the sharpshooter, his name should be placed immediately after the introductory phrase, which rules out choices **a** and **c**. Choice **d** is awkwardly constructed and unclear.

33. c. This is the only choice that is clear and logical. Choice **a** reads as though the eyes are in the third or fourth grade. Choices **b** and **d** are unclear.

34. a. The subject *recession* agrees in number with its verb *is*; in the other choices, the subjects and verbs do not agree.

35. a. The word *despite* establishes a logical connection between the main and subordinate clauses. *Whereupon* and *so that* (choices **b** and **c**) make no sense. Choice **d** is both illogical and ungrammatical.

36. c. The subordinator *because* in choice **c** establishes the logical causal relationship between subordinate and main clauses; choices **a** and **b** do not make sense. Choice **d** has faulty construction.

37. c. The subordinator *although* shows a logical contrasting relationship between subordinate and main clause. The other choices do not make sense.

38. d. *Although* means "despite the fact that" or "even though." Even though strip mining is cheap, it is harmful. The other choices do not convey this meaning.

39. a. *However* indicates an impending contradiction; it is the best choice because the two clauses compare tastes. In this case, the comparison contrasts Joelle's preference to Chelsea's.

40. d. This is the only choice that results in a complete and logical sentence. Choice **a** is illogical; choices **b** and **c** result in sentence fragments.

41. a. 5,280 feet = 1 mile, so 10,560 feet = 2 miles. To solve, divide the total 2 mile distance by the interval, 0.2 miles: $2 \div 0.2 = 10$.

42. c. Here, you are given a 2:3 ratio. You know one part: There are 360 nonunion workers. You can set up a proportion in order to calculate the unknown part: $\frac{2}{3} = \frac{?}{360}$. Cross multiply to get $360 \times 2 = 3 \times ?$, or $720 = 3 \times ?$. Divide both sides by 3 to get $? = 240$. This is the missing part: the number of union workers. Finally, add the number of union workers to nonunion workers to get the whole: $360 + 240 = 600$.

43. a. Rounding off the numbers will show that choice **a** is less than 600 and choices **b**, **c**, and **d** are all over 600 pounds.

44. a. First, multiply the amount of coins (or bills) by the value of the coin (or bill): 10 twenty-dollar bills = $10 \times \$20 = \$200$

3 five-dollar bills = 3 × $5 = $15

98 one-dollar bills = 98 × $1 = $98

88 quarters = 88 × $.25 = $22

52 dimes = 52 × $.10 = $5.20

200 nickels = 200 × $.05 = $10

125 pennies = 125 × $.01 = $1.25

Next, add up all the money: $200 + $15 + $98 + $22 + $5.20 + $10 + $1.25 = $351.45.

45. a. 120 yards ÷ 4 hours = 30 yards per hour; 30 yards ÷ 10 yards per hour = 3 people.

46. b. Let x = the number sought. Begin by breaking up the problem into smaller pieces: *two times a number* = $2x$, *seven times a number* = $7x$, and *seven times a number is taken away from 99* = $99 - 7x$. Next, combine the terms, $2x = 99 - 7x$, and simplify, $9x = 99$. Thus, $x = 11$.

47. c. Anthony can complete $\frac{1}{8}$ of the task in 1 hour. You know this because he completes the entire task in 8 hours. Together, Anthony and Dave complete $\frac{1}{3}$ of the task in 1 hour. (Thus, they are done in 3 hours.) Convert both fractions into *twenty-fourths*. $\frac{8}{24}$ per hour (both men) $- \frac{3}{24}$ per hour (just Anthony) $= \frac{5}{24}$ per hour (just Dave). Thus, Dave completes $\frac{5}{24}$ of the task per hour. It will take him $\frac{24}{5}$ hours to complete the entire task; $\frac{24}{5} = 4\frac{4}{5}$ hours.

48. c. $\frac{1}{8}$ of the $120 went to Suzanne: $\frac{1}{8} \times 120 = $15. This means there was 120 − 15 = $105 left. $\frac{1}{4}$ of the $105 went to Darlene: $\frac{1}{4} \times 105 = $26.25. Thus, the amount remaining is 105 − 26.25 = $78.75.

49. b. This is a three-step problem involving multiplication, subtraction, and addition. First find out how many fewer minutes Officer Jozwiak jogged this week than usual: 5 hours × 60 minutes = 300 minutes − 40 minutes missed = 260 minutes jogged. Now add back the number of minutes Officer Jozwiak was able to make up: 260 + 20 + 13 = 293 minutes. Now subtract again: 300 − 293 = 7 minutes jogging time lost.

50. d. Multiply the number of coins by the value of the coin:

120 quarters = 120 × $.25 = $30

300 dimes = 300 × $.10 = $30

600 nickels = 600 × $.05 = $30

500 pennies = 500 × $.01 = $5

Next, add all of the dollar amounts up: $30 + $30 + $30 + $5 = $95. The only choice that represents $95 is **d**: 1 fifty-dollar bill, 2 twenty-dollar bills, and 1 five-dollar bill.

51. a. First, calculate the total amount of money: $4,000 + $3,500 + $4,500 = $12,000. He puts 30% of the $12,000, or 0.30 × $12,000 = $3,600, into the savings account.

52. c. Five monitors will cost $175 × 5 = $875; three printers will cost $120 × 3 = $360; eight surge suppressors will cost $18 × 8 = $144. Before the discount, this adds to: $875 + $360 + $144 = $1,379; 12% of $1,379 = 0.12 × 1379 = $165.48. Thus, the final cost will be $1,379 − 165.48 = $1,213.52.

53. b. If 1 inch on the map denotes 1.5 km, then 31 inches on the map would represent 46.5 kilometers.

54. c. 1 kilometer = 1,000 meters. Use $D = RT$ with $D = 1,000$, $R = 2.5$ m/sec, and T as the unknown. Rearrange $D = RT$ to $T = \frac{D}{R} = \frac{1000}{2.5} = 400$ seconds.

55. c. Rearrange $D = RT$ into $R = D \div T$ by dividing both sides of the equation by T. Amy's rate is then $R = 8$ mi ÷ 40 min = 0.2 mi/min. Next, calculate Sharon's rate in the same units of miles per minute. This means you need to convert the 1 hour into 60 min. Sharon's rate is then $R = 12$ mi ÷ 60 min = 0.2 mi/min.

56. d. With the left turn, your unit will be heading in the same direction you were originally driving when your unit was on the interstate.

57. b. Two left turns will take State Trooper Levin in the opposite direction as he was originally driving.

58. c. Your unit will be heading in the same direction you were originally driving.

59. b. Taking the most direct legal route, you will be making four turns: right onto Pine Street, right onto Seminole Boulevard, right onto Swiss Street, and left onto Hampton Way.

60. b. If State Trooper DeSiervo turns left onto Castles Street, he will be facing south.

61. b. This is the most direct route because it requires the fewest turns. All the other choices require your unit to go the wrong way on one-way streets.

62. a. It is the only correct choice based on the directional coordinate shown on the map.

63. b. Selden, Coram, and Middle Island are all located along Route 25; in the other answer choices, at least one of the towns named is not located along an east-west highway.

64. b. Both towns are shown directly on Route 27a. Choices **a** and **c** are incorrect; they are the same roadway, which takes you too far away from either town. Choice **d** is incorrect; although Shirley is located on this route, it is nowhere near East Patchogue.

65. d. The easternmost portion of Longwood Road is shown going directly to the laboratory.

66. b. It is the only correct choice based on the directional coordinate shown on the map.

67. c. It is the only roadway that runs adjacent to each campus. The other local roads are near one campus or the other, but are not near both.

68. b. The first turn after heading west on Washington is to turn south onto Parker Road, then east to Lincoln Road, which will put the officer at the scene of the collision.

69. d. Officer Watson is heading east on Main Street and if he makes a U-turn, he will be heading west. If he turns onto Third Street, the only way he can turn will have him heading north. If he makes a second U-turn, he will now be facing south.

70. c. This is the best option to get to Ash Road and Church Street without going the wrong way on any one-way streets.

71. c. The colors in the other answer choices are not mentioned in the passage.

72. d. Choice **a**, Lang, is not mentioned in the passage. White and Tuttle, choices **b** and **c**, are working with Rodriguez, not training him.

73. b. Choice **a**, 15, is not mentioned in the passage. The number 14, choice **c**, is mentioned in the passage, but not in relation to the maximum number of inmates allowed into the visitors' room at one time. Twelve was the day of the month when Rodriguez reported to his new assignment in the visitors' room, but this is not what the question is asking for, so choice **d** is also incorrect.

74. a. The first sentence of the second paragraph says: *At 8 A.M. sharp, Officer Rodriguez reported to duty.*

75. b. This information is contained in the last paragraph of the passage.

76. c. Choice **a**, 10, is not mentioned in the passage. The number 12, choice **b**, is mentioned in the passage, but not in relation to the painted line. Twelve was the day of the month when Rodriguez reported to his new assignment in the visitors' room. Choice **d** is also incorrect; the number 16 is the maximum number of inmates allowed in the visitors' room.

77. b. The other days are not mentioned in the passage. Remember, test writers often target times and dates when creating memory questions.

78. c. Although these are all types of searches, only choice **c** is mentioned in the passage.

79. d. The times in the other answer choices are not mentioned in the passage. Remember to always pick up on any number in passages testing your memory skills.

80. a. Choice **b** is incorrect because the room, not the ceiling, is white. The line around the room is red, choice **c**, but the ceiling is not red. The passage does not mention the color blue, choice **d**.

81. b. Statement 8 indicates a direct link between Francis Onitsha and the making of ivory figurines.

82. d. In Statement 6, Michelle Eseka may be trying to focus the investigation away from her and toward Onitsha.

83. c. Margaret Woo referred only to the paperwork and did not actually check the contents of crates. Her story can easily be checked through her supervisor.

84. a. Statement 9 presents the possibility that Rosemary Ndele is working in concert with Freddy Jones. Because Jones is a primary suspect, her association with him makes her information of questionable value.

85. d. Statement 7 indicates that Eseka's business is in financial trouble; that could be a motive for engaging in a lucrative smuggling scheme.

86. c. Statements 5 and 6 provide a possible motive for William Calabar (a gambling debt) and indicate that he disregarded a direct order from his boss.

87. c. Statement 10 states that Cameroon officials provided U.S. investigators information from official records.

88. b. Statement 9 indicates the possibility that Jones sought out Mandara Exports and that he knows an employee there. This is a deviation from the normal course of business.

89. a. Statement 2 states that the bill of lading contains what is now known to be inaccurate information about the shipment. Statement 10 indicates that Cameroon customs was avoided, because officials there might check the shipment against the bill of lading.

90. b. Statements 7 and 10 both provide information about a member of the public, who may be the person mentioned in Statement 4.

91. d. Statement 8 indicates that Alan Pip may be somewhat unstable.

92. a. Statements 1 and 3 provide information about White's ability to access a locked postal box, along with the information that the envelope may not have gone through the U.S. Postal Service, but may instead have simply been placed with the mail.

93. c. Merely doing work to get more people to vote does not cast suspicion on a volunteer. Statements 1 and 3 might cast a little suspicion on Edna, and Statement 8 could be an attempt by Edna to divert attention from herself.

94. b. Even if Lawe had been making angry comments about the president and her student loans, it is doubtful that would be a serious threat.

95. d. Statements 3 and 7 taken together refer to the involvement of local police and Secret Service in preparations for the president's visit and the threat investigation.

96. d. Statement 2 provides no information that would further the investigation.

97. d. Step 2 says the officer should have asked the security guard to fill out a witness statement and a complaint form.

98. c. Officer Smits is stationed south of Officer Foster. Officer Walters cannot be farthest north, because Foster is north of Walters. Balboa is south of Foster, but may or may not be south of Walters; therefore, Balboa may not be farthest south, nor south of Walters.

99. c. Step 2 instructs the officer not to move any objects until photos are taken of them as they first appeared when the officer arrived.

100. b. Edgar burgled a warehouse before Nelson stole a car. Baker robbed a bank after Nelson stole a car; Mitchell assaulted a police officer after Baker robbed a bank and Nelson stole a car.

15 ▶ State Trooper Practice Test 5

CHAPTER SUMMARY

This is the fifth practice test in the book based on the most commonly tested areas on the state trooper exam.

The practice test consists of 100 multiple-choice questions in the following areas: reading comprehension, writing and information ordering, mathematics, spatial and directional orientation, memory and observation, and problem solving. Allot two hours to take this practice test.

This practice test is available through the LearningExpress online link, if you prefer to take it on the computer.

State Trooper Practice Test 5

1.	a	b	c	d		36.	a	b	c	d		71.	a	b	c	d
2.	a	b	c	d		37.	a	b	c	d		72.	a	b	c	d
3.	a	b	c	d		38.	a	b	c	d		73.	a	b	c	d
4.	a	b	c	d		39.	a	b	c	d		74.	a	b	c	d
5.	a	b	c	d		40.	a	b	c	d		75.	a	b	c	d
6.	a	b	c	d		41.	a	b	c	d		76.	a	b	c	d
7.	a	b	c	d		42.	a	b	c	d		77.	a	b	c	d
8.	a	b	c	d		43.	a	b	c	d		78.	a	b	c	d
9.	a	b	c	d		44.	a	b	c	d		79.	a	b	c	d
10.	a	b	c	d		45.	a	b	c	d		80.	a	b	c	d
11.	a	b	c	d		46.	a	b	c	d		81.	a	b	c	d
12.	a	b	c	d		47.	a	b	c	d		82.	a	b	c	d
13.	a	b	c	d		48.	a	b	c	d		83.	a	b	c	d
14.	a	b	c	d		49.	a	b	c	d		84.	a	b	c	d
15.	a	b	c	d		50.	a	b	c	d		85.	a	b	c	d
16.	a	b	c	d		51.	a	b	c	d		86.	a	b	c	d
17.	a	b	c	d		52.	a	b	c	d		87.	a	b	c	d
18.	a	b	c	d		53.	a	b	c	d		88.	a	b	c	d
19.	a	b	c	d		54.	a	b	c	d		89.	a	b	c	d
20.	a	b	c	d		55.	a	b	c	d		90.	a	b	c	d
21.	a	b	c	d		56.	a	b	c	d		91.	a	b	c	d
22.	a	b	c	d		57.	a	b	c	d		92.	a	b	c	d
23.	a	b	c	d		58.	a	b	c	d		93.	a	b	c	d
24.	a	b	c	d		59.	a	b	c	d		94.	a	b	c	d
25.	a	b	c	d		60.	a	b	c	d		95.	a	b	c	d
26.	a	b	c	d		61.	a	b	c	d		96.	a	b	c	d
27.	a	b	c	d		62.	a	b	c	d		97.	a	b	c	d
28.	a	b	c	d		63.	a	b	c	d		98.	a	b	c	d
29.	a	b	c	d		64.	a	b	c	d		99.	a	b	c	d
30.	a	b	c	d		65.	a	b	c	d		100.	a	b	c	d
31.	a	b	c	d		66.	a	b	c	d						
32.	a	b	c	d		67.	a	b	c	d						
33.	a	b	c	d		68.	a	b	c	d						
34.	a	b	c	d		69.	a	b	c	d						
35.	a	b	c	d		70.	a	b	c	d						

▶ State Trooper Practice Test 5

Directions: Read the following passage, then answer questions 1 through 3.

From the time of death, the temperature of a dead body decreases at the rate of one degree per hour until it reaches the surrounding environmental temperature. Normal body temperature is 98° F. Rigor mortis (the stiffening of muscles and joints) commences approximately four hours after death, progresses slowly for 16 hours, and gradually subsides for an additional 16 hours until it has completely dissipated.

1. Detective Ellis and Medical Examiner Slate respond to the scene of a homicide and examine the body of the victim. They note that the room temperature is 70°, the body's temperature is 88°, and the body is in partial rigor mortis. Which of the following would be the most reasonable inference?
   a. The time of death was about two hours before the examination.
   b. The time of death was about ten hours before the examination.
   c. The time of death was about 24 hours before the examination.
   d. The time of death was more than 48 hours before the examination.

2. Detective Ellis and Medical Examiner Slate respond to the scene of a homicide and examine the body of the victim. They note that the room temperature is 38°, the body's temperature is 60°, and the body has no rigor mortis. Which of the following would be the most reasonable inference?
   a. The time of death was about two hours before the examination.
   b. The time of death was about ten hours before the examination.
   c. The time of death was about 38 hours before the examination.
   d. The time of death was about 48 hours before the examination.

3. Detective Ellis and Medical Examiner Slate respond to the scene of a homicide and examine the body of the victim. They note that the room temperature is 90°, the body's temperature is 90°, and the body has no rigor mortis. Which of the following would be the most reasonable inference?
   a. The time of death was about eight hours before the examination.
   b. The time of death was about two hours before the examination.
   c. The time of death was about 24 hours before the examination.
   d. The time of death was more than 36 hours before the examination.

Directions: Read the following passage, then answer questions 4 and 5.

A lawful arrest must be based on probable cause, which is defined as facts and circumstances based on apparently reliable information that would lead a person of reasonable intelligence, experience, and common sense to conclude that an offense has been, is being, or will be committed by a particular person. Reasonable suspicion about a crime may be enough to stop and question a person, but without probable cause it is not enough to make a lawful arrest.

4. A trooper could make a lawful arrest based on which of the following?
- **a.** A bank manager approaches the trooper, points to a man sitting in a car across the street from the bank, and tells the officer that the man appears to have been watching the entrance to the bank for more than an hour.
- **b.** A trooper observes a man walk quickly out of a bank, enter a double-parked car, and drive away rapidly.
- **c.** An obviously intoxicated person approaches the trooper, points to a bank located across the street, and tells the officer to arrest the bank manager for stealing all the money out of his savings account.
- **d.** A bank manager approaches the trooper, points to an obviously intoxicated person, and tells the officer that the person reached over the bank counter and stole money from the bank teller.

5. A trooper could make a lawful arrest based on which of the following?
- **a.** reasonable suspicion by a trained trooper that a crime may have been committed
- **b.** an anonymous letter alleging a crime and who committed it
- **c.** hearsay information about a person with a reputation for criminal conduct
- **d.** the observation of a person who begins to run from the scene of crime as he sees the police approaching

Directions: Read the following passage, then answer questions 6 through 8.

A person is guilty of criminal trespass when he or she knowingly enters or remains unlawfully in a building. He or she enters or remains unlawfully when he or she does so without permission, license, or privilege. A person is guilty of burglary when he or she knowingly enters or remains unlawfully in a building with intent to commit a crime therein. A person is guilty of assault when with intent to cause physical injury to another person he or she causes such physical injury.

6. Charlotte Cooper received a call from her son's teacher, Mrs. Stoker, who told her that her son was going to fail his courses. Ms. Cooper immediately went to the school and entered the building through the front door, passing under the signs that say "No Trespassing" and "All Persons Must Stop at Security." She passed the security desk without stopping and proceeded to Mrs. Stoker's classroom. Cooper asked for an explanation from Stoker, but a heated argument developed and Cooper grabbed Stoker by the neck, choked her for a few seconds, and pushed her into a chair. Stoker was not injured. The school principal filed a complaint, and Trooper Cook arrested Cooper. Regarding charges against Cooper, which of the following is correct?
   a. She is guilty of criminal trespass for unlawfully entering the building, because she did not stop at the security desk.
   b. She is not guilty of criminal trespass because she was the parent of a student and had legitimate business in the school.
   c. She is guilty of assault because she choked Stoker.
   d. She is guilty of burglary for unlawfully entering the school with intent to commit a crime therein.

7. Assume the same facts as question 6, but, in addition, as Cooper was leaving the classroom, she noticed the teacher's grade book on the desk. She went into the women's bathroom and hid there, waiting for Stoker to leave so that she could take the grade book and destroy it. When Stoker left, Cooper entered the classroom, took the grade book, ripped out the pages, and threw them into a trash can. Regarding charges against Cooper, which of the following is incorrect?
   a. She is guilty of criminal trespass for unlawfully entering or remaining in the building without license or privilege.
   b. She is not guilty of burglary because she did not have the intent to commit a crime when she first entered the school, and the intent to steal and destroy the grade book was formulated after she entered.
   c. She is guilty of burglary for unlawfully entering or remaining in the school with intent to commit a crime therein, i.e., the larceny and destruction of the grade book.
   d. She is guilty of both criminal trespass and burglary.

8. Assume the same facts as in questions 6 and 7, but, in addition, as Cooper left her house to go to the school, she told her neighbor that she was going to beat the heck out of her son's teacher. Regarding charges against Cooper, which of the following is NOT true?
   a. She is guilty of criminal trespass for unlawfully entering or remaining in the school without license or privilege.
   b. She is guilty of assault because she entered the school with the intent to assault Mrs. Stoker.
   c. She is guilty of burglary for unlawfully entering or remaining in the school with intent to commit a crime therein, i.e., assault.
   d. She is guilty of both criminal trespass and burglary.

Directions: Read the following passage, then answer questions 9 and 10.

Traffic laws are enacted to enhance the orderly flow of traffic, to regulate motor vehicles and drivers, and to promote public safety. The number of vehicles, drivers, and roads far exceeds the number of law enforcement personnel available for regulatory duties.

9. To achieve the goals of traffic law, it is most effective for a police agency to enforce traffic laws in a manner to
   a. ensure that summonses are issued for all violations.
   b. concentrate only on the most serious violations.
   c. encourage the public's voluntary compliance with the traffic laws.
   d. raise as much revenue as possible.

10. A trooper observes a motorist pass a steady red light. The trooper should issue a summons in all of the following circumstances, except when the
   a. motorist did not intentionally drive through the light.
   b. motorist appears to be an upstanding, law-abiding citizen.
   c. motorist intentionally drove through the light but had looked both ways before proceeding.
   d. motorist carefully drove through the light because of an exteme emergency.

Directions: Read the following passage, then answer questions 11 through 15.

Corpus delicti means the body of the crime. In a homicide case, the *corpus delicti* consists of the fact that a human being is dead and that the death was caused by the criminal act or agency of another person, and was not suicide, natural, or accidental. In an arson case, the *corpus delicti* consists of the fact that a building was burned and that the fire was caused by the criminal act or agency of another person, and was not accidental.

11. In a possible homicide case, which of the following types of evidence would most likely serve the purpose of establishing *corpus delicti*?
   a. a suicide note by the deceased person
   b. fingerprints of a stranger at the crime scene
   c. evidence of sudden heart failure
   d. evidence of a caustic foreign substance in the decedent's mouth and throat

12. In a possible homicide case in which a dead body was found with a bullet wound to the head, which of the following types of evidence would most likely serve the purpose of establishing *corpus delicti*?
   a. The gun from which the bullet was fired was found in the victim's hand.
   b. The gun from which the bullet was fired was found ten feet from where the body fell.
   c. The victim has other gunshot wounds to the forearms and palms of the hands.
   d. The victim has another graze gunshot wound to the head.

13. In a possible arson case, which of the following types of evidence would most likely serve the purpose of establishing *corpus delicti* of arson?
a. The building was insured.
b. The fire started in one spot while the building was in use.
c. The fire started in more than one spot while the building was closed.
d. The sprinkler system did not work.

14. In a possible arson case, which of the following types of evidence would most likely serve the purpose of establishing *corpus delicti* of arson?
a. A body was found at the scene of the fire and the victim was the owner of the building.
b. A body was found at the scene of the fire and the victim died from the fire.
c. A body was found at the scene of the fire and the victim died of natural causes shortly before the fire.
d. A body was found at the scene of the fire and the victim was murdered shortly before the fire.

15. In a possible murder case in which a body was found in the remains of a building destroyed by fire, which of the following facts in evidence would most likely serve the purpose of establishing *corpus delicti* for the murder?
a. The victim had bruises and had no carbon dioxide in the lungs.
b. The victim had bruises and had substantial carbon dioxide in the lungs.
c. The victim had no bruises and had substantial carbon dioxide in the lungs.
d. The fire was intentionally set and the victim had substantial carbon dioxide in the lungs.

Directions: Read the following passage, then answer questions 16 and 17.

When questioning a witness to a crime or an accident, a trooper should ask questions in a manner to elicit the witness's best observation and memory. Sometimes, an officer has to press for answers, but he or she should not ask questions in a manner that suggests answers to the witness.

16. It would be most correct to state that a trooper investigating a vehicle accident that occurred at an intersection should NOT ask a witness which of the following questions?
a. Did you hear the vehicles collide?
b. Where were you looking when you heard the vehicles collide?
c. Did you see what color the traffic lights were when the vehicles collided?
d. Did you see that the light was red as the first vehicle went through the intersection?

17. It would be most correct to state that a trooper investigating a fight between Mr. Ko and Ms. Lang should NOT ask a witness which of the following questions?
a. Did you see the knife in Mr. Ko's hand before he slashed at Ms. Lang?
b. Were you present when the fight began?
c. Did you see a knife?
d. Who had the knife?

18. Grand larceny from the person is a less serious crime than grand larceny by extortion. Robbery is more serious than grand larceny from the person, but less serious than kidnapping. Kidnapping is more serious than grand larceny by extortion. Which crime is the most serious?
a. grand larceny from the person
b. grand larceny by extortion
c. robbery
d. kidnapping

19. Grand larceny by extortion is a more serious crime than grand larceny from the person. Robbery is less serious than kidnapping, but more serious than grand larceny from the person. Kidnapping is more serious than grand larceny by extortion. Which crime is the least serious?
   a. grand larceny by extortion
   b. grand larceny from the person
   c. robbery
   d. kidnapping

20. A trooper assigned as a station house watch officer receives an anonymous telephone call. The caller states that he has information about a serious crime that had been recently reported in the newspapers. The caller states that he does not want to be identified, and he does not give any information regarding his motive or reliability. Of the following, the best way for the trooper to handle the call would be to
   a. insist that the caller identify himself before continuing the conversation.
   b. put the caller on hold while attempting to contact the detectives assigned to the case.
   c. note the information given and attempt to get more details by pointing out the discrepancies between the caller's story and other available information.
   d. get all the details possible from the caller without providing the caller with any other available information.

21. Three of the sentences below contain one or more grammatical or spelling errors. Select the answer choice that is correct as is.
   a. There was a time when a woman were frowned on for expressing their desire to become police officers.
   b. There was a time when a woman was frowned upon for expressing her desire to become a police officer.
   c. There was a time when women were frowned on for expressing her desire to become a Police Officer.
   d. There was a time when women was frowned on for expressing a desire to become police officers.

22. Three of the sentences below contain one or more grammatical or spelling errors. Select the answer choice that is correct as is.
   a. Robert and Robin wanted to become troopers because they wanted to be a part of a well-respected organization.
   b. Robert and Robin wanted to become a trooper because they wanted to be a part of a well-respected organization.
   c. Robert and Robin wanted to become troopers because they wanted to be apart of a well-respected organization.
   d. Robert and Robin wanted to become Troopers because he/she wanted to be part of a well-respected organization.

23. Three of the sentences below contain one or more grammatical or spelling errors. Select the answer choice that is correct as is.

   a. In many cities in the United States, the tenor of a mayor is four years before they must run for reelection.

   b. In many city's in the United States, the tenure of a mayor is four years before he or she must run for reelection.

   c. In many cities in the United States, the tenure of a mayor is four years before he or she must run for reelection.

   d. In many citys in the united states, the tenure of a mayor is four years before he or she must run for reelection.

24. Three of the sentences below contain one or more grammatical or spelling errors. Select the answer choice that is correct as is.

   a. Sergeant Harper asked Trooper Stedman whether she wanted to run an extra mile on Friday mornings.

   b. Sergeant Harper asked Trooper Stedman did she want to run a extra mile on Friday mornings.

   c. Sergeant Harper ask Trooper Stedman if she want to run an extra mile on Friday mornings.

   d. Sergeant Harper asked Trooper Stedman why she don't want to run an extra mile on Friday mornings.

25. Three of the sentences below contain one or more grammatical or spelling errors. Select the answer choice that is correct as is.

   a. The amount of summons that Trooper Busby wrote in March was 42.

   b. The amount of summonses that Trooper Busby wrote in March were 42.

   c. The number of summons that Trooper Busby wrote in March was 42

   d. The number of summonses that Trooper Busby wrote in March was 42.

26. Three of the sentences below contain one or more grammatical or spelling errors. Select the answer choice that is correct as is.

   a. The severity of Trooper Prentiss's injury was not known.

   b. The severeness of Trooper Prentisses injury was not known.

   c. The severity of Trooper Prentise's injury was not known.

   d. The severeness of Trooper Prentiss's injury was not known.

27. Three of the sentences below contain one or more grammatical or spelling errors. Select the answer choice that is correct as is.

   a. Trooper Allen and Trooper Biaz likes his/her job.

   b. Trooper Allen and Trooper Biaz like their job.

   c. Trooper Allen and Trooper Biaz like his and her jobs.

   d. Trooper Allen and Trooper Biaz like their jobs.

28. One of the sentences below contains one or more grammatical or spelling errors. Select the answer choice that contains an error.

   a. Although state police patrol methods have remained similar over the years regardless of some people's call for changes.

   b. State police patrol methods have remained similar over the years regardless of some people's call for changes.

   c. Although state police patrol methods have remained similar over the years, some people have called for changes.

   d. State police patrol methods have remained similar over the years despite some politicians' calls for changes.

29. One of the sentences below contains one or more grammatical or spelling errors. Select the answer choice that contains an error.
a. Troopers need to keep their strength up during training.
b. Troopers need to keep their strengths up during training.
c. A trooper needs to keep his or her strength up during training.
d. Each trooper needs to keep his or her strength up during training.

Directions: For questions 30 through 35, choose the word or phrase that best fills the blank to properly complete the sentences.

30. Trooper Vitry injured her ankle in training; _____, she was excused from the mile rule for three days.
a. therefore
b. regardless
c. because of which
d. however

31. This month, Trooper Zeno issued _____ summonses than ever before.
a. less
b. fewer
c. not as many
d. lesser

32. Trooper Thomas is trying to become a better swimmer before the date of the physical education test _____.
a. will have arrived
b. had arrived
c. will arrive
d. arrives

33. The training sergeant gave each trooper considerable _____ attention.
a. personnel
b. personal
c. personable
d. personnell

34. The instructor during the lecture on questioning witnesses said it was important to _____ those you wanted to question so everyone did not give the same answer.
a. seperate
b. separate
c. take apart
d. separate

35. When making a traffic stop, a trooper should always remember to ask the driver for his or her _____.
a. lysence
b. lesence
c. license
d. licence

36. Identify the sentence that contains a mistake in capitalization, punctuation, grammar, or spelling. If you find no mistakes, select choice **d.**
a. John Jones has always wanted to be a Trooper.
b. My uncle took me to Yankee Stadium.
c. Suzanne took her dog Princess to see Dr. Doogie.
d. no mistakes

37. Identify the sentence that contains a mistake in capitalization, punctuation, grammar, or spelling. If you find no mistakes, select choice **d**.
  a. Juan was elected vice president of his academy class.
  b. Suzanne's nickname is Frenchie because she was born in Martinique.
  c. Trooper Goodcup issued two Summonses to a Motorist.
  d. no mistakes

Directions: Read the paragraph below and answer questions 38 through 40.

When a trooper provides physical descriptions of suspects for a dispatcher to broadcast, some information is more important than other portions of the description. Items that should be given out include:

  1. Color and length of hair
  2. Headgear (hat, cap, scarf, etc.) the suspect might have been wearing
  3. Race and sex
  4. Weapons the suspect displayed or may be carrying
  5. Approximate height and weight
  6. Upper body clothing such as coat, jacket, or shirt
  7. Lower body clothing (long or short pants, skirt, etc.)
  8. Footwear

38. Select the most appropriate order for providing information to be broadcast.
  a. 3, 4, 5, 7
  b. 6, 5, 1, 3
  c. 8, 1, 6, 2
  d. 3, 2, 6, 7

39. Select the least appropriate order for providing information to be broadcast.
  a. 8, 1, 6, 4
  b. 2, 6, 1, 7
  c. 4, 3, 5, 7
  d. 3, 4, 7, 8

40. Trooper Pitty is taking a report of a chain-snatch from a teenager at the bus terminal. The teen says the person who snatched his chain from around his neck was a chubby white male wearing a red bandana, white sneakers, and a dark-colored windbreaker, and was the same height as the teen (5′9″). He also recalled that the snatcher was wearing blue jeans, and had in his hand something that looked like a knife but might have been a box cutter.

What is the first thing Trooper Pitty should mention in his description?
  a. The suspect was wearing a red bandana.
  b. The suspect was chubby.
  c. the suspect's race and sex
  d. the suspect's height

Directions: Read the paragraph below and answer questions 41 through 43.

A trooper responds to take a report of a burglary at Ron's Discount Tire Store. Ron believes that someone must have driven a truck up to his store to take the tires because a large number have been taken. According to Ron, six Silver Edition touring tires were stolen, six Pathfinder Truck/SUV tires were stolen, and four each of the All Season Regular and All Season Ultra tires were stolen.

The tires are valued at:

- Silver Edition touring tires: $66 each
- Pathfinder Truck/SUV tires: $111 each
- All Season Regular tires: $41.99 each
- Al Season Ultra tires: $83.99 each

41. What is the total value of the Pathfinder Truck SUV tires reported by Ron?
  a. $600
  b. $666
  c. $444
  d. $335.96

42. What is the total value of the All Season Ultra tires reported by Ron?
  a. $600
  b. $666
  c. $503.94
  d. $335.96

43. What is the total value of all the tires reported by Ron?
  a. $1,565.92
  b. $1.655.96
  c. $1,229.96
  d. $899.96

Directions: Read the paragraph below and answer questions 44 through 46.

Trooper Suki is sent on a three-day training exercises that requires her to travel to the state's capital city. She will take her personal car and receive mileage reimbursement of 49.5 cents a mile. She will also receive reimbursement of expenses for meals at the per diem rate of $49 per day, with 75% reimbursement for her two travel days. The total mileage Trooper Suki put on her vehicle was 250 miles.

44. Trooper Suki's reimbursement for mileage is
  a. $12.37
  b. $123.75
  c. $122.50
  d. $12.50

45. Trooper Suki's reimbursement for meals is
  a. $220.50
  b. $245
  c. $183.75
  d. none of the above

46. Trooper Suki's total reimbursement for the training trip is
  a. $257.37
  b. $353
  c. $344.25
  d. none of the above

47. Trooper Acton drives his marked car 80 miles on Sunday, 50 miles on Monday, 50 miles on Tuesday, 80 miles on Wednesday, and 60 miles on Thursday. What is the average number of miles driven?
  a. 80 miles
  b. 50 miles
  c. 58 miles
  d. 64 miles

48. Seventy-five percent of the summonses issued by the officers in Troop X were for speeding. If 460 summonses were issued in the month of April, how many were NOT for speeding?
   a. 100
   b. 115
   c. 230
   d. There is not enough information to answer the question.

49. Trooper Rosen is taking the train from his headquarters to a meeting at the state capitol. The train trip takes three hours; his meeting is at 2 P.M., and it takes about 30 minutes to get from headquarters to the train station. To be sure to get to his meeting on time but not more than 30 minutes early, Trooper Rosen should plan to take a train that leaves at what time?
   a. 11:30 A.M.
   b. 11:00 A.M.
   c. 10:30 A.M.
   d. 10:00 A.M.

Directions: Read the paragraph below and answer questions 50 through 52.

Trooper Addison responds to take a report of a burglary at Bette's Beauty Supply Store. According to Bette, both personal items and beauty supply items were missing when she opened the store on Saturday morning. Among the personal items were her portable tape player, valued at $57; four compact disks (CDs), valued at $12.99 each; her leather jacket, valued at $450, and $125 in cash. Store items that were missing included:

   ▪ 10 boxes of combs and hair ornaments, each box valued at $112
   ▪ 9 boxes of hair color, each box valued at $90
   ▪ 6 boxes of sunscreen, each box valued at $80
   ▪ 5 boxes of lipsticks, each box valued at $55

50. What is the total value of the personal items reported missing by Bette?
   a. $626.96
   b. $632
   c. $683.96
   d. $783.96

51. What is the total value of all the store items reported missing by Bette?
   a. $2,685
   b. $1,565
   c. $1,875
   d. $1,975

52. What is the total value of Bette's personal items and store items that were reported missing?
   a. $2,197
   b. $2,601.96
   c. $3,368.96
   d. $3,468.96

Directions: Read the paragraph below and answer questions 53 through 55.

Many police departments use military time to ensure that officers are not confused when reporting for duty or writing reports. Military time uses a 24-hour clock. One minute after midnight is 0001 hours; one minute after noon is 1201 hours, one P.M. is 1300 hours, two P.M. is 1400 hours, and so on until the clock strikes midnight (2400 hours).

53. Trooper Oliver works an eight-hour shift that begins at 1500 hours. In nonmilitary time, this means that she works from
   a. 5 P.M. to 1 A.M.
   b. 3 P.M. to 11 P.M.
   c. 1:50 P.M. to 9:50 P.M.
   d. 1:30 A.M. to 9:30 A.M.

54. Trooper Smyth arrived at work at 0814 hours, but Trooper Tomlin did not arrive until 0940 hours. How long was Trooper Smyth at work before Trooper Tomlin arrived?
   a. one hour and 26 minutes
   b. one hour and 54 minutes
   c. two hours and six minutes
   d. two hours and 36 minutes

55. The department is considering changing from a schedule of five eight-hour to four ten-hour tours each week. If the new schedule is implemented, troopers who report to work at 0600 hours will get off duty at
   a. 2 P.M.
   b. 3 P.M.
   c. 4 P.M.
   d. 5 P.M.

Directions: Use the following map to answer questions 56 through 60.

Center City is laying out the route of its new light rail system. The map legend shows you the proposed route (called *alignment* on the map), and uses an X to show where streets will be closed and a O to show where the tracks will cross a street that will also be open to vehicle traffic. For these questions, you may ignore whether the route will be grade separated with the light rail train (LRT) going over or under the street crossing.

56. The total number of *grade separated crossings* from Federal Bd to Kipling St is
   a. two.
   b. three.
   c. four.
   d. five.

57. W. Jewell Av intersects the proposed rail route at which point?
a. Alameda Av
b. Exposition Av
c. Kipling St
d. It does not intersect the proposed rail route at all.

58. The total number of grade separated crossings on 6th Av is
a. one.
b. two.
c. three.
d. four.

59. How many times will a vehicle traveling on Federal Bd from Exposition Av to 23rd Av cross the alignment?
a. one
b. two
c. three
d. zero

60. According to the map, the alignment will affect I-25 in what way?
a. by creating a grade separation somewhere between 10th Av and 8th Av
b. by creating a grade separation somewhere between Colfax Av and 8th Av
c. by creating a grade crossing somewhere between 8th Av and 6th Av
d. I-25 will not be affected by the alignment.

Directions: Read the paragraph below and answer questions 61 through 70.

At about 5:00 A.M., a trooper, driving on a two-way north-south road, is directed by the radio dispatcher to respond forthwith to the town of Middletown, New York. He knows that Middletown is west of Bear Mountain, which is east of the trooper's location and on the same approximate latitude as Middletown. He also knows that the road on which he is currently driving is east of Middletown. On all roads that the trooper might travel on, the speed limit is 60 miles per hour.

61. If the trooper is driving north and reaches a two-way east-west road that leads to Middletown, he should
a. keep going straight.
b. turn right.
c. turn left.
d. turn around and head south.

62. If the trooper is driving south and reaches an east-west road that leads to Middletown, he should
a. keep going straight.
b. turn right.
c. turn left.
d. turn around and head north.

63. If the trooper is driving north and he is located north of Middletown and Bear Mountain when he receives the call, he should
a. keep going straight.
b. turn right at the next intersection.
c. turn left at the next intersection.
d. turn around and head south.

64. If the trooper is driving south and he is located south of Middletown and Bear Mountain when he receives the call, he should
a. keep going straight.
b. turn right at the next intersection.
c. turn left at the next intersection.
d. turn around and head north.

65. If the trooper makes a turn on the two-way east-west road and sees a sign that Bear Mountain is ahead, he should
  a. keep going straight.
  b. turn around, return to the north-south road, and head north.
  c. turn around, return to the north-south road, and head south.
  d. turn around and continue past the north-south road.

66. If Middletown is 20 miles west of the north-south road and the trooper is 20 miles south of the east-west road when he receives the call, traveling at the speed limit, he could correctly estimate that he could reach Middletown in
  a. 20 minutes.
  b. 30 minutes.
  c. 40 minutes.
  d. 60 minutes.

67. If Middletown is 20 miles west of the north-south road and the trooper is 40 miles north of the east-west road when he receives the call, traveling at the speed limit, he could correctly estimate that he could reach Middletown in
  a. 20 minutes.
  b. 40 minutes.
  c. 60 minutes.
  d. 80 minutes.

68. If Middletown is 20 miles west of the north-south road and the trooper is 30 miles north of the east-west road, heading north when he receives the call, he could correctly estimate that he could reach Middletown in
  a. 30 minutes.
  b. 40 minutes.
  c. 50 minutes.
  d. 70 minutes.

69. If Middletown is 20 miles west of the north-south road and the trooper is 20 miles south of the east-west road, heading north when he receives the call, traveling at 30 miles per hour, he could correctly estimate that he could reach Middletown in
  a. 20 minutes.
  b. 40 minutes.
  c. 60 minutes.
  d. 80 minutes.

70. Middletown is 20 miles west of the north-south road. The trooper is driving north on the north-south road and is 40 miles south of the east-west road when he receives the call. The trooper turns right at the east-west road and drives for 5 miles before realizing he is going in the wrong direction. He turns around and proceeds to Middletown. Traveling at the speed limit, approximately how long did it take him to reach Middletown?
  a. 50 minutes
  b. 60 minutes
  c. 70 minutes
  d. 80 minutes

Directions: Study the photo below, then answer questions 71 through 76 without looking back at the photo.

71. Based on the photo, the number of people crossing the street in front of the train is
a. one.
b. two.
c. three.
d. undeterminable from the photo.

72. Based on the photo, the number of people who are crossing the street while wearing a personal music device is
a. one.
b. two.
c. three.
d. undeterminable from the photo.

73. Other than those seen crossing the street in front of the train, how many other people or non-transit vehicles can be observed in the photo?
a. one person and no vehicles
b. one person and one vehicle
c. two persons and no vehicle
d. two persons and one vehicle

74. What is the total number of people who are seen in the photo?
a. three
b. four
c. five
d. six

75. The two people coming toward the photographer appear to be
a. women dressed casually.
b. men dressed in jeans.
c. in conversation with each other.
d. women in business attire.

76. Based on the photo, how many sets of tracks do the pedestrians appear to be crossing?
a. one
b. two
c. three
d. undeterminable from the photo.

77. Compare the sets and select the answer from the choices below.
94726179   j94726179   94726179
a. All three names or numbers are exactly alike.
b. Only the first and second names or numbers are exactly alike.
c. Only the first and third names or numbers are exactly alike.
d. Only the second and third names or numbers are exactly alike.

78. Compare the sets below.
94726179   j94726179   94726179
The difference between the sets would best be described as which of the following?
a. The middle combination begins with a letter and the others do not.
b. The last two digits of all three are different.
c. The first two numbers of all three are different.
d. None of the statements is correct.

79. Compare the sets and select the answer from the choices below.
Rodriquez24
Rodriquez24
Rodrigues24
Rodriques24
a. All four names or numbers are exactly alike.
b. Only the first and second names or numbers are exactly alike.
c. Only the first and fourth names or numbers are exactly alike.
d. Only the second and third names or numbers are exactly alike.

80. Trooper Garcia broke her leg playing softball and has been assigned to perform clerical work in the Records Section. Sergeant West has asked her to alphabetize some contact cards. She must place the name in capital letters in the correct place in the files.

RICHOT, ALLAN

Names already in the file are:
Rachot, Allen
Riache, Allan
Ricehot, Alain
Ricehot, Allen

Where in the card file will Trooper Garcia place *Richot, Allan*?
a. before all the other names
b. between *Rachot, Allen* and *Riache, Allan*
c. between *Ricehot, Alain* and *Ricehot, Allen*
d. after *Ricehot, Allen*

Directions: Read the passage below and answer questions 81 through 84.

To properly perform their police duties, troopers need to understand the fundamental rules of evidence. They need to understand the hearsay rule and the exceptions to it.

Unless an exception applies, hearsay evidence will not be admissible at trial. Hearsay is a statement made out of court that is offered in court for the truth of the fact asserted in the statement. Consequently, to prove a defendant committed a crime, a police officer could not testify at trial that a witness told him or her the defendant had committed the crime. To avoid the hearsay rule, the witness would have to take the stand and testify to his or her direct observations.

When an out-of-court statement is offered in court not for the truth of its content but for another purpose such as impeaching a witness by showing prior inconsistent statements, it is not hearsay and may be admitted.

Several exceptions to the hearsay rule apply, such as spontaneous declarations and excited utterances. Spontaneous declarations and excited utterances are statements made close in time to a startling event, while the person making the statement is under the stress of excitement caused by the event, and before there is an opportunity for the person to reflect or to contrive a self-serving statement. Under some circumstances in which these exceptions apply, a trooper may testify about a statement made out of court to prove the fact asserted in the statement.

81. A trooper is called to a family dispute. When he arrives, a woman runs toward him, screaming, "My husband tried to choke me to death." The trooper notices red marks around the woman's throat. After a brief investigation, the trooper arrests the husband. Later, at the police station while the trooper is filling out paperwork, the woman calls the trooper over and makes a second statement to him, "I pretended to be dead so he would stop." The husband is charged with attempted murder and assault. However, at the trial, the woman refuses to testify against her husband, and the trooper is called to the stand. Regarding the trooper's testimony, which of the following would be correct?
a. The trooper would be allowed to testify only about his observation of the red marks on the woman's throat.
b. He would be allowed to testify about both statements the woman made, because she was under extreme emotional stress when she made the statements.
c. He would be allowed to testify about his observation of the red marks and about the first statement the woman made but not the second statement.
d. He would be allowed to testify about his observation of the red marks and about the second statement the woman made, because the woman had calmed down by the time she made that statement.

82. When the trooper investigated the woman's complaint, he found the husband sitting in a chair, smoking a cigarette, and watching a football game. The trooper asked the husband what had happened, and the husband answered, "I didn't choke her. She was choking me." During the trial, the husband claimed self-defense, and his lawyer questioned the trooper. Regarding the trooper's testimony, which of the following would be correct?

a. The trooper would be allowed to testify about the husband's statement because it was a spontaneous statement.

b. The trooper would be allowed to testify about the husband's statement because it was an excited utterance.

c. The trooper would not be allowed to testify about the husband's statement because it was in response to a question.

d. The trooper would not be allowed to testify about the husband's statement because it was made after the husband had an opportunity to reflect or to contrive.

83. During the trial, the husband testified in his own defense. He testified that he and his wife had had an argument but that no physical contact had occurred between them. He testified that she accused him because she was jealous of his relationship with another woman. After the husband's testimony, the trooper was recalled to the witness stand as a rebuttal witness. Regarding the trooper's testimony, which of the following would be correct?

a. The trooper would be allowed to testify about the husband's statement because it was a spontaneous statement.

b. The trooper would be allowed to testify about the husband's statement because it was an excited utterance.

c. The trooper would be allowed to testify about the husband's statement because the wife had refused to testify.

d. The trooper would be allowed to testify about the husband's statement because the testimony was offered not for the truth of the fact asserted in the statement, but to impeach the husband's credibility by showing that he had made a prior inconsistent statement.

84. Which of the following statements most likely would NOT be admissible as a spontaneous declaration or excited utterance exception to the hearsay rule?

a. Immediately after an automobile accident, one of the drivers stated, "I'm sorry, I should have been paying more attention."

b. Immediately after an automobile accident, a bystander said to one of the drivers, "You idiot. Why did you go through the light?"

c. A half-hour after an automobile accident, one of the drivers stated, "I had the right of way. The other guy went through the stop sign."

d. When a stabbing victim fell to the ground and was asked what was wrong, he answered, "Mildred stabbed me."

Directions: Read the paragraph below and answer questions 85 through 95.

In many state police agencies, the first trooper to arrive at the scene of a serious crime is often the same trooper who will be responsible for taking photographs to preserve the scene and for collecting evidence. The trooper should take the following steps in the order listed:

1. Make sure the crime scene is secure and assign another trooper to be responsible for who comes in and out of the area.
2. Leave the crime scene as it is, not moving any objects or specific items of evidence until photographs can be taken of the scene.
3. Take a photograph of the overall crime scene area, and then take more specific photos of all pertinent pieces of potential evidence.
4. After the first set of photographs is taken, take another set that includes a ruler to provide a sense of scale.
5. Place the film in a container and mark the container with the case number, the date and location, and the trooper's identity.
6. Collect pertinent pieces of evidence. The trooper should mark the evidence pieces directly by scratching his or her initials into the object, or place the pieces into containers and mark the container with the case number, the date and location, and the officer identification.
7. Preserve a chain of custody for all evidence and limit the custodians to as few persons as possible.
8. Deliver the photographs and evidence to the department laboratory.

Trooper Fitzpatrick and Trooper Hanson respond to a past burglary at a private residence. Trooper Fitzpatrick has been trained as an evidence technician. Trooper Hanson is a rookie and has not received such training yet. They are met at the residence by the owner, a distraught woman, who tells them that her home has been ransacked and many of her personal items have been destroyed. Hanson listens while Fitzpatrick asks the woman questions. Fitzpatrick tells Hanson to wait by the front door. The woman leads Fitzpatrick through the house and shows him her china dishes that were broken, old photographs that were ripped up, and food in her kitchen that was partially eaten and thrown about the floor. She tells him that her jewelry has been stolen, and opens her jewelry boxes to show him that they are empty. They find a back window that was pried open, and they see several smoked cigarette stubs on the floor.

As Fitzpatrick begins to take photographs of the residence, Hanson comes in and asks whether he needs any help. Fitzpatrick takes first a set of overall photos of each room, and then takes a set of photos of specific, pertinent items. He takes specific photographs of the pried-open window, the jewelry boxes, the broken dishes, and the torn photographs. While he does this, Trooper Hanson checks out the rest of the house with the owner. As Fitzpatrick finishes the second set of photographs, Hanson approaches him and says, "Look what I found. This was in the backyard." She is holding a small crowbar. She places the crowbar on the marks where the window had been pried open to see whether the crowbar fits with the marks. She says, "Yeah. It's about the right size. Should we take this as evidence?" Hanson puts the crowbar on the windowsill, and Fitzpatrick takes a photograph of it.

After a few minutes, the woman's relatives arrive, and they begin cleaning up the mess in the kitchen. The woman says, "Look, they ate half of my apple," and she throws the apple in the garbage. Trooper Fitzpatrick asks the relatives to stop cleaning up because he wants to see whether any fingerprints have been left.

Trooper Fitzpatrick attempts to find fingerprints in the kitchen and where the back window was pried open, but he does not find any useable prints. He takes the crowbar as evidence, taping a note to it with the date and his name. Then, Trooper Fitzpatrick goes off duty, and sends Trooper Hanson to deliver the photographs and the crowbar to the department laboratory.

85. Which action or actions of Trooper Fitzpatrick were improper?
   a. telling Trooper Hanson to wait by the front door
   b. allowing the woman into the house with him
   c. allowing the woman to lead him through the house
   d. allowing the woman to open the jewelry boxes to show him they were empty

86. Which action or actions of Trooper Fitzpatrick were improper?
   a. taking overall photographs of each room before taking specific photographs
   b. taking photographs of the pried-open window
   c. taking a photograph of the crowbar on the windowsill
   d. taking photographs of the broken china and torn photographs

87. Which action or actions of Trooper Hanson were proper?
   a. offering to help Trooper Fitzpatrick
   b. checking out the rest of the house with the owner
   c. picking up the crowbar
   d. listening as Fitzpatrick questioned the woman

88. Which action or actions of Trooper Hanson were improper?
   a. picking up the crowbar before it was photographed where it was found
   b. placing the crowbar on the marks where the window had been pried
   c. placing the crowbar on the windowsill to be photographed
   d. all of the above

89. Which action or actions of Trooper Hanson most seriously impaired the evidence gathering process?
   a. finding the crowbar
   b. picking up the crowbar before a photograph was taken
   c. placing the crowbar on the marks where the window had been pried
   d. placing the crowbar on the windowsill to be photographed

90. Considering that Trooper Fitzpatrick was the senior officer and had been trained as an evidence technician, which of his actions was improper?
   a. his failure to clearly instruct Hanson to stay at the front door and to prevent unauthorized persons from entering the crime scene
   b. his failure to stop Hanson from placing the crowbar on the marks, which could have destroyed or marred the evidentiary value of the marks
   c. photographing the crowbar on the windowsill when it was found at a different location
   d. all of the above

91. Considering that Trooper Fitzpatrick was the senior officer and had been trained as an evidence technician, which of his actions was improper?
   a. his failure to take a second set of photographs with a ruler included in the photos
   b. his failure to take photographs of the cigarette stubs
   c. his failure to take photographs of the partially eaten food, including the apple
   d. all of the above

92. Considering that Trooper Fitzpatrick was the senior officer and had been trained as an evidence technician, which of his actions was improper?
a. asking the relatives not to clean up the food in the kitchen
b. attempting to find fingerprints in the kitchen
c. attempting to find fingerprints on the back window
d. allowing the woman to throw the apple pie in the garbage

93. Regarding the apple, Trooper Fitzpatrick's best action would have been to
a. allow the woman to throw the apple in the garbage, because it was perishable.
b. photograph the apple before disposing of it.
c. take a sample of it to the laboratory.
d. collect, preserve, and deliver it to the laboratory for possible DNA recovery or possible bite mark comparisons.

94. Considering that Trooper Fitzpatrick was the senior officer and had been trained as an evidence technician, which of his actions was proper?
a. taking the crowbar as evidence
b. marking the crowbar as evidence by taping a note to it with the date and his name
c. not instructing Hanson to initial the crowbar
d. sending Hanson to deliver his photographs to the department laboratory

95. Regarding the crowbar, Trooper Fitzpatrick's best action would have been to
a. put the crowbar back where it was found in the backyard and photograph it there.
b. place the crowbar on the marks on the window and take close photographs of the match.
c. mark the crowbar as evidence by taping a note to it with the date and his name.
d. instruct Trooper Hanson to scratch her initials into the crowbar because she found it.

Directions: Read the paragraph below and answer questions 96 through 100.

A trooper responding to a robbery in progress must act in accordance with the public safety purposes of protecting life and property, avoiding unnecessary injury to the public, apprehending criminals, and collecting and preserving evidence.

While patrolling in his radio patrol car, Trooper Evans was notified of a silent alarm indicating that a robbery was taking place at the National Bank located at Broad and Main Streets. Trooper Evans was approximately one mile from the bank. He turned on his overhead lights and constant siren and sped to the bank, slowing to approximately 20 miles per hour as he proceeded through red lights at intersections. When he arrived at the bank, he angle-parked the radio car in front of the entrance, leaving on the turret light and siren, drew his gun, and rushed in the front door of the bank. Inside, he found that the robbers had already fled. Evans questioned the bank manager, and the following exchange occurred:

Evans: "Which way did they go?"
Manager: "They left by the front door."
Evans: "How many were there?
Manager: "Three."
Evans: "Were they white or black?"

Manager: "I'm not sure. I think they were Hispanic."
Evans: "What kind of guns did they have?"
Manager: "I'm not sure."

Trooper Evans went to his car and radioed the following message to the radio dispatcher: "Be on the lookout for three Hispanic males, armed with guns, who fled the National Bank at Broad and Main Streets, approximately two minutes ago."

Trooper Evans returned to the bank, sat at the bank manager's desk, and asked the bank manager to describe what happened. The bank manager told him that she had been sitting at her desk when a male and a female came into his office and sat down. They asked about a loan. Shortly thereafter, a very tall Hispanic male joined them, saying he was a relative. After a minute, the taller male moved behind the bank manager, and the shorter male stood up, leaned on the desk, and put a knife against the manager's neck. The shorter male told the manager to take them behind the tellers' counter or he would cut her throat. The manager agreed and escorted them behind the tellers' counter. The tall male filled a tan canvas bag with money, and the three robbers left. At that point, one of the tellers pressed the silent alarm button.

96. Which of the following actions taken by Trooper Evans was proper and in accordance with the purposes of public safety?
   a. speeding with his overhead lights and siren on directly to the front of the bank
   b. slowing down to approximately 20 miles per hour as he proceeded through red lights at intersections
   c. angle parking in front of the bank entrance and leaving on his overhead lights and siren
   d. drawing his gun as he entered the bank

97. During Trooper Evans's initial questions to the bank manager, what was the most improper, leading, and suggestive question that he asked?
   a. Which way did they go?
   b. How many were there?
   c. Were they white or black?
   d. What kind of guns did they have?

98. Which part of the message that Trooper Evans transmitted to the radio dispatcher was supported by the information he had received from the bank manager?
   a. three Hispanic males
   b. armed with guns
   c. fled the National Bank at Broad and Main Streets
   d. about two minutes ago

99. What information would have been important to give to the radio dispatcher?
   a. One robber was a very tall Hispanic male.
   b. The robbers were carrying a canvas bag filled with money.
   c. One robber was a female, and one robber had a knife.
   d. all of the above

100. Regarding the collection and preservation of evidence, for which action could Trooper Evans be most criticized?
   a. transmitting an inaccurate description of the robbers
   b. asking leading and suggestive questions before letting the bank manager describe what had occurred
   c. sitting in the bank manager's chair
   d. failing to immediately set up a crime scene

► Answers

1. b. The body temperature dropped 10°, corresponding to ten hours, during the progress of rigor mortis. Choices **a**, **c**, and **d** do not correctly apply the formula of body temperature loss and the time factors involved.

2. c. The body temperature dropped 38°, corresponding to 38 hours, after rigor mortis dissipated. Choices **a**, **b**, and **d** do not correctly apply the formula of body temperature loss and the time factors involved.

3. d. No rigor mortis was present; therefore, the correct answer must be either less than four hours or more than 36 hours. Choices **a**, **b**, and **c** are incorrect. Because the body temperature dropped 8°, corresponding to eight hours, the answer could not be less than four hours and must be more than 36 hours.

4. d. The bank manager appears to be a reliable complainant with credible information about the crime. Choices **a** and **b** are incorrect because, though the conduct could raise a reasonable suspicion, the people involved more than likely had innocent explanations. Choice **c** is incorrect because the intoxicated person's complaint, without further information, appears farfetched.

5. d. Running from the police under these circumstances satisfies the standards of probable cause to make an arrest. Choice **a** is incorrect because reasonable suspicion alone is not enough to make a lawful arrest. Choice **b** in itself is not reliable. Choice **c** is incorrect because a reputation for criminal conduct does not amount to a crime.

6. a. Cooper entered the school unlawfully because she was not licensed or privileged to enter the school. Choice **b** is incorrect because parents must stop at the security desk. Choice **c** is incorrect because Stoker was not physically injured. Choice **d** is incorrect

because Cooper did not have the intent to commit a crime when she entered the school.

7. b. This is the only choice that provides an incorrect charge, because Cooper remained in the school with intent to commit a crime therein. Choices **a**, **c**, and **d** are correct answers because she unlawfully entered and she unlawfully remained with the intent to commit a crime therein.

8. b. This is the only choice that provides an untrue charge; Cooper is not guilty of assault because Stoker was not physically injured. Choice **c** is true because Cooper entered the building with the intent to commit a crime therein. Choices **a** and **d** are also true.

9. c. The traffic system can work only with the public's cooperation and voluntary compliance. Not enough troopers are available to issue summonses for every violation, so choice **a** is incorrect. Choice **b** is incorrect because troopers should not ignore the less serious violations when they are committed in their presence. Choice **d** is incorrect because revenue is not the primary consideration.

10. d. This is the best answer because all laws are qualified by the need to act in genuine emergencies. Choice **a** is incorrect because traffic laws are designed not only for intentional violators, but also for negligent or careless violators. Choice **b** is incorrect because traffic laws are enforced against all citizens to encourage them to drive carefully. Choice **c** is incorrect because looking both ways does not excuse the violation.

11. d. Choice **d** is correct because it most likely could be evidence of poisoning. Choice **a** is incorrect; a suicide note would lead away from an inference of homicide. Choice **b** is incorrect; without more information, a person's presence established by fingerprints does not establish that the person committed a crime. Choice **c** is incorrect; it is more likely evidence of death by natural causes.

12. c. Such defensive wounds indicate that the victim was trying to defend himself or herself from an assault. Choice **a** is incorrect; it would lead to an inference of suicide. Choice **b** is incorrect; although the gun found ten feet away could lead to an inference of homicide, it is not conclusive because the person could have staggered away from the spot of the shooting or thrown the gun as a reaction to the shot. Choice **d** is incorrect because the person could have been attempting suicide and missed with the first shot.

13. c. A fire started in more than one spot is not likely to have been accidental, especially when it occurred while the building was closed. Choice **a** is incorrect because most buildings are insured. Choice **b** is incorrect because it is less likely to have been arson than choice **c**. Choice **d** is incorrect in that it is a lesser factor for suspicion than choice **c**.

14. d. The murder of the victim could have been the motive to set the fire in order to cover up the murder. Choices **a**, **b**, and **c** are incorrect because they offer no evidence to infer that arson occurred.

15. a. It is most likely to serve in establishing *corpus delicti*; because the victim had no carbon dioxide in the lungs, he or she must have died before the fire, and the bruises indicate physical force. Choices **b** and **c** are less likely because the victim had carbon dioxide and could have died accidentally from the fire. Choice **d** is incorrect; although the fire was intentionally set, no evidence is given of who set the fire (it may have been the victim) or whether it was set with the intention of killing the victim.

16. d. It assumes that the light was red and suggests the answer to the witness. Choices **a**, **b**, and **c** are proper non-leading questions.

17. a. The question assumes that there was a knife and that Mr. Ko slashed at Ms. Lang. It is a leading question that suggests the answer to the witness. Choices **b**, **c**, and **d** are proper non-leading questions.

18. d. Kidnapping is more serious than robbery and also more serious than grand larceny by extortion, which is more serious than grand larceny from the person.

19. b. Grand larceny from the person is less serious than grand larceny by extortion and robbery, both of which are less serious than kidnapping.

20. d. The details obtained may be helpful to the investigation. Choices **a** and **b** are incorrect because both actions could cause the caller to hang up. Choice **c** is incorrect because the officer should not provide information to the caller about the case that the caller may not know.

21. b. *Woman* is singular and requires a singular possessive (*her*).

22. a. The words that pertain to *Robert and Robin* are all plural to agree with the plural subject.

23. c. In choice **a**, *a mayor* does not agree in number with *they*. Choices **b** and **d** spell *cities* incorrectly for this sentence's intended meaning. Choice **d** also incorrectly lowercases *United States*.

24. a. Choices **b**, **c**, and **d** each contain one or more grammatical or tense errors.

25. d. Use *number* with nouns that can be counted: number of summonses, number of cars. Also, *summonses* is the correct plural of the noun *summons*. In addition, *was* is the proper verb to use with the singular number.

26. a. The correct word is *severity; severeness* and *severness* are not words. *Trooper Prentiss's* is the proper possessive form; *Prentisses* is not a possessive.

27. d. The compound noun requires a plural verb and plural object.

28. a. This is a sentence fragment. Choices **b**, **c**, and **d** are grammatically correct sentences.

29. b. This sentence unnecessarily makes *strength* plural. Choices **a**, **c**, and **d** are grammatically correct sentences.

30. a. *Therefore* indicates that the ankle injury resulted in Trooper Vitry's being excused.

31. b. Use *fewer* with nouns that can be counted: fewer summonses, fewer cars, fewer dogs and cats, etc. Use *less* with nouns that cannot be counted: less time, less money, etc.

32. d. The appropriate verb tense is the present.

33. b. Choices **a** and **c** are incorrect; *personnel* is spelled with one *l* and is not a synonym for *personal*. Choice **c** is incorrect because is an adjective that is appropriately used to modify only a person's personality or character traits. Choice **d** is not a word.

34. b. *Separate* is the correct spelling.

35. c. *License* is the correct spelling.

36. a. *Trooper* is not a proper noun and, therefore, should not be capitalized.

37. c. Both *summonses* and *motorist* are common nouns; there is no need to capitalize either.

38. a. This includes personal descriptors that a suspect is not likely to be able to alter and provides safety information as to whether the suspect may have been armed.

39. b. This includes descriptors that the suspect may most easily alter within a short period of time. Headgear and upper body outerwear may be easily discarded. The suspect may have been wearing a wig. Lower body outerwear is not so easily discarded but is often very general (e.g., blue jeans, black slacks).

40. c. Although the description is very general, it is the most important piece of information, followed by choices **d** and **b**. Choice **a** provides the least useful information because the suspect can easily discard the bandana, but it may be useful in conjunction with the other information.

41. b. You calculated 6 × 111. Choice **a** is an incorrect multiplication. Choice **c** is most likely based on recalling four rather than six tires having been taken. Choice **d** is the value of the All Season Ultra tires.

42. d. You calculated 4 × $83.99. Choice **a** is an incorrect multiplication. Choice **b** is the value of the Pathfinder Truck SUV tires. Choice **c** is most likely based on recalling six rather than four tires having been taken.

43. a. $1,565.92 is the sum of all the tire values. (6 × 66) + (6 × 111) + (4 × 41.99) + (4 × 83.99). Choice **b** reverses numbers and results in an addition error. Choice **c** omits the value of the All Season Ultra Tires. Choice **d** omits the value of the Pathfinder Truck/SUV tires.

44. b. $123.75 is determined by solving 0.495 × 250 mile. Choices **a**, **c**, and **d** are arrived at by incorrectly placing the decimal point or rounding up or down the 49.5 cents a mile.

45. a. Choice **a** is determined by solving $49 × 3 for the days of travel, which totals $147. You must then determine that 75% of $49 is $36.75, which is the reimbursement for each of the two travel days. The total reimbursement is $147 + $73.50, which totals $220.50. Choice **b** is based on Trooper Suki receiving $49 for all five days. Choice **c** is based on Trooper Suki receiving $36.75 for all five days, and choice **d** is incorrect because a correct answer is available.

46. c. Choice **c** is determined by adding the correct mileage reimbursement to the correct meal reimbursement ($123.75 + $220.50 = $344.25). Choices **a** and **b** are derived from earlier incorrect calculations.

47. d. This is a two-step problem. First, add the five numbers: 80 + 50 + 50 + 80 + 60 = 320. Now, divide the sum by 5 (the number of days) to find the average: 320 ÷ 5 = 64.

48. b. First, determine what percent of the summonses were not for speeding by subtracting: 100% − 75% = 25%. Change 25% to a decimal (0.25) and solve 0.25 × 460.

49. d. Trooper Rosen's decision is based on a three-hour train ride, about 30 minutes to get from the station to his meeting site, and another 30 minutes of extra time, for a total of four hours. If he is on the 10 A.M. train, he will have four hours to reach his destination.

50. c. You must multiply the value of the CDs by four and then correctly add the other items to derive the total.

51. a. Choice **a** is the sum of all the values. (10 × $112) + (9 × $90) + (6 × $80) + (5 × $55) = $2,685.

52. c. Choice **c** is the sum of Bette's personal items plus the value of the store's items ($683.96 + $2,685 = $3,368.96).

53. b. 1500 hours is 3 P.M.; an eight-hour shift that begins at 3 P.M. would end at 11 P.M.

54. a. 0814 is the same as 8:14 A.M. and 0940 is the same as 9:40 A.M. The elapsed time between them is one hour and 26 minutes.

55. c. Troopers who begin ten-hour tours at 0600 will complete their tours at 1600 hours, which is 4 P.M.

56. c. The map legend shows grade-separated crossings at Federal Bd, Sheridan Bd, Wadsworth Bd, and Kipling St.

57. d. The map shows that part of W Jewell Av runs parallel to the proposed rail route, but it does not intersect it anywhere along the route.

58. c. The map shows three separated crossings, one at Union Bd, one at Simms St, and one between Simms and Oak Streets.

59. a. The vehicle traveling on Federal Bd from Exposition Av to 23rd Av will cross the alignment at the intersection of 10th Av and Federal Bd.

60. b. Although the map does not indicate the name of every avenue, these can be identified in the area of the I-25 grade crossing. Choice **a** is incorrect because 10th Av is shown as ending at Federal Bd. Choice **c** is incorrect because neither 8th Av nor 6th Av shows a crossing planned for the places at which they

intersect with I-25. Choice **d** is incorrect because the map shows that I-25 will be affected by the alignment.

61. c. Turning left would be turning west, and Middletown is west of the road. Choice **a** is incorrect because continuing north would not bring him west. Choice **b** is incorrect because turning right would be turning to the east. Choice **d** is incorrect because heading south would not bring him west.

62. b. Turning right would be turning west, and Middletown is west of the road. Choice **a** is incorrect because continuing south would not bring him west. Choice **c** is incorrect because turning left would be turning to the east. Choice **d** is incorrect because heading north would not bring him west.

63. d. He must head south to the east-west road before turning west. Choice **a** is incorrect because continuing north would not bring him west. Choice **b** is incorrect because turning right would be turning to the east. Choice **c** is incorrect because although he would be heading west, he would be north of Middletown, and this would not be as efficient as proceeding to the east-west road on the same latitude as Middletown.

64. d. He must head north to the east-west road before turning west. Choice **a** is incorrect because continuing south would not bring him west. Choice **b** is incorrect because although he would be heading west, he would be south of Middletown, and this would not be as efficient as proceeding to the east-west road on the same latitude as Middletown. Choice **c** is incorrect because turning left would be turning to the east.

65. d. Because Bear Mountain was east of his location, he must turn around and head west to Middletown. Choice **a** is incorrect because going straight would be continuing east and

Middletown is west. Choice **b** is incorrect because heading north would not bring him west. Choice **c** is incorrect because heading south would not bring him west.

66. c. The trooper is 20 + 20 = 40 miles from Middletown when he receives the call. Traveling at 60 mph, which is one mile per minute, he could reach Middletown in 40 minutes.

67. c. 20 + 40 = 60. 60 miles at 60 mph = 60 minutes.

68. c. 20 + 30 = 50. 50 miles at 60 mph = 50 minutes.

69. d. 20 + 20 = 40 miles. 30 mph = one-half mile per minute. 40 miles at one-half mile per minute = 80 minutes to travel 40 miles.

70. c. 20 + 40 + 5 + 5 = 70. 70 at 60 mph = 70 minutes.

71. c. Three people are seen crossing the street in the photo.

72. a. The woman in the center of the photo closest to the viewer is wearing headphones that appear to be connected to a personal music device.

73. d. On the right-hand side of the photo, two people are in the corner of the photo, one partially hidden by a wall and the other crouched in front of the wall. One vehicle can be seen in the background moving in the direction opposite the train.

74. c. Three people are seen crossing the tracks and two people are visible in the left-hand portion of the photo.

75. a. The two people coming toward the photographer appear to both be women who are dressed casually.

76. b. The train is on one set of tracks and another set can be seen where the woman with the personal music device is walking.

77. c. The first and third numbers are exactly alike.

78. a. All the numbers are the same; the difference is that the middle combination is preceded by the letter *j*.

79. b. The first and second names and numbers are exactly alike.

80. d. When the first letter is the same, names are alphabetized based on each succeeding letter. In this example, the first names are not relevant.

81. c. The woman's first statement appears to have been an excited utterance because it was made while she was running and screaming after she had just been choked. The choking was evidenced by the red marks. Choice **a** is incorrect because the trooper would be allowed to testify to the first statement. Choices **b** and **d** are incorrect; the trooper would not be allowed to testify to the second statement, because it was made after considerable time had passed and the woman had had time to calm down and reflect.

82. d. The husband made the statement after considerable time had passed; he apparently was calm and had had time to reflect and to contrive a self-serving answer. Choices **a**, **b**, and **c** are incorrect because the statement was neither a spontaneous declaration nor an excited utterance.

83. d. Out-of-court statements may be admissible when they are not offered for the truth of the fact asserted in the statement. Here it was offered to attack the husband's credibility by showing his prior inconsistent statement. Choices **a**, **b**, and **c** are incorrect because the statement was neither a spontaneous declaration nor an excited utterance.

84. c. It would not be admissible because considerable time had passed and the driver had had time to reflect and to contrive a self-serving answer. Choices **a**, **b**, and **c** are incorrect because they may be admissible, because they were made in response to and immediately after startling events.

85. d. This is improper because nothing should be touched until photographs are taken and the item is examined for fingerprints. Choices **a**, **b**, and **c** were proper.

86. c. This is improper because they did not find the crowbar on the windowsill but in the backyard. Choices **a**, **b**, and **d** were proper.

87. d. Because Trooper Hanson is a rookie, it was proper for her to let Fitzpatrick take the lead. Choices **a** and **b** were improper; she should have remained at the front door as instructed. Choice **c** was improper; she picked up evidence and moved it before it was photographed.

88. d. Choices **a**, **b**, and **c** were all improper handling of evidence.

89. c. This is the most serious impairment because by placing the crowbar on the marks, she may have destroyed or marred the evidentiary value of the initial marks. Choice **a** is not a serious impairment, though finding the crowbar without picking it up would have been beneficial. Choices **b** and **d** are impairments, but not as serious as choice **c**.

90. d. Choices **a**, **b**, and **c** were all improper.

91. d. Choices **a**, **b**, and **c** were all improper.

92. d. The apple could be evidence to identify the perpetrator. It could be possible to recover DNA evidence from the perpetrator's saliva on the apple. It could also be possible to photograph and preserve the apple to match the bite with a suspect's teeth. Choices **a**, **b**, and **c** were all proper actions.

93. d. This is the best action. Choices **a**, **b**, and **c** were all improper because potential evidence was destroyed.

94. a. The crowbar is potential evidence. Choice **b** is improper because a note can be lost; he should have scratched his initials into the crowbar. Choice **c** is improper because Hanson found the crowbar and should have been the one to initial it for identification. Choice **d** is improper because he should have deliv-

ered the photographs himself to preserve and limit the chain of evidence.

95. d. Because Hanson found the crowbar and will have to be the one to identify it in court, she will need to identify it with her initials. Choice **a** is incorrect because the crowbar has already been moved from its initial crime scene placement. Choice **b** is incorrect because placing the crowbar could damage the existing marks and/or create new marks. Choice **c** is incorrect because a taped note can be easily lost.

96. d. Because the trooper decided to enter the bank, it was reasonable for him to draw his gun as he approached the potentially dangerous situation. Choices **a** and **c** are incorrect because approaching the bank with the siren on would alert the robbers that the police were coming. Choice **b** is incorrect because going through red lights at 20 miles per hour recklessly endangers the public. A trooper should come to a full stop before proceeding through a red light.

97. d. This is the most improper because the question assumed the fact that the robbers had guns. Choice **c** was improper but less so than choice **d**. Choices **a** and **b** were proper questions.

98. c. It is the only choice with correct information. Choices **a**, **b**, and **d** contain erroneous information.

99. d. Choices **a**, **b**, and **c** each provided useful descriptive information.

100. c. By sitting in the bank manager's chair where part of the crime occurred, the trooper may have destroyed fingerprints or other evidence. Choice **d** is not the best answer because although the trooper failed to set up a crime scene, it was not as severe an error as **c**. Choices **a** and **b** are not the best answers because they do not directly relate to preservation of evidence.

16 ▶ State Trooper Practice Test 6

CHAPTER SUMMARY

This is the sixth and final practice test in the book based on the most commonly tested areas on the state trooper exam.

T he practice test consists of 100 multiple-choice questions in the following areas: reading comprehension, writing and information ordering, mathematics, spatial and directional orientation, memory and observation, and problem solving. Set aside two hours to take this practice test.

This practice test is available through the LearningExpress online link, if you prefer to take it on the computer.

State Trooper Practice Test 6

1.	ⓐ	ⓑ	ⓒ	ⓓ
2.	ⓐ	ⓑ	ⓒ	ⓓ
3.	ⓐ	ⓑ	ⓒ	ⓓ
4.	ⓐ	ⓑ	ⓒ	ⓓ
5.	ⓐ	ⓑ	ⓒ	ⓓ
6.	ⓐ	ⓑ	ⓒ	ⓓ
7.	ⓐ	ⓑ	ⓒ	ⓓ
8.	ⓐ	ⓑ	ⓒ	ⓓ
9.	ⓐ	ⓑ	ⓒ	ⓓ
10.	ⓐ	ⓑ	ⓒ	ⓓ
11.	ⓐ	ⓑ	ⓒ	ⓓ
12.	ⓐ	ⓑ	ⓒ	ⓓ
13.	ⓐ	ⓑ	ⓒ	ⓓ
14.	ⓐ	ⓑ	ⓒ	ⓓ
15.	ⓐ	ⓑ	ⓒ	ⓓ
16.	ⓐ	ⓑ	ⓒ	ⓓ
17.	ⓐ	ⓑ	ⓒ	ⓓ
18.	ⓐ	ⓑ	ⓒ	ⓓ
19.	ⓐ	ⓑ	ⓒ	ⓓ
20.	ⓐ	ⓑ	ⓒ	ⓓ
21.	ⓐ	ⓑ	ⓒ	ⓓ
22.	ⓐ	ⓑ	ⓒ	ⓓ
23.	ⓐ	ⓑ	ⓒ	ⓓ
24.	ⓐ	ⓑ	ⓒ	ⓓ
25.	ⓐ	ⓑ	ⓒ	ⓓ
26.	ⓐ	ⓑ	ⓒ	ⓓ
27.	ⓐ	ⓑ	ⓒ	ⓓ
28.	ⓐ	ⓑ	ⓒ	ⓓ
29.	ⓐ	ⓑ	ⓒ	ⓓ
30.	ⓐ	ⓑ	ⓒ	ⓓ
31.	ⓐ	ⓑ	ⓒ	ⓓ
32.	ⓐ	ⓑ	ⓒ	ⓓ
33.	ⓐ	ⓑ	ⓒ	ⓓ
34.	ⓐ	ⓑ	ⓒ	ⓓ
35.	ⓐ	ⓑ	ⓒ	ⓓ

36.	ⓐ	ⓑ	ⓒ	ⓓ
37.	ⓐ	ⓑ	ⓒ	ⓓ
38.	ⓐ	ⓑ	ⓒ	ⓓ
39.	ⓐ	ⓑ	ⓒ	ⓓ
40.	ⓐ	ⓑ	ⓒ	ⓓ
41.	ⓐ	ⓑ	ⓒ	ⓓ
42.	ⓐ	ⓑ	ⓒ	ⓓ
43.	ⓐ	ⓑ	ⓒ	ⓓ
44.	ⓐ	ⓑ	ⓒ	ⓓ
45.	ⓐ	ⓑ	ⓒ	ⓓ
46.	ⓐ	ⓑ	ⓒ	ⓓ
47.	ⓐ	ⓑ	ⓒ	ⓓ
48.	ⓐ	ⓑ	ⓒ	ⓓ
49.	ⓐ	ⓑ	ⓒ	ⓓ
50.	ⓐ	ⓑ	ⓒ	ⓓ
51.	ⓐ	ⓑ	ⓒ	ⓓ
52.	ⓐ	ⓑ	ⓒ	ⓓ
53.	ⓐ	ⓑ	ⓒ	ⓓ
54.	ⓐ	ⓑ	ⓒ	ⓓ
55.	ⓐ	ⓑ	ⓒ	ⓓ
56.	ⓐ	ⓑ	ⓒ	ⓓ
57.	ⓐ	ⓑ	ⓒ	ⓓ
58.	ⓐ	ⓑ	ⓒ	ⓓ
59.	ⓐ	ⓑ	ⓒ	ⓓ
60.	ⓐ	ⓑ	ⓒ	ⓓ
61.	ⓐ	ⓑ	ⓒ	ⓓ
62.	ⓐ	ⓑ	ⓒ	ⓓ
63.	ⓐ	ⓑ	ⓒ	ⓓ
64.	ⓐ	ⓑ	ⓒ	ⓓ
65.	ⓐ	ⓑ	ⓒ	ⓓ
66.	ⓐ	ⓑ	ⓒ	ⓓ
67.	ⓐ	ⓑ	ⓒ	ⓓ
68.	ⓐ	ⓑ	ⓒ	ⓓ
69.	ⓐ	ⓑ	ⓒ	ⓓ
70.	ⓐ	ⓑ	ⓒ	ⓓ

71.	ⓐ	ⓑ	ⓒ	ⓓ
72.	ⓐ	ⓑ	ⓒ	ⓓ
73.	ⓐ	ⓑ	ⓒ	ⓓ
74.	ⓐ	ⓑ	ⓒ	ⓓ
75.	ⓐ	ⓑ	ⓒ	ⓓ
76.	ⓐ	ⓑ	ⓒ	ⓓ
77.	ⓐ	ⓑ	ⓒ	ⓓ
78.	ⓐ	ⓑ	ⓒ	ⓓ
79.	ⓐ	ⓑ	ⓒ	ⓓ
80.	ⓐ	ⓑ	ⓒ	ⓓ
81.	ⓐ	ⓑ	ⓒ	ⓓ
82.	ⓐ	ⓑ	ⓒ	ⓓ
83.	ⓐ	ⓑ	ⓒ	ⓓ
84.	ⓐ	ⓑ	ⓒ	ⓓ
85.	ⓐ	ⓑ	ⓒ	ⓓ
86.	ⓐ	ⓑ	ⓒ	ⓓ
87.	ⓐ	ⓑ	ⓒ	ⓓ
88.	ⓐ	ⓑ	ⓒ	ⓓ
89.	ⓐ	ⓑ	ⓒ	ⓓ
90.	ⓐ	ⓑ	ⓒ	ⓓ
91.	ⓐ	ⓑ	ⓒ	ⓓ
92.	ⓐ	ⓑ	ⓒ	ⓓ
93.	ⓐ	ⓑ	ⓒ	ⓓ
94.	ⓐ	ⓑ	ⓒ	ⓓ
95.	ⓐ	ⓑ	ⓒ	ⓓ
96.	ⓐ	ⓑ	ⓒ	ⓓ
97.	ⓐ	ⓑ	ⓒ	ⓓ
98.	ⓐ	ⓑ	ⓒ	ⓓ
99.	ⓐ	ⓑ	ⓒ	ⓓ
100.	ⓐ	ⓑ	ⓒ	ⓓ

▶ State Trooper Practice Test 6

Directions: Read the following passage, then answer questions 1 and 2.

The Police Benevolent Association (PBA) has developed a monthly newsletter for academy class 15. The newsletter will be created using new desktop computer equipment and software that the PBA recently purchased with members' dues money. In the future, the PBA may use the same equipment to create additional newsletters and to print business cards for officers, as well as brochures publicizing its activities on behalf of its members.

1. The paragraph best supports the statement that the PBA
   a. has increased the amount of dues it collects from each member.
   b. has developed a newsletter for one specific academy class.
   c. offers a wide variety of benefits to its members.
   d. currently makes business cards available to all its members.

2. From the paragraph you are able to determine
   a. that academy classes 1 to 14 also had newsletters developed for them.
   b. that the PBA has never before developed newsletters for academy classes.
   c. that the PBA never had computers before this purchase.
   d. none of the above

Directions: Read the following passage, then answer questions 3 through 14.

According to law, a trooper, in the course of effecting an arrest or preventing the escape from custody of a person whom he or she reasonably believes to have committed a crime, may use deadly physical force to effect the arrest or prevent the escape when and to the extent he or she reasonably believes such to be necessary only when he or she reasonably believes the crime was:

1. A felony or attempt to commit a felony involving the use or attempted use or threatened imminent use of physical force against a person; or
2. Kidnapping, arson, escape in the first degree, burglary in the first degree or any attempt to commit such a crime; or
3. A felony, and in the course of resisting arrest or attempting to escape from custody, the person who committed the felony is armed with a firearm or deadly weapon.

Regardless of the particular offense which is the subject of the arrest or attempted escape, the use of deadly physical force is necessary to defend the police officer or another person from what the trooper reasonably believes to be the use or imminent use of deadly physical force.

State police department policies emphasize that troopers use deadly physical force only as a last resort and only when reasonable and necessary.

3. Robbery is a crime involving the use or attempted use or threatened imminent use of physical force against a person. A trooper on patrol near a school has observed a 16-year-old youth threaten a smaller youth. The 16-year-old yelled that he would punch the younger boy in the face if the boy did not give him his lunch money. When the trooper approaches, the 16-year-old runs. The trooper tries to catch him, but cannot. What action should the trooper NOT take?
  a. Use deadly physical force to effect the arrest.
  b. Ask the smaller youth whether he knows the name of the 16-year-old.
  c. Transmit a radio description of the 16-year-old.
  d. Prepare a report and refer the case to the detective division for further investigation.

4. Felonious assault is a crime involving the use or attempted use or threatened imminent use of physical force against a person. A trooper responds to a 911 call of a family fight in a private house. When he enters the house, a woman tells him that her husband severely beat her. She is bruised and bleeding. She tells the trooper her husband is in the kitchen, and she wants him arrested. As the trooper enters the kitchen, the husband runs out a back door. The trooper chases him, but the husband jumps in his car and starts to drive away. As the husband passes the trooper, the trooper should
  a. shoot at him before the car picks up speed.
  b. shoot the windshield so the husband will not be able to drive away.
  c. shoot one of the tires to disable the car.
  d. get the plate number of the car and transmit a radio description of the car and the husband.

5. Murder is a crime involving the use of physical force against a person. A trooper responds to a 911 call of a family fight in a private house. When she enters the house, she finds the body of a recently deceased woman. The deceased has stab wounds to her torso. The trooper determines that the woman's husband is still in the house and is carrying a knife. The trooper finds the husband sitting on a chair in a bedroom. The husband refuses to surrender and refuses to drop the knife. The trooper should
  a. call for backup and try to keep the husband contained until assistance arrives.
  b. shoot the husband if he starts to get out of the chair.
  c. try to shoot the knife out of his hand.
  d. shoot him if he tries to jump out of the bedroom window.

6. A trooper responds to a 911 call outside an apartment building regarding a past rape. When he arrives, the parents of a 13-year-old female complain to the trooper that their daughter had sexual intercourse with a 20-year-old male who lives in a different apartment in the same building. The trooper enters the building to arrest the male, but the male flees. The trooper chases the male, but the male outruns him and is about to get away. What action should the trooper take?
  a. The trooper should shoot the male in the legs to prevent his escape.
  b. The trooper should shoot only if he cannot radio for the assistance of other troopers.
  c. The trooper should let the male get away rather than shoot at him.
  d. The trooper should fire warning shots over the head of the male.

7. A trooper responds to a 911 call regarding a suspicious man at a playground. As the trooper arrives, several women run toward her, shouting that a man just dragged a little girl into a parking lot. The man threatened the women with a knife. He was wearing a gray sweatshirt. The trooper runs into the parking lot and sees a man wearing a gray and white sweatshirt slam the trunk of a car closed. The man hurries to the driver's door and begins to open the door with car keys. The trooper shouts to the man to stop, but the man turns the key in the door. What action would be improper for the trooper to take?
  a. to refrain from shooting, because she cannot be sure that it is the same man the women described or that the girl is in the trunk
  b. to run to the man and attempt to prevent him from getting in the car
  c. to immediately shoot the man if she does not believe that by using other means, she can prevent the man from driving away
  d. to take the plate number and transmit a radio description of the car and the man

8. Burglary first degree is a crime involving the use or attempted use or threatened imminent use of physical force against a person. In which of the following circumstances might a trooper be justified in using deadly physical force if reasonable and necessary to arrest or prevent escape from custody?
  a. when a person has committed burglary third degree
  b. when a person has committed burglary second degree
  c. when a person has committed burglary first or second degree
  d. when a person has committed burglary first degree

9. In which of the following circumstances might a trooper be justified in using deadly physical force if reasonable and necessary to arrest or prevent escape from custody?
  a. when a person has committed escape third or second degree
  b. when a person has committed escape second degree
  c. when a person has committed escape first or second degree
  d. when a person has committed escape first degree

10. It would be most accurate to state that a trooper might be justified in using deadly physical force if reasonable and necessary to arrest or prevent escape from custody of a person who committed
  a. arson third or second degree.
  b. arson second degree.
  c. arson first degree.
  d. arson first, second, or third degree.

11. It would be most accurate to state that a trooper might be justified in using deadly physical force if reasonable and necessary to arrest or prevent escape from custody in which of the following circumstances?
  a. to arrest a person who committed a felony
  b. to arrest a person who committed a felony and who resists arrest by running away
  c. to arrest a person who committed a felony and who resists arrest by threatening to use physical force
  d. to arrest a person who committed a misdemeanor and who resists arrest by threatening to use deadly physical force

12. It would be most accurate to state that a trooper might be justified in using deadly physical force if reasonable and necessary to arrest or prevent escape from custody in which of the following circumstances?
   a. to arrest a person who committed a felony
   b. to arrest a person who committed a felony and who resists arrest by running away
   c. to arrest a person who committed a misdemeanor and who, while resisting arrest, is armed with a deadly weapon
   d. none of the above

13. It would be most accurate to state that a trooper might be justified in using deadly physical force if reasonable and necessary to arrest or prevent escape from custody in which of the following circumstances?
   a. to arrest a person who committed the felony of burglary third degree and who resists arrest by running away
   b. to arrest a person who committed the felony of burglary third degree and who, while resisting arrest, is armed with a deadly weapon
   c. to arrest a person who committed the felony of burglary second degree and who resists arrest by running away
   d. to arrest a person who committed the felony of burglary second degree and who resists arrest by threatening to use physical force

14. It would be most accurate to state that a trooper might be justified in using deadly physical force if reasonable and necessary to arrest or prevent escape from custody in which of the following circumstances?
   a. to arrest a person for an offense when the person threatens to punch the officer in the face
   b. to arrest a person for an offense when the person refuses to put his or her hands behind his back to be handcuffed
   c. to arrest a person for an offense when the person backs away from the officer while holding a knife
   d. to arrest a person for an offense when the person refuses to comply with the officer's directions to freeze, takes a combat stance, reaches into his or her waistband, and removes an object that appears to be a weapon

Directions: Read the following passage, then answer questions 15 through 20.

Many troopers are eager to prevent crime, often at the expense of their own safety. State police departments, on the other hand, often prefer that troopers take less dangerous actions and rather observe and report possible criminal behavior and even, sometimes, allow a possible suspect to leave the scene to assure the protection of life first, whether the trooper's or someone else's.

15. At ten minutes to midnight, Trooper Gold from his patrol car observes two men standing outside a liquor store. He has not seen these men in the neighborhood before, and Gold knows that the liquor-store owner usually closes at midnight and takes the day's receipts home with him. Which of the following would be the most appropriate action for Gold to take?
   a. Immediately stop and frisk the men for weapons.
   b. Chase the two men away from the store.
   c. Pay no more attention to them since they may have a perfectly innocent explanation for standing outside the store.
   d. Observe the men until the store owner closes the store and leaves safely.

16. Assume in connection with question above that Trooper Gold had decided the two men outside the liquor store were probably there for innocent purposes, and Gold drove away because he was off duty at midnight. Assume further that at ten minutes after midnight, as Gold was parking his patrol car at the station house, a report of a robbery at the liquor store was broadcast over the police radio. Which of the following would be the best action for Gold to take?
   a. Park the car, sign out, and go home.
   b. Prepare a report regarding what he had seen and leave it for the next shift.
   c. Immediately call the sergeant and tell her what he had done.
   d. Contact the radio dispatcher to ascertain what had happened at the robbery scene and, if appropriate, advise the dispatcher of the description of the two men he had observed.

17. A trooper is aware of several vicious robberies that have occurred in her area of responsibility. She is dispatched to a reported robbery in a liquor store, and when she arrives she finds the store manager bleeding profusely from a stab wound to the upper arm. The manager tells her that the robber stabbed him and just ran out the back door that leads to an alleyway. The trooper should immediately
   a. run after the robber before he or she gets too far away.
   b. get a description from the manager and transmit it over the police radio.
   c. because the manager is cut only in the upper arm, run after the robber, but transmit a request for an ambulance as she runs.
   d. render medical aid to the manager.

18. In a busy commercial area, a trooper stops two men who fit the description of two robbers who had robbed a fast-food store at gunpoint. The trooper draws her weapon and directs the men to place their hands against the wall in a spread-eagle fashion. One man, who is on the left, complies, placing his hands far apart and keeping his legs spread apart. However, the other man, who is on the right, keeps moving about, pushing off the wall, and bringing his legs together. In considering issues of safety, what is the best course of action for the trooper to take?

   a. The trooper, keeping her gun trained on the men, should take cover and not attempt to frisk the men until backup arrives.

   b. The trooper, with her gun in her right hand, should approach the man on the right and attempt to frisk him with her left hand.

   c. The trooper, with her gun in her right hand, should approach the man on the left and attempt to frisk him with her left hand.

   d. The trooper should direct the man on the right to turn around so she can see whether the man is armed or not.

19. Trooper Green encounters two intoxicated men fighting on the street. Each of the men has a broken beer bottle in his hand. The trooper orders them to drop the beer bottles and to stop fighting, but they continue to circle each other and continue to swing the beer bottles at each other. What should Trooper Green do next?

   a. Get between the two men so that cannot strike each other.

   b. Stay away from the men, call for help, and wait for backup to arrive.

   c. Take out his gun and threaten to shoot the men if they do not stop.

   d. Do not get in between the men, but wait for an opportunity to safely disarm them.

20. Considering her own and the public's safety, which of the following would be the most appropriate circumstances for a trooper to respond to a radio call, using the overhead lights and siren of her vehicle to bypass traffic signals?

   a. responding to a robbery in progress

   b. responding to a burglary in progress

   c. responding to a fight among high school students

   d. responding to a past murder

21. Three of the sentences below contain one or more grammatical or spelling errors. Select the answer choice that is correct as is.

   a. Trooper Rasheed responded to a report from the dispatcher that someone had tripped and fallen in Newtown Mall, and discovered a 10-year-old boy who was hurt bad.

   b. Trooper Rasheed responded to a report from the dispatcher that someone had tripped and had fell in Newtown Mall, and discovered a 10-year-old boy who was hurt bad.

   c. Trooper Rasheed responded to a report from the dispatcher that someone had tripped and had fell in Newtown Mall, and discovered a 10-year-old boy that was badly hurt.

   d. Trooper Rasheed responded to a report from the dispatcher that someone had tripped and fallen in Newtown Mall, and discovered a 10-year-old boy who was badly hurt.

22. Three of the sentences below contain one or more grammatical or spelling errors. Select the answer choice that is correct as is.
  a. Troopers are expected to have his/her uniforms neat, clean, and pressed whenever he/she are on duty.
  b. Troopers are expected to have their uniforms neat, clean, and pressed whenever they are on duty.
  c. A trooper is expected to have their uniform neat, clean and pressed whenever they are on duty.
  d. Troopers are expected to have one's uniforms neat, clean, and pressed whenever one is on duty.

23. Three of the sentences below contain one or more grammatical or spelling errors. Select the answer choice that is correct as is.
  a. Each morning during training, Sergeant Hardy leaded the rookies in a one-mile run at the academy.
  b. Each morning during training, Sergeant Hardy lead the rookies in a one-mile run at the academy.
  c. Each morning during training, Sergeant Hardy led the rookies in a one-mile run at the academy.
  d. Each morning during training, Sergeant Hardy leded the rookies in a one-mile run at the academy.

24. Three of the sentences below contain one or more grammatical or spelling errors. Select the answer choice that is correct as is.
  a. Trooper Alonzo had a better assignment then Trooper Berra.
  b. Trooper Alonzo has a better assignment then Trooper Berra.
  c. Trooper Alonzo has a better assignment than Trooper Berra.
  d. Trooper Alonzo had a betterer assignment than Trooper Berra.

25. Three of the sentences below contain one or more grammatical or spelling errors. Select the answer choice that is correct as is.
  a. Each week, the training sergeant gave the award to the trooper that had the best test scores.
  b. Each week, the Training Sergeant gave the award to the Trooper who had the best test scores.
  c. Each week, the training sergeant gave the award to the trooper who had the best test scores.
  d. Each week, the training sergeant gave the award to the trooper which had the best test scores.

26. Three of the sentences below contain one or more grammatical or spelling errors. Select the answer choice that is correct as is.
  a. Many people believe the community center should be run like a business.
  b. Many people believe the community center should be ran like a business.
  c. Many people believe the community center should be run as a business.
  d. Many people believe the community center should be ran as a business.

27. Three of the sentences below contain one or more grammatical or spelling errors. Select the answer choice that is correct as is.
  a. Sergeant Senior was impressed by the way they do their job.
  b. Sergeant Senior was impressed by the way they did their jobs.
  c. Sergeant Senior was impressed by the way they did their job.
  d. Sergeant Senior was impressed by the way they done their jobs.

28. One of the sentences below contains one or more grammatical or spelling errors. Select the answer choice that contains an error.
   a. The media has a major role in how society portrays women in police forces.
   b. The media have a major role in how women are viewed as police officers.
   c. The media play a major role in how the public views women police officers.
   d. The media have a major role in how women police officers are viewed by members of a community.

29. One of the sentences below contains one or more grammatical or spelling errors. Select the answer choice that contains an error.
   a. The two troopers and two sergeants was sick yesterday.
   b. Two troopers and two sergeants were sick yesterday.
   c. Two troopers and the two sergeants were sick yesterday.
   d. Two troopers and two sergeants reported sick yesterday.

Directions: For questions 30 through 33, choose the word or phrase that best fills the blank to properly complete the sentences.

30. To better respond to calls for police service, the department would like to employ _____ troopers.
   a. many more
   b. much more
   c. a lots more
   d. increased

31. The department sends troopers to college job fairs because it would like to _____ college graduates.
   a. higher
   b. hirer
   c. hire
   d. hyre

32. Trooper Ames knew that she was not to _____ confidential police information to her friends and neighbors.
   a. disclose
   b. close in on
   c. disrobe
   d. disclosure

33. Trooper Campbell makes _____ of felony arrests.
   a. a large number
   b. a largest amount
   c. too many
   d. lot's

34. Identify the sentence that contains a mistake in capitalization, punctuation, grammar, or spelling. If you find no mistakes, select choice **d.**
   a. Juan is the best student. Although he was not born in the United States.
   b. Suzanne is short, but she is able to climb the fence easily.
   c. The academy instructors expect everyone to do well on the first test.
   d. no mistakes

35. Identify the sentence that contains a mistake in capitalization, punctuation, grammar, or spelling. If you find no mistakes, select choice **d**.
   a. John could have did the work quicker than Mary.
   b. John could have done the work more quickly than Mary did it.
   c. John could have done the work quicker than Mary.
   d. no mistakes

36. Identify the sentence that contains a mistake in capitalization, punctuation, grammar, or spelling. If you find no mistakes, select choice **d**.
   a. It is a long drive from Albany to New York City.
   b. It's a long drive from Albany to New York City.
   c. Its' a long drive from Albany to New York City.
   d. no mistakes

37. Identify the sentence that contains a mistake in capitalization, punctuation, grammar, or spelling. If you find no mistakes, select choice **d**.
   a. Suzanne and Margaret both sing well.
   b. Suzanne and Margaret both sing good.
   c. Suzanne and Margaret are both good singers.
   d. no mistakes

Directions: Read the paragraph below and answer questions 38 through 40.

Troopers Chen and Vann were directed by the dispatcher to respond to a private house to take a report of a past burglary. At the scene, the homeowner informed them that she was gone all day on Monday, May 8, that the address for her house was 200 Vee Lane, that her name was Suzie Katzie, and that she had no idea who could have entered her home in the time she left in the morning and returned that evening. She said the intruder took her laptop computer, which was in the house when she left, but is now the only item she has so far determined to be missing.

38. Trooper Chen, the senior officer, is writing up the crime report. Select the answer that expresses the facts reported to her most clearly and accurately.
   a. Suzie Katzie reported that her home at 200 Vee Lane was broken into on May 8 and that her laptop computer is now missing.
   b. Susanne Katz reported that she wasn't home on May 8 and that she lost her laptop computer sometime during her travels that day.
   c. Suzanne Katze reported that her home at 200 V Lane was broken into on May 8 and that her laptop computer is now missing.
   d. Suzie Katzie reported that she went to the mall to buy a dress and that when she came home after stopping along the way for groceries she entered her home at 200 Vee Lane and discovered that her computer wasn't there any more.

39. In the same incident, Troopers Chen and Vann also learn from Suzie Katzie that she had left her front door unlocked because she was expecting a guest, Annie Martin, from out of town, but that Annie had not arrived. Based on this additional information, Trooper Chen decides that her next best action is to do what?
   a. not to take a report because it is obvious that Annie Martin arrived and borrowed the laptop
   b. request a description of Annie Martin and inform the dispatcher that Martin is wanted in connection with a house burglary
   c. lecture Suzie Katzie about the perils of leaving her front door unlocked
   d. none of the above

40. In the same incident, later that night, Trooper Vann explains to her friend that she responded to a call involving a robbery in which a woman named Annie Martin living at 20 Vee Lane reported her laptop was taken. How many facts of the case did Trooper Vann confuse?
a. one
b. two
c. three
d. four

Directions: Read the paragraph below and answer questions 41 through 43.

Trooper King has been advised by the dispatcher to respond to the central bus station to take a complaint from Ms. Danner. When Trooper King interviews Ms. Danner, he learns that she is waiting to take the bus to Center City to visit her children. She explains that her bus ticket cost $49 and she intends to see her grandchild perform in the high school play. After leaving the waiting room to purchase coffee and a sandwich, she returned to the waiting room to find her suitcase missing. There were numerous small clothing and toiletry items in her suitcase for which she could not give an exact value, but she did know the value of a number of the larger items. Among those items, she listed one dress valued at $140, another dress valued at $65, one pantsuit valued at $99.95, one pair of earrings valued at $200, one ring valued at $89, and one yellow metal chain and charm with the initial *S* valued at $560.

41. What is the total value of all the items reported by Ms. Danner?
a. $1,173.95
b. $1,174
c. $849
d. $1,222.95

42. What is the total value of the clothing items reported by Ms. Danner?
a. $849
b. $49
c. $234.95
d. $1,173.95

43. What is the total value of the jewelry items reported by Ms. Danner?
a. $289
b. $849
c. $1,222.95
d. $1,173.95

44. Troop J received ten boxes of yellow crime scene tape to be used to mark off locations from which the public is barred. Each box contains three dozen rolls of tape. How many roles of tape did Troop J receive?
a. 360 rolls
b. 300 rolls
c. 240 rolls
d. There is not enough information to answer the question.

45. Trooper Jackson is assigned to keep track of the summonses issued by Troop B and to mail them to headquarters. In March, he had 400 summonses to mail. Each summons must first be packed into an envelope that holds 20 summonses. How many envelopes will Trooper Jackson need to package the summonses written in March?
a. 80 envelopes
b. 40 envelopes
c. 20 envelopes
d. 10 envelopes

46. Trooper Jackson received a memo from headquarters informing him that in the future, summonses will be packed in envelopes that contain only 15 summonses. Based on his having the same 400 summons as in the question above, how many envelopes will Trooper Jackson need for the summonses written in March?
   a. 80 envelopes
   b. 45 envelopes
   c. 27 envelopes
   d. 18 envelopes

Directions: Read the paragraph below and answer questions 47 and 48.

Troopers Allen and Reedy have been advised by the dispatcher to respond to an apparent burglary at the Experts Are Us computer store. When they arrive, they interview the owner, Mr. Smithfield, who says he locked up on Sunday afternoon and arrived on Monday morning to find the following items missing:

- 3 telephone sets, each valued at $150
- 3 laptop computers, each valued at $2,000
- 2 desktop computers, each valued at $960
- 2 monitors, each valued at $500
- 10 flash drives, each valued at $45

47. What is the total value of all the items reported by Mr. Smithfield?
   a. $3,820
   b. $8,820
   c. $9,370
   d. $9,820

48. On Tuesday, Mr. Smithfield calls the troopers and reports that the telephone sets were not stolen; he found them in a trash can behind the store and believes the thieves left them behind because the other items were more valuable. When Troopers Allen and Reedy file their follow-up report, the total value of items reported missing should be reduced by
   a. $150
   b. $300
   c. $450
   d. nothing, because the sets were removed from the store.

49. Trooper Doyle has been assigned to work with the local elementary school students on arts and crafts projects during antidrug week activities. She spent some of her own money for supplies and the captain has given her permission to request reimbursement. She spent $10 on crayons, $12 on drawing paper, $12.50 on pens, and $26.80 on cutouts and puppets for the students' presentations. What is the total amount that Trooper Doyle is entitled to receive?
   a. $49
   b. $49.30
   c. $61.30
   d. $73.80

50. According to the Casper *Star-Tribune*, in 2005, the Wyoming Highway Patrol issued about 55,000 speeding tickets, 73% of which were issued to men. Assuming the number to have been exactly 55,000 speeding tickets, how many of the speeding tickets were issued to men?
   a. 40,000
   b. 40,150
   c. 40,300
   d. 40,450

Directions: Read the paragraph below and answer questions 51 through 53.

Many police departments use military time to ensure that officers are not confused when reporting for duty or writing reports. Military time uses a 24-hour clock. One minute after midnight is 0001 hours; one minute after noon is 1201 hours, one P.M. is 1300 hours, two P.M. is 1400 hours, and so on until the clock strikes midnight (2400 hours).

51. Trooper Parker works an eight-hour shift that begins at 1700 hours. In non-military time, this means that he works from
   a. 3 P.M. to 11 A.M.
   b. 5 P.M. to 1 A.M.
   c. 6 P.M. to 2 A.M.
   d. 7 P.M. to 3 A.M.

52. Trooper Watts arrived at work at 1924 hours but Trooper Brown did not arrive until 2050 hours. How long was Trooper Watts at work before Trooper Brown arrived?
   a. one hour and 26 minutes
   b. one hour and 54 minutes
   c. two hours and six minutes
   d. two hours and 36 minutes

53. The department is considering changing back from a schedule of four ten-hour tours to its original schedule of five eight-hour tours. When the schedule reverts to the old one, troopers who report for work at 0800 hours will get off duty at
   a. 2 P.M.
   b. 3 P.M.
   c. 4 P.M.
   d. 5 P.M.

Directions: Read the paragraph below and answer questions 54 and 55.

The average starting salary for troopers is $38,000. Rookie troopers spend their first six months in the academy, during which time they earn no overtime pay. Troopers are generally able to earn about 10% over their salary once they are on patrol. In addition, they receive a 4.5% increase at the end of their first full year as troopers.

54. Trooper Altieri should probably expect to earn _____ during her first year.
   a. $38,000
   b. $39,000
   c. $39,900
   d. $41,000

55. The base salary for Trooper Altieri will be _____ during her second year as a trooper.
   a. $39,100
   b. $39,710
   c. $42,000
   d. $55,100

Directions: The city of Pittsburgh is laying out the route for an extension of its existing transit system. The map legend shows you which portions of the new lines will be underground, which will be above ground, and the locations of existing and new stations. A number of major sections of the city and major attractions within those sections are also indicated on the map. Use this map to answer questions 56 through 58.

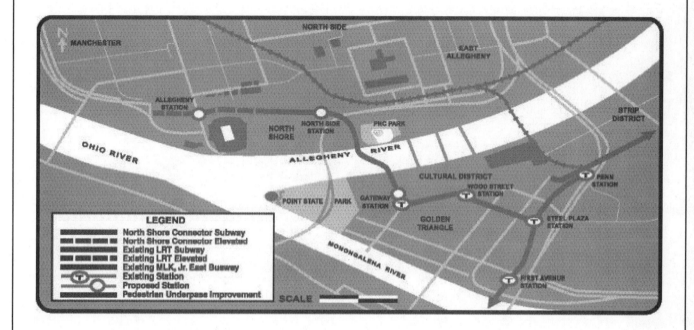

56. East Allegheny is in what direction in relation-ship to the existing Gateway Station?

a. northeast

b. northwest

c. southeast

d. southwest

57. The closest station to PNC Park will be

a. Allegheny Station.

b. North Side Station.

c. Gateway Station.

d. none of the above.

58. The rivers that meet at Point State Park are the

a. Ohio and Allegheny rivers.

b. Allegheny and Monongahela rivers.

c. Ohio and Monongahela rivers.

d. Ohio, Allegheny, and Monongahela rivers.

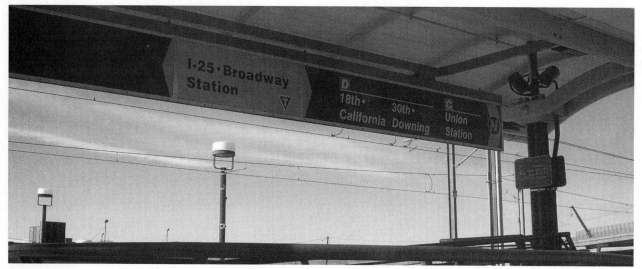

Directions: Use the photo above to answer questions 59 through 61.

59. From the photo, it is most logical to presume that the Broadway Station intersects with highway

a. D 18.

b. C Union.

c. 30th Route.

d. I-25.

60. The number of destinations other than Broad-way Station that are shown in the photo is

a. one.

b. two.

c. three.

d. zero.

61. Based on the directional arrows on the signage at Broadway Station, a rail rider could correctly assume that the train will be heading _____ from Broadway Station to Union Station.

a. south

b. north

c. east

d. west

Directions: The map provides you with locations and routes in south Florida. Lauderdale by the Sea is the northernmost town on the coast; Hallendale Beach is the southernmost; Sunrise is the westernmost. Use this map to answer questions 62 through 66.

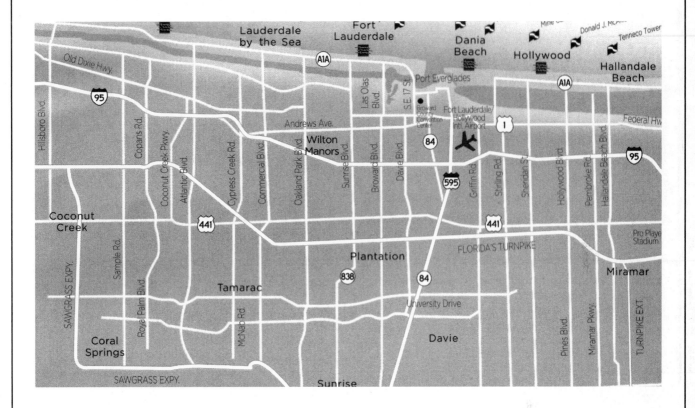

62. To travel from the Broward County Convention Center to Fort Lauderdale/Hollywood International Airport, you would need to go in which direction?
a. northeast
b. southwest
c. southeast
d. northwest

63. The Florida Turnpike runs roughly parallel to U.S. 441 between
a. Coconut Creek Parkway and Pembroke Road.
b. Cypress Creek Road and Hollywood Boulevard.
c. Oakland Park Boulevard and Hollywood Boulevard.
d. Oakland Park Boulevard and Pembroke Road.

64. Old Dixie Highway crosses Interstate 95 at
    a. Copans Road.
    b. Coconut Creed Parkway.
    c. Atlantic Boulevard.
    d. no point.

65. The local road that appears to take you closest to Fort Lauderdale/Hollywood International Airport is
    a. Griffin Road.
    b. Stirling Road.
    c. Davie Boulevard.
    d. S.E. 15th Street.

66. To travel south from Tamarac to Miramar with a minimum of route changes, a driver would be advised to travel on
    a. University Drive.
    b. the Florida Turnpike.
    c. Interstate 95.
    d. US 441.

Directions: Use the map below and answer questions 67 through 70.

67. Martin Luther King Blvd. intersects with I-70 at which of the following intersections?
    a. Peoria
    b. Havana
    c. Colfax
    d. none of the above

68. The most direct way to get from Arapahoe Rd. to Hampden and University Blvd. is to take
    a. Colorado Blvd. to County Line Rd., turn onto University Blvd., and proceed to Hampden.
    b. Arapahoe Rd. to University Blvd. and proceed to Hampden.
    c. Arapahoe Rd. to I-25, take I-25 to I-225, and proceed to Hampden and University Blvd.
    d. Arapahoe Rd. to Broadway, take Broadway to Hampden, and proceed on Hampden to University Blvd.

69. For the portion of the two routes shown on the map, I-70 runs _____ to Colfax.
    a. perpendicular
    b. on a 90-degree angle
    c. parallel
    d. on a 70-degree angle

70. At no point on the map does I-225 appear to cross
    a. Colfax.
    b. Martin Luther King Blvd.
    c. Yosemite St.
    d. Leetsdale Parker Rd.

Directions: Study the scene below and answer questions 71 through 75 without referring back to the picture.

71. How many people can you see in the karate school through the window?
a. five
b. three
c. one
d. two

72. How many adults are currently crossing the street?
a. five
b. two
c. one
d. three

73. How many police officers are at the scene?
a. two
b. three
c. none
d. one

74. How many vehicles are involved in the accident?
a. one
b. two
c. three
d. four

75. What business is directly above the 23rd Bakery?
a. National Bank
b. Bait Shop
c. Karate
d. none

Directions: Use the following paragraph to answer questions 76 and 77.

In response to complaints by merchants of thefts from cars parked in a strip mall of fewer than eight stores, Trooper Sassoon has been assigned to patrol the area. He hears and sees the following:

1. Two well-dressed women exit a minivan, pick up dry cleaning from one of the shops, reenter the minivan and drive away.
2. A man honks his car horn continuously until a teenager comes out of the video store, tosses a small package into the car, and enters the car. The man then drives away.
3. A man leaves the corner sporting goods store carrying a bulky item and runs toward a car parked along the mall but not in the parking area.
4. A woman pushing an empty baby carriage engages in conversation with a shabbily dressed man who has been standing in front of the mall liquor store for approximately an hour.

76. Sergeant Eng later asked Trooper Sassoon to list what he observed during his patrol in the order of most suspicious to least suspicious. Select the most appropriate order for Trooper Sassoon's list.
a. 1, 2, 3, 4
b. 2, 3, 4, 1
c. 4, 3, 2, 1
d. 3, 4, 2, 1

77. After Trooper Sassoon filed his report, he and Sergeant Eng double-checked earlier reports and learned that some merchants had reported that items were missing from their stores after women shoppers had departed. Had Trooper Sassoon known that, he might have altered his above report to give
   a. higher priority to the two well-dressed women.
   b. higher priority to the woman pushing an empty baby carriage.
   c. lower priority to the man leaving the sporting goods store.
   d. all of the above

Directions: Read the paragraph below and answer questions 78 through 80.

Trooper Gallagher broke her wrist and has been assigned to perform clerical work in the Records Section. Sergeant Torelli has asked her to alphabetize some contact cards. She must place the name in capital letters in the correct place in the files.

SARGANT, SUSAN

Names already in the file are:
Saegent, Suzie
Sergent, Susie
Sergent, Suzanne
Sugant, Sally

78. Where in the card file will Trooper Gallagher place *Sargant, Susan*?
   a. after *Saegent, Suzie* but before *Sergent, Susie*
   b. after *Sergent, Susie* but before *Sergent, Suzanne*
   c. after *Sergent, Suzanne* but before *Sugant, Sally*
   d. after *Sugant, Sally*

79. When Trooper Gallagher begins to actually file the cards she has alphabetized, she learns that SARGANT, SUSAN is an incorrect name and that the name of the contact is actually SARGANTE, SUSAN
Based on this new information, where will she now file the card?
   a. before *Saegent, Suzie*
   b. before *Sergent, Susie*
   c. after *Sergent, Suzanne*
   d. after *Sugant, Sally*

80. Trooper Gallagher has discovered yet another error. The correct spelling of SARGANT, SUSAN is actually SAREGANTE, SUSAN. Based on this even newer information, where will she finally file the card?
   a. before *Saegent, Suzie*
   b. before *Sergent, Susie*
   c. after *Sergent, Suzanne*
   d. after *Sugant, Sally*

Directions: Read the following paragraphs and answer questions 81 through 83.

Many state police departments deploy a portion of their personnel to plainclothes anticrime patrol. Being dressed in plainclothes, rather than in uniform, allows these officers a better opportunity to observe criminal activity and to apprehend criminals before or immediately after a criminal act. Plainclothes patrol requires certain adjustments in police procedures, and rules for communicating with uniformed officers have been developed.

An elderly man hurriedly approaches a uniformed trooper and reports that he was mugged by a young man wearing a blue sweatshirt, blue jeans, and sneakers who just ran around the corner. The mugger took the elderly man's watch and wallet. The uniformed trooper runs around the corner, and from a distance, he believes he sees someone enter an abandoned building.

He transmits over his portable radio a description of the mugger and the address of the abandoned building. Two anticrime officers in plainclothes respond and meet the uniformed trooper at the building, which is a three-story building with boarded-up windows. The first anticrime officer says that she will cover the back and she immediately runs down an alleyway along the side of the building. The second anticrime officer says to the uniformed trooper, "Let's go," and they enter the building to search for the suspect, both taking out their firearms. The plainclothes officer attaches his police badge to his left breast pocket where it can be seen.

The building is dark inside except for dim light coming through some of the broken boarded-up windows. The uniformed trooper has a large flashlight, but the anticrime officer has only a small penlike flashlight. The uniformed trooper goes up the stairs to search the upper two floors while the anticrime officer waits at the bottom of the stairs. As the anticrime officer waits at the bottom of the stairs, he hears something that he believes is coming from under the stairs. With his small flashlight he steps around behind the staircase and finds a trap door to the basement. He lifts the trap door, but it is heavy, and he drops it. Just as he drops it, two backup uniformed troopers enter the building. They hear the trap door drop and see the anticrime officer jump away with his gun in his hand. They shout to him to drop the gun. He is surprised and turns toward them. They shoot at him 12 times, striking him twice.

81. Which of the following is the most serious mistake made by the first uniformed trooper?
   a. transmitting a description of the mugger before he obtained complete information from the victim
   b. transmitting the address of the abandoned building based on only his belief that he saw someone enter it
   c. entering the abandoned building with the plainclothes officer
   d. leaving the plainclothes officer alone in the abandoned building

82. Which of the following is the most serious mistake made by the second anticrime officer?
   a. entering the building with the uniformed trooper
   b. entering the building with only a small penlike flashlight
   c. attaching his badge to his breast pocket rather than holding it up in his hand
   d. failing to transmit to the radio dispatcher that a plainclothes officer was entering the abandoned building

83. Which of the following is the most accurate statement regarding the actions of the two backup uniformed troopers?
   a. It was a mistake to enter the building.
   b. It was a mistake to fire at the plainclothes officer before identifying him.
   c. It was a mistake to fire so many bullets at the plainclothes officer.
   d. Based on the available information, it would be unfair to criticize their actions.

Directions: Read the paragraph below and answer questions 84 and 85.

Traffic laws are enacted to enhance the orderly flow of traffic, to regulate motor vehicles and drivers, and to promote public safety. The number of vehicles, drivers, and roads far exceeds the number of law enforcement personnel available for regulatory duties.

84. To achieve the goals of traffic law, it is most effective for a police agency to enforce traffic laws in a manner to
   a. ensure that summonses are issued for all violations.
   b. concentrate only on the most serious violations.
   c. encourage the public's voluntary compliance with the traffic laws.
   d. raise as much revenue as possible.

85. A trooper observes a motorist pass a steady red light. The trooper should issue a summons in all of the following circumstances, except when the motorist
   a. did not intentionally drive through the light.
   b. appears to be an upstanding, law-abiding citizen.
   c. intentionally drove through the light but had looked both ways before proceeding.
   d. carefully drove through the light because of an extreme emergency.

Directions: Read the following paragraphs and answer questions 86 through 91.

Criminally negligent homicide occurs when a person causes the death of another person through criminal negligence. Manslaughter occurs when a person recklessly causes the death of another person. Murder occurs when a person, under circumstances evincing a depraved indifference to human life, recklessly engages in conduct that creates a grave risk of death to another person and thereby causes the death of another person.

Assault third degree occurs when a person, through criminal negligence, causes physical injury to another person by means of a deadly weapon or dangerous instrument. Assault second degree occurs when a person recklessly causes serious physical injury to another person by means of a deadly weapon or dangerous instrument. Assault first degree occurs when a person, under circumstances evincing a depraved indifference to human life, recklessly engages in conduct that creates a grave risk of death to another person and thereby causes serious physical injury to another person.

A person acts with criminal negligence with respect to a result defined as an offense when he fails to perceive a substantial and unjustifiable risk that such result will occur. The risk must be of such nature and degree that the failure to perceive it constitutes a gross deviation from the standard of care that a reasonable person would observe in the situation.

A person acts recklessly with respect to a result defined as an offense when he or she is aware of and consciously disregards a substantial and unjustifiable risk that such result will occur.

86. Danny Donovan is 25 years old. He buys a new .22 caliber rifle and takes it to the countryside to test-fire it. He drives to an apparently uninhabited area, parks his car on the side of a country road, and walks deep into the woods. Surrounded by trees, he fires the gun at tree trunks and branches. He does not know that a hundred yards beyond the woods is the soccer field of an elementary school. One of the bullets he fires travels out of the woods and strikes a child playing soccer. The child suffers a minor grazing wound to his leg. Donovan is unaware of this, and as he returns to his car, he is arrested for shooting the child. The most serious and appropriate charge of which Donovan would be guilty is
   a. criminally negligent homicide.
   b. assault third degree.
   c. assault second degree.
   d. none of the above.

87. Danny Donovan is 25 years old. He buys a new .22 caliber rifle and takes it to the countryside to test-fire it. Driving to the countryside, he notices a few houses scattered in the heavily wooded area. He parks his car on the side of a country road and walks into a wooded area. Surrounded by trees, he fires the gun at tree trunks and branches. He does not know that a hundred yards beyond the wooded area is the soccer field of an elementary school. One of the bullets he fires travels out of the woods and strikes a child playing soccer. The child suffers a minor grazing wound to his leg. Donovan is unaware of this, and as he returns to his car, he is arrested for shooting the child. The most serious and appropriate charge of which Donovan would be guilty is
   a. criminally negligent homicide.
   b. assault third degree.
   c. assault second degree.
   d. none of the above

88. Danny Donovan is 25 years old. He buys a new .22 caliber rifle and takes it to the countryside to test-fire it. Driving to the countryside, he notices houses and residential developments scattered in the area. He parks his car on the side of a road and walks into a wooded area. He considers that there might be houses or buildings in the area, but he assumes that they are far enough away to test-fire his gun. Surrounded by trees, he fires the gun at tree trunks and branches. A hundred yards beyond the wooded area is the soccer field of an elementary school. One of the bullets he fires travels out of the woods and strikes a child playing soccer. The child suffers a serious injury to his leg. Donovan is unaware of this, and as he returns to his car, he is arrested for shooting the child. The most serious and appropriate charge of which Donovan would be guilty is
   a. criminally negligent homicide.
   b. assault third degree.
   c. assault second degree.
   d. assault first degree.

89. Danny Donovan is 25 years old. He buys a new .22 caliber rifle and takes it to the countryside to test-fire it. Driving to the countryside, he notices houses and residential developments scattered in the area. He parks his car on the side of a road and walks into a wooded area. He considers that there might be houses or buildings in the area, but he assumes that they are far enough away to test-fire his gun. Surrounded by trees, he fires the gun at tree trunks and branches. A hundred yards beyond the wooded area is the soccer field of an elementary school. One of the bullets he fires travels out of the woods and strikes a child playing soccer. The child is struck between the eyes and dies. Donovan is unaware of this, and as he returns to his car, he is arrested for shooting the child. The most serious and appropriate charge of which Donovan would be guilty is
  a. assault first degree.
  b. criminally negligent homicide.
  c. manslaughter.
  d. murder.

90. Danny Donovan is 25 years old. He buys a new .22 caliber rifle and takes it to the countryside to test-fire it. Driving to the countryside, he notices houses and residential developments scattered in the area. He parks his car on the side of a road and walks into a wooded area. Surrounded by trees, he fires the gun at tree trunks and branches. Not satisfied with testing the gun in the enclosed wooded area, Donovan walks to the end of the woods and sees the soccer field of an elementary school. A few kids are practicing on the soccer field. To see how far his bullets will travel and to see whether the kids can hear where the shots were coming from, Donovan fires at the goal post near where the kids are playing. One of the bullets travels past the goal post and strikes a child. The child suffers a serious injury to his leg. Donovan is unaware of this, and as he returns to his car, he is arrested for shooting the child. The most serious and appropriate charge of which Donovan would be guilty is
  a. criminally negligent homicide.
  b. assault third degree.
  c. assault second degree.
  d. assault first degree.

91. Danny Donovan is 25 years old. He buys a new .22 caliber rifle and takes it to the countryside to test-fire it. Driving to the countryside, he notices houses and residential developments scattered in the area. He parks his car on the side of a road and walks into a wooded area. Surrounded by trees, he fires the gun at tree trunks and branches. Not satisfied with testing the gun in the enclosed wooded area, Donovan walks to the end of the woods and sees the soccer field of an elementary school. A few kids are practicing on the soccer field. To see how far his bullets will travel and to see whether the kids can hear where the shots were coming from, Donovan fires at the goal post near where the kids are playing. One of the bullets travels past the goal post and strikes a child. The child is struck between the eyes and dies. Donovan is unaware of this, and as he returns to his car, he is arrested for shooting the child. The most serious and appropriate charge of which Donovan would be guilty is
a. assault first degree.
b. criminally negligent homicide.
c. manslaughter.
d. murder.

Directions: Read the paragraphs below and answer questions 92 through 98.

Trooper Acosta responds to the scene of a robbery at a convenience store. The store clerk tells the officer that a man came in with a gun and robbed her of all the money in the cash register. The robber had threatened her with the gun, saying that he would blow the clerk's head off if she did not give him the money. Three customers saw the robber leave.

The witnesses each described what they saw of the gun. The store clerk said she only saw a barrel pointed at her and that is all she can remember. The first witness said it was a silver automatic pistol. The second witness said it was a revolver. The third witness said he saw only that it was black.

The store clerk said the robber was a black male about 30 years old, about six feet tall and 160 pounds, wearing blue pants and a gray sweatshirt with a hood. The first witness said the robber was a Hispanic male, dark skinned, between 5′8″ and 5′10″ and 170 pounds, about 25 years old, wearing blue pants and a blue sweatshirt with a hood. The second witness said the robber was a Hispanic male about 20 years old, between 5′8″and 5′10″ and 160 pounds, wearing black pants and a gray jacket. The third witness said the robber was a Hispanic male, dark skinned, about 6′2″ and 180 pounds, between 20 and 30 years old, wearing blue jeans and a gray sweatshirt.

92. The store clerk and the three customers each gave descriptions of the robber. Which description of the robber is most likely correct?
a. He wore blue pants and a gray sweatshirt with a hood.
b. He wore blue pants and a blue sweatshirt with a hood.
c. He wore black pants and a gray jacket.
d. He wore blue jeans and a gray sweatshirt.

93. The store clerk and the three customers each gave descriptions of the robber. Which description of the robber is most likely correct?
a. He was a black male about 30 years old.
b. He was a Hispanic male, dark skinned, about 25 years old.
c. He was a Hispanic male about 20 years old.
d. He was a Hispanic male, dark skinned, between 20 and 30 years old.

94. The store clerk and the three customers each gave descriptions of the robber. Which description of the robber is most likely correct?
   a. He was about six feet tall and 160 pounds.
   b. He was between 5′8″ and 5′10″ and 170 pounds.
   c. He was between 5′8″ and 5′10″ and 160 pounds.
   d. He was about 6′2″ and 180 pounds.

95. The witnesses each described what they saw of the gun. Which description of the gun is most likely correct?
   a. It was an automatic pistol.
   b. It was a revolver.
   c. It was black.
   d. It was a handgun of unknown type and color.

96. Trooper Acosta should transmit which of the following as the most accurate be-on-the-lookout (BOLO) report?
   a. BOLO for a Hispanic male, approximately 30 years old, six feet tall, 160 pounds, wearing blue pants and a gray sweatshirt with a hood—and armed with a gun.
   b. BOLO for a Hispanic male, dark skin, approximately 30 years old, six feet tall, 160 pounds, wearing blue pants and a gray sweatshirt with a hood—and armed with a gun.
   c. BOLO for a Hispanic male, dark skin, approximately 20 years old, between 5′8″ and 5′10″ tall, 160 pounds, wearing a gray sweatshirt—and armed with a handgun.
   d. BOLO for a Hispanic male, dark skin, approximately 30 years old, between 5′8″ and 5′10″ tall, 160 pounds, wearing blue pants and a gray sweatshirt with a hood—and armed with a handgun.

97. Trooper Acosta was aware of four other store robberies that occurred in the past year. He returned to the station house and reviewed the reports for those robberies to see whether the description of the convenience store robber matched the description of any of the suspects in the prior robberies.

Suspect in Robbery #1: Black male, 35 years old, six feet tall, 200 pounds, wearing a white T-shirt—and armed with a black automatic pistol.

Suspect in Robbery #2: Hispanic male, 25 years old, 5′10″ tall, 160 pounds, wearing a gray sweatshirt—and armed with an automatic pistol.

Suspect in Robbery #3: Hispanic male, dark skin, between 20 and 25 years old, between 5′8″ and 5′10″ tall, between 160 and 180 pounds, wearing blue pants and a gray sweatshirt with a hood—and armed with a handgun.

Suspect in Robbery #4: White or Hispanic male, approximately 20 years old, six feet tall, 140 pounds, wearing a black shirt and black pants—and armed with a knife.

Of the following choices, which descriptions of the prior robbery suspects most closely match the description of the suspect in the robbery of the convenience store?
   a. #1 and #2
   b. #2 and #3
   c. #3 and #4
   d. only #2

98. Trooper Acosta also reviewed the prior robbery reports to see what language the suspects used when confronting the robbery victim.

Suspect in Robbery #1 said: "Hand me all the money before I use this."

Suspect in Robbery #2 said: "I don't want to hurt you. Just give me the money."

Suspect in Robbery #3 said: "Gimme the money or I'll blow your head off."

Suspect in Robbery #4 said: "I'm gonna cut you if you don't give it up."

Of the following choices, which language of the prior robbery suspects most closely matches the language of the suspect in the robbery of the convenience store?
a. #1 and #2
b. #2 and #3
c. #3 and #4
d. only #3

Directions: Read the paragraph below and answer questions 99 and 100.

At 11:00 P.M., a trooper responds to a noise complaint in a park playground. When she arrives, she finds approximately 20 teenagers in the playground, which has posted signs indicating the playground closes 30 minutes after sunset. As she approaches the teenagers, she smells marijuana emanating from a group of five teenagers who quickly walk away and try to exit the playground.

99. The best action the trooper should take is to
a. arrest all the teenagers for being in the park after hours.
b. draw her weapon and run after the five teenagers who are walking away.
c. call out to the teenagers and order them to stay where they are.
d. call for help and wait for backup to arrive before approaching any of the teenagers.

100. If the five teenagers run away in different directions, the action the trooper should take is to
a. run after all five of them.
b. pick out one that she thinks she can catch, and run after him or her.
c. fire a warning shot in the air so that no one else runs.
d. hold the other teenagers for investigation to determine whether crimes or offenses have been committed.

► Answers

1. b. The paragraph states that the newsletter has been developed specifically for academy class 15. Choices **a** and **c** are not discussed in the paragraph and choice **d** contradicts what is stated in the paragraph.

2. d. The paragraph says nothing about earlier newsletters, so choices **a** and **b** cannot be determined. Choice **c** is probably untrue. The paragraph says the PBA purchased new equipment, but it could have previously owned some other computer equipment.

3. a. It would *not* be reasonable and necessary to use deadly physical force to arrest the youth under these circumstances. Choices **b**, **c**, and **d** are all proper actions for the trooper to take.

4. d. The husband's identity is known and other police units will most likely be able to stop his car or locate him. It is unreasonable and unnecessary to shoot him. Choices **a**, **b**, and **c** would each be dangerous, unreasonable, and ineffective.

5. a. Nothing has been shown that would necessitate shooting the husband. Choices **b** and **d** are incorrect; unless the husband attacks the trooper, nothing has happened that would necessitate shooting him. Choice **c** is incorrect because it is an unreasonable action.

6. c. This is a statutory rape without any indication of the use or threatened use of physical force. Therefore, the trooper is unauthorized to use deadly physical force. Choices **a** and **b** are incorrect because this situation does not warrant shooting. Choice **d** is incorrect because warning shots are dangerous, unnecessary, and unjustified.

7. c. It would be improper to immediately shoot the man without first attempting to stop him and investigate further. Choices **a**, **b**, and **d** are incorrect because they are all proper courses of action to take under the circumstances.

8. d. Burglary first degree is one of the offenses for which the use of deadly physical force can be justified. Choices **a**, **b**, and **c** are incorrect; they are not among the offenses for which the use of deadly physical force can be justified.

9. d. Escape first degree is one of the offenses for which the use of deadly physical force can be justified. Choices **a**, **b**, and **c** are incorrect; they are not among the offenses for which the use of deadly physical force can be justified.

10. d. All of the degrees of arson are among the offenses for which the use of deadly physical force can be justified.

11. d. A trooper can defend himself or herself against the threat of deadly physical force. Choice **c** is incorrect because the threat was of physical force, but not deadly physical force. Choices **a** and **b** are incorrect because they would require the person to be armed with a deadly weapon while resisting in order to justify the use of deadly physical force.

12. d. Choices **a** and **b** are incorrect because they would require the person to be armed with a deadly weapon while resisting in order to justify the use of deadly physical force. Choice **c** is incorrect because, though the person is armed with a deadly weapon, the underlying crime is only a misdemeanor, not a felony.

13. b. Deadly physical force can be justified when the person committed a felony and is armed with a deadly weapon when he resists arrest. Choices **a** and **c** are incorrect because burglary second or third degree does not involve the use of physical force, and deadly physical force is authorized only for burglary first degree. Choice **d** is incorrect because the threat was of only physical force, not deadly physical force.

14. d. The trooper could reasonably believe the person was going to shoot at him or her. Choice **a** is incorrect because without more information, this is a threat of only physical force, not deadly physical force. Choice **b** is incorrect; a trooper could use physical force to make the person comply, but not deadly physical force. Choice **c** is incorrect because the person may potentially use deadly physical force, but while he or she is backing away, it is not imminent. If he or she moved toward the trooper, the trooper may be justified to use deadly physical force.

15. d. It is the most reasonable, prudent, and lawful action to take. Choices **a** and **b** are incorrect. Based on the circumstances, the trooper did not have lawful authority to frisk or chase the men. Choice **c** is incorrect because the trooper would be derelict in his duties were the men in fact contemplating a crime.

16. d. The trooper's information and description of the possible suspects may be helpful in apprehending the suspects. Choice **a** is incorrect because the trooper would be derelict in his duties if he did not ascertain whether the two men he observed were possible suspects. Choice **b** is incorrect because time is of the essence in attempting to apprehend the perpetrators of a robbery. Choice **c** is incorrect because it is more important to broadcast a description of the men, and he could tell the sergeant at the first practicable opportunity.

17. d. A trooper's first duty is to protect life. The manager was bleeding profusely and could have been bleeding from an artery. Choices **a**, **b**, and **c** are incorrect because they are of secondary importance to saving life.

18. a. This is the safest course of action; it would be too risky for one trooper to attempt to frisk these potentially dangerous and armed criminals. Choices **b** and **c** are not safe courses of action for the trooper. Choice **d** is incorrect because it is a better and safer tactic to keep the suspect facing away from the trooper.

19. d. This maintains the trooper's safety while he remains close enough to resolve the situation when the opportunity arises. Choice **a** is a poor tactic that exposes the trooper to injury. Choice **b** is incorrect. Although the trooper must be cautious, he cannot ignore the situation. Choice **c** is incorrect; unless the trooper

is personally threatened or one of the men is clearly assaulting the other, the trooper should not shoot or threaten to shoot.

20. c. Upon hearing the sirens, the students might stop fighting. Choices **a** and **b** are incorrect because each would warn a criminal that the police were on the way and would prevent the police from apprehending the criminal. Choice **d** is incorrect. The murder was in the past, so the circumstances do not warrant the use of these emergency devices.

21. d. Choice **a** needs the adverb *badly* instead of the word *bad*. Choices **b** and **c** each contain a verb tense error. *Fell* should be *fallen*.

22. b. Choices **a**, **c**, and **d** each contain number agreement errors.

23. c. Choices **a** and **b** use the wrong verb tense of *to lead*. Choice **d** uses *leded*, which is not a form of *to lead*.

24. c. Choices **a** and **b** are incorrect. The comparative is *than*, not *then*. In choice **d**, *betterer* is not a word.

25. c. The word *trooper* describes a person and requires the use of *who* or *whom* rather than *that* or *which*. Choices **a**, **b**, and **d** each have one or more grammatical or usage errors.

26. a. The sentence calls for use of the present verb tense. It also calls for the word *like* rather than *as*.

27. b. The sentence requires a past tense, so choices **a** and **d** can be ruled out. Choice **c** is wrong; the word *jobs* should be plural because *their* is plural.

28. a. This choice presumes the word *media* is singular, which is incorrect. It also says that society portrays women, not that the media do. Choices **b**, **c**, and **d** are grammatically correct sentences.

29. a. The subject of the sentence is plural and, therefore, requires a plural verb.

30. a. It is the only grammatically correct sentence.

31. c. *Hire* is a synonym for *employ*.

32. a. Confidential information should not be told to those who have no need for it. *Disclose* is a synonym for *tell*.

33. a. Use *number* with nouns that can be counted. Choice **b** is incorrect because it uses *amount* and *a largest*, which is grammatically wrong. Choice **c** is incorrect because the phrase *too many of* is not grammatically correct. Choice **d** is incorrect because *lot's* is a possessive of the noun *lot*.

34. a. *Although he was not born in the United States* is not a complete sentence; it is a phrase and should be part of the sentence before it.

35. a. *John could have did* uses the simple past rather than the past participle form of the verb *to do*.

36. c. *Its'* contains an apostrophe in the incorrect place. Choice **a** is preferred. Although choice **b** uses a contraction (*it's*), this would be acceptable in informal speech.

37. b. *Good* is not an adverb; it cannot be used to modify the verb *to sing*.

38. a. This choice provides all the correct information in a concise report. Choice **b** is incorrect because the victim's name is changed and because the report implies that her laptop computer was not in the house at the time of the burglary. Choice **c** is incorrect because the victim's name is changed and the address is incorrectly reported. Choice **d** is incorrect because it provides information that is not relevant to the incident.

39. d. Choice **a** is incorrect because Trooper Chen must take the report even if she suspects the laptop was borrowed and will eventually be located. Choice **b** is incorrect because if Martin has the laptop as Trooper Chen suspects, based on what the trooper was told, there is a good chance Martin is not a burglar. Choice **c** is incorrect because, though Trooper Chen might mention that leaving one's door unlocked is unwise, it is not her role to lecture citizens who are reporting what they believe to be crimes.

40. d. Four elements of the situation were not properly recalled: the name of the victim, the type of crime reported, the address, and whose laptop was missing.

41. a. This is the sum of the total value of all the items Ms. Danner reported. Choice **b** is incorrect because it rounds up the value of the items. Choice **c** is incorrect because it is the value of only the jewelry. Choice **d** is incorrect because it includes the value of the bus ticket, which Ms. Danner did not report missing.

42. c. This is the sum of the clothing items Ms. Danner reported. Choice **a** is incorrect because it is the value of the jewelry. Choice **b** is incorrect because it is the value of the bus ticket. Choice **d** is incorrect because it is the total value of the all the items Ms. Danner reported missing.

43. b. This is the sum of the jewelry items Ms. Danner reported. Choice **a** is incorrect because it excludes the value of the chain and charm with the initial *S*. Choice **c** is incorrect because it includes the value of all items plus the bus ticket. Choice **d** is incorrect because it is the value of all items reported by Ms. Danner.

44. a. To develop the correct answer you must know that 12 rolls of tape constitute a dozen; thus, each box contains 36 rolls of tape. To derive the answer, multiply the number of rolls by the number of boxes ($36 \times 10 = 360$).

45. c. Divide the total number of summonses by the number that can be packed into each envelope: $400 \div 20 = 20$.

46. c. Divide the total number of summonses by the number that can be packed into each envelope ($400 \div 15 = 26.6$). Round 26.6 up to the next whole number, 27.

47. d. This is the sum of the total value of all the items Mr. Smithfield reported. You must multiply the value of each item by the number reported missing and then add the subtotals. Choices **a**, **b**, and **c** each leave out some of the items that Mr. Smithfield reported missing.

48. c. The three telephone sets, with a total value of $450, were no longer missing. Therefore, they should not be included in the value of the missing property.

49. c. Add all the expenses to determine Trooper Doyle's reimbursement.

50. b. To calculate 73% of 55,000, multiply 0.73 by 55,000.

51. b. 1700 hours is 5 P.M. An eight-hour shift that begins at 5 P.M. would end at 1 A.M.

52. a. 1914 is the same as 7:14 P.M. and 2040 is the same as 8:40 P.M. The elapsed time between these times is 1 hour and 26 minutes.

53. c. Troopers who begin eight-hour tours at 0800 will complete their tours at 1600 hours, which is 4 P.M.

54. c. There are three steps involved in solving this calculation. First, convert 10% to a decimal: 0.10. Multiply $19,000 (one-half the annual salary) by 0.10 (the percent to be earned). Then, add this amount ($1,900) to the annual salary.

55. b. There are three steps involved in solving this calculation. First, convert 4.5% to a decimal: 0.45. Multiply that by $38,000 to find the salary increase. Then, add the result ($1,710) to the original salary ($38,000).

56. a. The indicator in the upper left-hand corner orients you to north, from which you must determine that east is right, west is left, and south would be in the opposite direction that the arrow is pointing.

57. b. PNC Park is located on the north side of the Allegheny River, and North Side Station will be the closest station to it once it opens.

58. d. All three rivers meet at Point State Park.

59. d. I-25 is prominent in the station name and is designated in the style common for the Interstate Highway System.

60. c. Three other station names are shown: 18th and California, 30th and Downing, and Union Station.

61. b. The arrow in the photograph indicates the train will be traveling north from the Broadway Station to Union Station.

62. b. Using the coordinates given to you in the description, the airport is southwest of the Convention Center.

63. c. This is the section of the Florida Turnpike that runs almost perfectly parallel to U.S. 441.

64. d. Old Dixie Highway and Interstate 95 follow a similar route, but they do not cross at any point shown on the map.

65. a. Griffin Road and U.S. 595 are shown closest to the airport. Of the two, Griffin Road is a local road and U.S. 595 is the interstate bypass.

66. b. Choice **a** is incorrect because University Drive does not go far enough south. Choice **c** is incorrect because it takes you out too far east. Choice **d** is incorrect because it takes you farther east than choice **b**.

67. d. Martin Luther King Blvd. is shown as a relatively short street that runs parallel to I-70.

68. b. It is the most direct route, requiring the least number of road changes.

69. c. I-70 can be seen at the top of the map; Colfax is below Martin Luther King Blvd. running parallel to I-70.

70. b. Martin Luther King Blvd. is a short street between I-70 and Colfax that does not intersect at any point on the map with I-225.

71. d. Two people are shown in the school's window.

72. b. Two people are shown crossing the street with a baby carriage. A man across the street appears to be looking at the accident, not crossing the street.

73. a. There is one police officer taking notes and another directing traffic.

74. b. There are two vehicles involved in the accident. The other vehicles—a police car, an ambulance, and a tow truck—are responding to the accident, but you may presume that they were not part of the accident.

75. d. The four windows above the 23rd Bakery do not have any commercial sign; it appears to be a residential property.

76. d. This places first the most suspicious action, namely the man leaving the store carrying a bulky item and not entering a car parked in the mall. Choices **a** and **b** list first activities that without further investigation appear to be normal mall behavior. Choice **c** lists first a behavior that is less common than those in choices **a** and **b**, but not as suspicious as the behavior listed first in choice **d**.

77. d. With additional information, Trooper Sassoon might have viewed the situations differently, particularly the activities involving the women.

78. a. When the first letter is the same, names are alphabetized based on each succeeding letter. In this example, the first names are not relevant.

79. b. When the first letter is the same, names are alphabetized based on each succeeding letter. The *e* added to *Sargente* does not change the name's place in the alphabetical listing.

80. b. When the first letter is the same, names are alphabetized based on each succeeding letter. The *e* added in the middle to create *Saregent* does not change the name's place in the alphabetical listing.

81. d. This is the most serious mistake because the uniformed trooper left the plainclothes officer alone in the dimly lit building, where he could easily be mistaken for the suspect. Choice **c** is a mistake but not as serious as choice **d**. Choices **a** and **b** were proper actions.

82. d. This is the most serious mistake. The officer should have foreseen that uniformed troopers would respond to the building and should have warned them of his presence inside the building. Choices **a** and **b** were mistakes, but were not as serious as choice **d**. Choice **c** was a proper action.

83. d. The troopers were unaware that a plainclothes officer was in the building and were suddenly faced with an unknown person who jumped and turned toward them with a gun in his hand. Choice **b** was not a mistake for the same reasons. Choice **c** was not a mistake since all the bullets did not strike the trooper. Choice **a** was not a mistake; the troopers were assisting the first uniformed trooper.

84. c. The traffic system can work only with the public's cooperation and voluntary compliance. Choice **a** is incorrect because not enough troopers are available to issue summonses for every violation. Choice **b** is incorrect because troopers should not ignore the less serious violations when they are committed in their presence. Choice **d** is incorrect because revenue is not the primary consideration.

85. d. All laws are qualified by the need to act in genuine emergencies. Choice **a** is incorrect because traffic laws are designed not only for intentional violators, but also for negligent or careless violators. Choice **b** is incorrect because traffic laws are enforced against all citizens to encourage them to drive carefully. Choice **c** is incorrect because looking both ways does not excuse the violation.

86. d. Although Donovan could be sued civilly for ordinary negligence, his conduct was not criminally negligent. Choice **a** is incorrect since the child did not die. Choice **b** is incorrect; from Donovan's perspective, the failure to perceive the soccer field was not a gross deviation from the standard of care a reasonable person would observe in the situation. Choice **c** is incorrect for the same reason as choice **b**, and also because the child did not suffer a serious injury.

87. b. The failure to perceive the reasonable possibility that people were in the area where he was shooting the gun was the kind of gross deviation that amounts to criminally negligent conduct. Choice **a** is incorrect because the child did not die. Choice **c** is incorrect because the child did not suffer a serious injury.

88. c. His awareness and conscious disregard of the substantial and unjustifiable risk that people were nearby constitutes reckless conduct, and the child suffered a serious injury. Choice **a** is incorrect because the child did not die. Choice **b** is incorrect because the conduct was more serious and culpable than criminal negligence and the child suffered serious injury.

89. c. His awareness and conscious disregard of the substantial and unjustifiable risk that people were nearby constitutes reckless conduct, and the child died. Choice **a** is incorrect because the child died. Choice **b** is incorrect because the conduct was more serious and culpable than criminal negligence.

90. d. Donovan's reckless conduct created a grave risk of death, evinced a depraved indifference to human life, and caused serious physical injury. Choice **a** is incorrect because the child did not die. Choices **b** and **c** are incorrect because Donovan's conduct was more serious and culpable than criminal negligence or recklessness.

91. d. Donovan's reckless conduct created a grave risk of death, evinced a depraved indifference to human life, and caused death. Choice **a** is incorrect because the child's death is a more serious result than serious physical injury. Choices **b** and **c** are incorrect since Donovan's conduct was more serious and culpable than criminal negligence or recklessness.

92. a. Blue pants, gray sweatshirt, and a hood are the elements repeated most often by the eyewitnesses and are therefore most likely correct.

93. d. Hispanic and dark skinned are the elements repeated most often by the eyewitnesses and are therefore most likely correct. The ages given in choices **a**, **b**, and **c** are different from the other answers; therefore, choice **d** is the best answer regarding age.

94. c. Between 5′8″ and 5′10″ and 160 pounds are the elements repeated most often by the eyewitnesses and are therefore most likely correct.

95. d. The witnesses agree only that it was a handgun. No other elements are repeated often enough to merit reliance on their accuracy.

96. d. This matches the most likely descriptions obtained above. Choices **a**, **b**, and **c** are incorrect because they include less likely descriptions obtained.

97. b. Descriptions #2 and #3 both match the suspect. Choice **a** is incorrect; although description #2 matches the suspect, #1 does not. Choice **c** is incorrect; although #3 matches the suspect, #4 does not. Choice **d** is incorrect; although #2 matches the suspect, it is not the only one that matches because #3 also matches.

98. d. Choice **d** is correct; the language used in robbery #3 most closely matches the language in the convenience store robbery. Choice **a** is incorrect because the language does not match. Choice **b** is incorrect; although #3 matches, #2 does not. Choice **c** is incorrect; although #3 matches, #4 does not.

99. c. It is a reasonable attempt to exercise her authority to investigate the matter. Choice **a** is incorrect; although the trooper might have the authority to arrest the teenagers, discretion should be considered in this situation, and she should focus on the five who were walking away. Choice **b** is incorrect; a trooper should draw his or her weapon only when it is warranted. Choice **d** is incorrect because the trooper should talk to the teenagers.

100. d. The trooper could obtain further information to determine whether additional action is required. Choice **a** is incorrect because it is impractical for one trooper to try to catch five individuals. Choice **b** is incorrect because it is impractical to engage in such a chase. Choice **c** is incorrect because firing a warning shot in this situation is unreasonable, unnecessary, and dangerous.

17 ▶ The Oral Appraisal Exam

CHAPTER SUMMARY

Not all state police agencies include an oral appraisal exam in their hiring procedures. The major reason for this is that it is a costly and time-consuming process to have each candidate questioned by an interview board at a centralized location. Agencies that do use an oral appraisal generally record the interview and retain the tape in the event a candidate lodges a challenge to this portion of the hiring process. One agency that includes an oral suitability interview in its hiring process is the ISP. The interview lasts an hour and applicants are ranked based on its results. The PSP also conducts an oral interview and provides detailed information about the process on its website.

Generally, even if there is not a formal board interview, candidates will have spoken to employees of the agency sometime during the hiring process. Although these conversations may seem informal, they are an opportunity for you to present yourself in the best possible way. Maybe you spoke with a human resources official when you sought information about the job; maybe you spoke with a trooper assigned to the recruitment unit at a job fair or received the application in person from the agency's headquarters. It may be true that these people make no employment decisions, but you have an opportunity to present yourself in a professional way and to get a sense of what behavior would be appropriate in the agency you hope to join. Look at how people are dressed; listen to how they speak to you. You have no way of knowing whether any of these initial contacts with the agency are people you will see again. Particularly in smaller departments, there is a good chance you will cross paths with these individuals again, and what is said about first impressions being lasting impressions is true.

▶ Physical Appearance

While there is no need to dress formally to go to head-quarters to pick up an application, you should look presentable. If you speak with a recruiter at a state fair, it is expected that you will dress differently than you would if the meeting were at a college job fair. Some colleges now require that students attend job fairs in business attire. Certainly if your selected agency conducts an oral appraisal exam, you should plan to dress in such attire. This may not mean a suit and tie every-where in the United States, but it means at least a button-down dress shirt and slacks with a pressed crease for men. A man should not appear at his oral interview in sneakers, a polo or T-shirt, or jeans. Women applicants need not wear a dress, but should also wear a button-down blouse and a skirt or a suit. Just as for men, sneakers, any polo or T-shirts, or jeans are inappropriate. For both men and women, hair should be tidy, shoes should be shined, and jewelry should be kept to a minimum.

The PSP advises candidates that business attire is expected at the oral and polygraph exams and for the background investigation interview, noting that gym attire is appropriate only for the physical fitness tests and the medical and psychological evaluations. Do not assume that this is the same for all agencies; check before you show up at any stage of the hiring process in gym or casual clothing rather than in business attire.

▶ Successful Interview Techniques

If your selected agency conducts an interview, you might consider practicing in front of a mirror or talking to adult businesspeople. You might even record yourself talking and try to eliminate from your speech habits known as *verbal tics*. Verbal tics include inject-ing into each sentence words such as *like, you know,* or *I mean.* Do not start sentences with the word *well,* and

do not use any curse words or racial, ethnic, or sexist slurs. Higher-pitched voices sometimes tend to sound more tentative than a voice in a lower timbre. Although you cannot totally change your speaking voice and style, you can minimize the tendency to sound unsure of yourself by not letting your voice go up at the end of each sentence to make it seem you are asking a question rather than answering one. You want to sound self-assured and confident without sounding like someone who knows it all.

Your posture is also important. Remember not to slouch or wiggle around in your seat. If you are more comfortable crossing your legs, do so at the ankle rather than swinging one leg across the knee of another.

▶ Answering Questions

While you will be asked factual questions at the inter-view about yourself, such as what you majored in at school and why, or why you want to become a law enforcement officer, the primary purpose of the oral interview is not to learn the answers to these questions as much as for agency personnel to see how you per-form under stress and to get a sense of your ability to analyze problems and converse with others. Some interviewers will ask probing questions that try to assess your character; some will ask you if you have any questions for them so that they can get a sense of your communications skills and of whether you have sincerely thought about what a career in law enforce-ment entails.

Listen carefully and learn the names of those on the appraisal board. When someone asks you a ques-tion, respond using the rank and last name of that person, and make eye contact with the questioner and with others on the panel. Do not look down at your shoes or at your fingers while you speak. Be sure also to get the name, its proper spelling, and the proper title of the person heading the interview panel, since you might want to follow up with a short note thanking the panel for the opportunity to meet with its members and reinforcing your interest in joining the agency.

Sample Interview Questions

Not all oral appraisals follow the same format, but some questions that you can be fairly sure you will be asked include:

- Why did you select this particular agency to apply to?
- What are your strengths?
- What are your weaknesses?
- What do you think you will be doing in this agency during your first year of service? Your fifth year of service?

Describing Yourself

You must be prepared for a general "tell us about yourself" question. Here, as in all the questions, you want to answer honestly and briefly. "Tell us about yourself" does not mean to replay every detail of your life up to this point. It is fine to talk briefly about your family, schooling or military experience, any jobs you've held, and why you want to be a state trooper. Similarly, when you discuss strengths and weaknesses, think about these in a professional sense. You might consider describing weaknesses that can be turned into strengths, because you want to illustrate that while you are not perfect, you also have the capacity to improve yourself.

Hypothetical Questions

Another line of questioning might be similar to the problem solving questions on the written exam. This means you might be asked a hypothetical question that gets to the point about how you would act at a crime scene or an assistance call.

You might be given a set of facts and asked what you would do first when you arrived at the scene. For instance:

- You are dispatched to a neighborhood park where young people are reported to have been noisy and possibly drinking alcohol and smoking marijuana. When they see you arriving, they disperse in a number of different directions. What would you do? How would you determine who to chase? Would you fire a warning shot into the air? Would you shoot at any of the fleeing youths? Would you take down the license number of a vehicle you see three of the youths get into and drive away?

Or you might be asked a question that delves into your personal ethics, such as:

- You overhear a colleague making racist or sexist remarks about a coworker; what would you do?
- You stop a motorist on a deserted stretch of the interstate and he offers you $100 not to write a ticket; what would you do?

Although you may have thought about these or similar types of questions, the oral appraisal may raise some issues you had not given thought to before. Try to answer carefully but honestly because if you lie, a later question may bring you back to the same situation, and you will find yourself stumped if you do not recall what you said earlier, or if it becomes obvious that your answer sounded good but doesn't reflect your beliefs at all.

Asking Questions

Generally, the last phase of the appraisal gives you an opportunity to question the interviewers on the panel. Try to have at least one good question to ask, because asking no questions may be interpreted as a lack of real interest in the agency. If you have nothing specific to ask, ask about the future steps in the hiring process, which shows your interest in continuing as a candidate. You might also consider making a short closing statement that reinforces your interest in the position and your belief that you will be able to fulfill the responsibilities of the position. However, you do not want this to sound too rehearsed, as if you'd practiced it word-for-word for the last month.

18▶ The Physical, Medical, and Psychological Exams

CHAPTER SUMMARY
Of these three exams, the physical is the only one that that a candidate can really "study" for. Since medical and psychological exams may differ, having a general knowledge of what these tests consist of will best prepare you for them.

Many agencies provide details about tests on their websites or in materials sent to candidates who have passed the earlier steps in the hiring process. However you obtain material from your agency of choice, read it carefully and follow the instructions provided. Many agencies place these steps late in the hiring process, so you will have already passed a number of hurdles on the way to employment. It would be unfortunate at this stage to be disqualified because you failed to follow instructions rather than because of any medical or psychological bar to employment.

▶ Physical Exam

For many applicants, especially women and candidates of both sexes who have been inactive for most of their lives, the physical exam may be as big—or even bigger—a hurdle than the written exam. Sometimes, even for those in good physical condition, the physical exam becomes a psychological barrier. But there is no reason for this; as with the written exam, you can study for the physical exam. In fact, some agencies post on their websites exactly what the physical exam will consist of, meaning that your studying for it can be even more directly targeted than your studying for the written exam.

Two agencies that tell candidates what will be expected of them at the physical are the NYSP and the PSP. Because these exams are fairly typical, and actually are on the more difficult end of the spectrum, their requirements will give you an excellent idea of what will be expected of you.

The NYSP calls its test physical ability testing, or PAT. The test is generally scheduled about six months prior to the start of an academy class. To do well, candidates need to start getting in shape about one year before they hope to enter an academy class. Candidates are invited to the PAT according to their rank order on the written exam, which means that you will be called sooner if you scored high on the written exam. The good part of this is that you have an early chance to move into an academy class. If you haven't been taking care of your physical conditioning, though, you will need to start a physical fitness program almost immediately upon receiving your score.

The NYSP assists candidates in passing the PAT by stressing training in three areas: stretching and flexibility, strength training, and a cardiovascular program. Generally, recruiting offices across New York state schedule seminars to help candidates prepare for the PAT and understand the techniques for performing the various physical tests.

The PSP provides one of the most detailed explanations of its physical testing requirements of any state police agency. It is also one of the most rigorous. Regardless of the agency you are interested in applying for, you should visit the PSP website (www.psp.state.pa.us) to gain an understanding of what your agency of choice may expect of you. The entry level physical standards for the PSP as of 2006 included completing a 300-meter run in 67 seconds, completing 30 sit-ups in one minute, completing 13 push-ups in one minute, obtaining a vertical jump of 14 inches, and completing a 1.5-mile run in just under 17 minutes. These are the standards for entry; you will be expected to have improved your fitness by the time you graduate so that you are able to complete the 300-meter run in 56 seconds, complete 37 sit-ups and 30 push-ups in one minute each, raise your vertical jump to 18 inches, and complete the 1.5-mile run in 14 minutes and five seconds.

Many state police agencies, unlike the vast majority of municipal police departments, expect you to maintain your physical ability throughout your career. Many troopers are tested annually for physical fitness. The NJSP, another agency with stringent physical standards, requires all troopers to take part in an annual fitness test, which includes a 1.5-mile run. This agency makes no adjustments for age or sex under the assumption that those running from the police do not stop to determine whether the trooper chasing them is young or old, or male or female.

Women have tended to do poorly on state police physical ability tests. To help them, as well as men who are not fit and agile, many agencies provide fact sheets on how to study for the physical exam and on the best techniques for mastering the skills required to pass. Although many candidates do not realize it, there are better and worse ways of running, jumping, and, particularly, making it over a five- or six-foot wall or dragging a 150-pound dummy. Knowing how to bend your body, when to rely on leg strength rather than upper body strength, and how to conserve energy for that last push of effort are things that can be learned. Healthy habits and diet to decrease your weight and increase your cardiovascular capacity can also be learned. A number of agencies also schedule pretraining sessions for candidates, and some conduct a pretest that is given under conditions similar to the actual test to give candidates an opportunity to learn what they do well in and what they might need to focus on before the actual test. This is an excellent reason to keep visiting the website of the agency you have applied to, because training sessions may be announced regularly.

Regardless of your physical condition, you must be prepared to undertake a fitness program to pass the majority of state police physical ability exams. Unlike applicants for local police departments, you may not be able to participate in pretraining that is conducted near your home. This means you will need to use the material provided by your agency to develop a program that you can work on alone. To maintain your motivation, you might consider joining a gym where you can obtain some assistance from professional trainers. If you are still in college, you might consider asking someone in the athletic department to guide you. You might also try to learn from your recruiter if there are other candidates in your immediate area so that you can form a workout group to help and to motivate one another.

▶ Medical Exam

If you were not tested for drug use during the physical ability portion of the applicant process, it is likely that this will be done during the medical exam. Although at one time, almost any drug use was an automatic disqualification for police employment, that is no longer the case. Different agencies have different policies regarding past experimentation with drugs, but you will not be hired by any agency if you test positive for drug use at the time of your medical exam. Find out the policy of the agency you are testing for so that you are prepared at the time of testing. If your agency accepts candidates who have experimented with drugs in the past, do not lie about the last time you used any of the permissible drugs, because the truth may be determined during your background investigation, and you will be automatically disqualified—not only for the drug experimentation, but also for having lied.

Many agencies once placed the medical exam early in the hiring process, but considerations based on the Americans with Disabilities Act (ADA) have moved it further along in the process. The ADA, which was signed into law in 1990, extended various protections to candidates who may have disabilities that do not preclude them from performing a full range of police tasks. To comply with this law, the PSP, for instance, in 2006 placed the medical exam as step six of seven steps prior to appointment. Prior to the medical exam, a candidate for the PSP will have completed an application, passed the qualifying written and oral exams, completed fitness tests (including drug screening), and passed a polygraph and a background investigation.

The PSP provides an applicant with detailed instructions for completing medical documentation by a physician of the applicant's choice and at the applicant's expense that includes a physical exam, a certificate of visual efficiency, a dental exam, a complete blood count, and a chest X-ray. The material is reviewed by the State Police Medical Officer. Although there are no specific height and weight requirements, applicants must pass audiometer screening, must have healthy gums and a full set of teeth, and must meet very specific vision standards. The PSP is unusual because it directs the applicant to go to a private physician to meet the medical requirements; many agencies expect the applicant to appear for a medical exam conducted by doctors employed by the agencies specifically for this purpose.

There are many reasons why police agencies want to hire only candidates who are in good health. The most immediate reason is that the academy is very strenuous, and it would not be a good use of time or money to hire candidates who were not in sufficiently good health to complete the training and accept assignment as officers. The longer-range reasons are to ensure that candidates are not injury-prone, and do not suffer their own medical emergencies while responding to police emergencies, and to minimize the number of officers who retire early due to illness at considerable cost to the agency. Recently, a small number of law enforcement agencies have sought to keep their employees healthy by prohibiting officers from smoking in public or even from smoking at all. If such a prohibition applies in the agency you are applying for, you will be told that not smoking is a condition of employment, and that if you claim not to smoke and are found to do so, you will face disciplinary action up to and including termination. A number of state courts have upheld these policies despite challenges by applicants, so you should inquire what health-related requirements (smoking, drinking, or other prohibitions) the agency you are applying for may have in place.

► Psychological Exam

The psychological assessment is another exam that it is almost impossible to study for. It is difficult to believe today that it has been only in the past thirty years that police agencies have relied heavily on psychological assessments of their candidates. Today it is common for applicants to be given a battery of paper-and-pencil tests and to undergo an interview with a licensed psychologist who is familiar with law enforcement officers' job responsibilities.

Although some agencies inform applicants of the tests that will be administered, the best advice is to answer questions honestly and not to try to be clever or cunning. Most of the tests ask the same questions more than once in slightly different formats, so it is virtually impossible to trick the test and lie consistently and successfully. Some of the more commonly used tests are the Minnesota Multiphasic Personality Inventory (MMPI), the California Personality Inventory (CPI), the Wechsler Adult Intelligence Scale—Revised (WISC-R), and the Inwald Personality Inventory (IPI). Questions are designed to ferret out those who have impulse control problems, lie or are evasive consistently, are substance abusers, have high levels of stress, or have difficulty managing anger. Many of the questions are also aimed at eliminating candidates who exhibit high levels of hypochondria; this is often a symptom of psychological problems and may also indicate that an applicant has a high possibility of being absent too often due to illness or injury, and then attempting to retire early.

Probably the best way to prepare for the psychological exam is to relax. Spending time at home or with loved ones, rather than socializing with those who may contribute to your uncertainty and concern, will reduce stress levels. Sleeping well and following a healthy diet and exercise regimen prior to the test may also aid you in being clear-minded and alert when filling out paper-and-pencil tests, and certainly when speaking with a trained psychologist or psychiatrist.

Special FREE Offer from LearningExpress!

**LearningExpress will help you be better prepared for,
and score higher on, the state trooper exam.**

Go to the LearningExpress Practice Center at www.LearningExpressFreeOffer.com, an interactive online resource exclusively for LearningExpress customers.

Now that you've purchased LearningExpress's *State Trooper Exam*, you have **FREE** access to:

- **Two full-length state trooper practice tests** that mirror official state trooper exams
- **Multiple-choice questions covering** memory and observation, math skills, reading comprehension, spatial and directional orientation, **and much more!**
- **Immediate scoring** and **detailed answer explanations**
- Benchmark your skills and focus your study with our **customized diagnostic reports**

Follow the simple instructions on the scratch card in your copy of *State Trooper Exam*. Use the individualized access code found on the scratch card and go to www.LearningExpressFreeOffer.com to sign in. Start practicing online for the state trooper exam right away!

Once you've logged on, use the spaces below to write in your access code and newly created password for easy reference:

Access Code: _____   Password: _____